World Health Organization

World Health Organization

by

Gian Luca Burci
Senior Legal Officer, World Health Organization

and

Claude-Henri Vignes
Former Legal Counsel, World Health Organization

This book was originally published as a monograph in the International
Encyclopaedia of Laws/Medical Law.

2004

KLUWER LAW INTERNATIONAL
THE HAGUE / LONDON / NEW YORK

Published by:
Kluwer Law International
P.O. Box 85889
2508 CN The Hague, The Netherlands
sales@kluwerlaw.com
http://www.kluwerlaw.com

Sold and Distributed in North, Central and South America by:
Aspen Publishers, Inc.
7201 McKinney Circle
Frederick, MD 21704, USA

Sold and Distributed in all other countries by:
Extenza-Turpin Distribution Services
Blackhorse Road
Letchworth
Hertfordshire SG6 1HN, United Kingdom

A C.I.P. Catalogue record for this book is available from the Library of Congress

Printed on acid-free paper

Cover design: The Bears Communications, Amsterdam

ISBN 90 411 22737

© 2004 Kluwer Law International

The Authors

Mr Gian Luca Burci was born on 11 May 1958 in Florence. An Italian national, Mr Burci holds a doctorate in law from the University of Genoa (Italy). Assistant, International Law Institute, University of Genoa (1986–1988). Mr Burci's career has largely taken place in several international organizations. He served as associate professional officer, Evaluation Section, Department for Technical Cooperation, International Atomic Energy Agency, Vienna (1988–1989); legal officer, Office of the Legal Counsel, Office of Legal Affairs, United Nations, New York (1989–1998). Since June 1998, Mr Burci is a senior legal officer in the Office of the Legal Counsel, World Health Organization. Mr Burci has published numerous articles on various topics of public international law, in particular on the law of United Nations economic sanctions, succession of states to treaties, and United Nations peace-keeping.

Mr Claude-Henri Vignes was born on 22 December 1930 in Marseilles. Undertook studies at the Faculty of Law Aix-en-Provence (1948–1953). Doctorate in law (1953). Called to the Bar in Marseilles (1954). Lecturer in Law, Faculty of Aix-en-Provence (1957–1960). Lecturer in Law, Faculty of Lyon (1960–1962). Associate Professor, Faculty of Law, Geneva (1975). Invited Professor, Institut d'Etudes Politiques, Grenoble (1978). Lectured at the Institut des Hautes Etudes Internationales (Paris), at the University of Paris I and the University of Aix-en-Provence. Joined the Legal Division of the World Health Organization (1961). Chief of the Unit of Constitutional and Legal Matters (1969). Appointed WHO Legal Counsel (1978). Personal representative of the Director-General for the occupied territories in the Middle East (1975–1985). Agent of the WHO before the ILO Administrative Tribunal. Agent of the WHO before the International Court of Justice in the Advisory Opinion 'Interpretation of the Agreement of 25 March 1951 between the WHO and Egypt' (1980) and in the Advisory Opinion 'Legality of the Use by a State of Nuclear

The Authors

Weapons in Armed Conflicts' (1996). Left the WHO (June 1991). Reappointed WHO Legal Counsel (July 1993–December 1995). Served as a consultant to the Office of the Legal Counsel (1996–1998). Author of a number of articles on international and administrative law. At present, provides advice on legal issues to public and private institutions.

Acknowledgements

The authors wish to express their gratitude and appreciation to the WHO officials who reviewed the various sections of this contribution and gave valuable comments. A substantial debt of gratitude is owed in particular to Thomas S.R. Topping, the Legal Counsel, who reviewed in detail this work notwithstanding his many commitments, and who gave many good and insightful suggestions in the process. Many thanks also to Denis Aitken for having timely reviewed the manuscript, as well as to Jim Akré, Douglas Bettcher, Max Hardiman, Hans Hogerzeil, Nick Jeffrey, André L'Hours, Anne Mazur, George Micod, Jonathan Quick, Clas Sandstrom, Jorgen Schlundt, Tokuo Yoshida. A special mention should be made of Valentina Milano of the Office of the Legal Counsel, who gave invaluable help on Chapters 6 and 8, and Beatrice Quadranti of the Graduate Institute of International Studies, Geneva, who took care of several ungrateful tasks with outstanding thoroughness and professionalism. Many thanks should also go to Anne Jaggi Poulsen, who typed and revised the manuscript in an impeccable fashion. Finally, Mr Burci would like to express all his gratitude to his wife Nalini and his daughter Priya, for their patience, understanding and support.

Acknowledgements

Table of Contents

Table of Contents

Table of Contents

Table of Contents

List of Abbreviations

AMRO	Regional Office of the Americas
APOC	African Programme for Onchocerciasis Control
CCO	Committee of Cosponsoring Organizations of UNAIDS
CDTI	Community-directed treatment with ivermectin
CEB	Chief Executives Board for Coordination
CMH	Commission on Macroeconomics and Health
CSA	Committee of Sponsoring Agencies
CVI	Children's Vaccine Initiative
DOTS	Directly Observed Treatment, Short-course
EAC	Expert Advisory Committee
EPTA	United Nations Expanded Programme of Technical Assistance
ESAC	Expert Scientific Advisory Committee
FCTC	Framework Convention on Tobacco Control
GAP	Gender Advisory Panel
GATB	Global Alliance on Tuberculosis Drug Development
GAVI	Global Alliance for Vaccines and Immunization
GDF	Global Drug Facility
GDEP	Global DOTS Expansion Plan
GLC	Green Light Committee
GPV	Global Programme for Vaccines and Immunization
HFA	Health for All
HRP	Special Programme on Research Training in Human Reproduction
IARC	International Agency for Research on Cancer
ICD	International Classification of Diseases
ICF	International Classification of Functioning, Disability and Health
ICIDH	International Classification of Impairments, Disabilities and Handicaps
IFPMA	International Federation of Pharmaceutical Manufacturers Association
IHR	International Health Regulations
INB	Intergovernmental Negotiating Body
INN	International Nonproprietary names
ISC	International Statistical Congress
ISI	International Statistical Institute
IUATLD	International Union against Tuberculosis and Lung Disease
JAC	Joint Action Forum
JCHP	Joint Committee on Health Policy
JCB	Joint Coordinating Board
JPC	Joint Programme Committee

List of Abbreviations

JECFA	Joint FAO/WHO Expert Committee of Food Additives
JMPR	Joint FAO/WHO Meeting on Pesticides Residues
LID	Long-term Institutional Development Grant
MIP	Meeting of Interested Parties
MMV	Medicines for Malaria Venture
MOU	Memorandum of Understanding
NCDs	Noncommunicable Diseases
NTP	National Tuberculosis Programme
OCP	Onchocerciasis Control Programme
OIHP	International Office of Public Hygiene
PAHO	Pan American Health Organization
PASB	Pan American Sanitary Bureau
PCB	Programme Coordinating Board
PCC	Policy and Coordination Committee
PPPs	Public-Private Partnerships
RAPs	Regional Advisory Panels
RBM	Roll Back Malaria Programme
RCS	Research capability strengthening
SERG	Scientific and Ethical Review Group
SPS	Agreement on the Application of Sanitary and Phytosanitary Measures
STAC	Scientific and Technical Advisory Committee
TBT	Agreement on Technical Barriers to Trade
TCC	Technical Consultative Committee
TDR	Special Programme for Research and Training in Tropical Diseases
UNAIDS	Joint United Nations Programme on HIV-AIDS
UNCND	United Nations Commission on Narcotic Drugs
UNDAF	United Nations Development Assistance Frameworks
UNDG	United Nations Development Group
UNDP	United Nations Development Programme
UN-ECE	United Nations Economic Commission for Europe
UNFPA	United Nations Fund for Population Activities
UNRRA	United Nations Relief and Rehabilitation Administration
WHA	World Health Assembly

Part I. Introduction

Chapter 1. Genesis

1. The idea of establishing a single international organization whose mandate would cover all fields of public health was launched, for the first time at the United Nations Conference on International Organization, which was convened in San Francisco from 25 April to 26 June 1945. During the Conference, the delegations of Brazil and China submitted a joint declaration recommending 'that a General Conference be convened within the next few months for the purpose of establishing an international health organization . . . [and] that the proposed international health organization be brought into relationship with the Economic and Social Council'.[1] The San Francisco Conference unanimously approved the declaration and, on 15 February 1946, the Economic and Social Council adopted a resolution calling 'an international conference to consider the scope of, and the appropriate machinery for, international action in the field of public health and proposals for the establishment of a single international organization of the United Nations'.[2] The task of preparing the agenda and proposals for the consideration of the conference was attributed to a Technical Preparatory Committee consisting of experts which met in Paris from 18 March to 5 April 1946. The Committee complied with its mandate and drew up an annotated agenda for the Conference as well as a draft Constitution for the future health organization. The International Health Conference was held in New York from 19 June to 22 July 1946 and was attended by 51 delegations from members of the United Nations and a number of observers. It adopted the Constitution for the future World Health Organization, together with several other documents. One of these established an Interim Commission which would prepare and convoke the first World Health Assembly, would perform certain urgent tasks and would carry out the surviving activities of the existing health institutions until the entry into force of the WHO Constitution. This required the deposit with the Secretary-General of the United Nations of the instruments of acceptance by 26 Members of the United Nations.[3] The other texts dealt mainly with the suppression of the existing health institutions and the carrying out of their surviving activities pending the final establishment of WHO.

1. *See* Official Records of the World Health Organization (hereafter OR) 1, p. 39.
2. *Ibid.*
3. Article 80 of the Constitution.

2. The birth of such an international organization was, however, the outcome of more than a century of concerted endeavours which had resulted in the establishment of a number of international bodies. But there was a need to unify action against the ever-growing spread of diseases caused by the development of inter-national trade. During the nineteenth century a number of international sanitary conferences had been convened,[1] the first in Paris in 1851 being generally considered as having opened a new era of international action in public health. Following the Eleventh International Sanitary Conference held in Paris in 1903, twelve states concluded an arrangement in Rome in 1907 which created the Paris-based Inter-national Office of Public Hygiene (OIHP), whose functions were to disseminate general information on public health amongst its members, particularly with regard to the most common communicable diseases, namely cholera, plague and yellow fever. The Health Organization of the League of Nations was established in 1920 by the London Conference on the basis of Article XXIII(f) of the Covenant of the League of Nations which provided that the members would 'endeavour to take steps in matters of international concern for the prevention and control of diseases'. This meant that during the period till after World War II, two international health organizations coexisted to which was added, later, the United Nations Relief and Rehabilitation Administration (UNRRA), which took over, from 1945, the respons-ibilities of the OIHP pertaining to international sanitary conventions.

1. Paris (1851), Paris (1859), Constantinople (1866), Vienna (1874), Washington (1881), Rome (1885), Venice (1892), Dresden (1893), Paris (1894), Venice (1897).

3. These organizations were, nonetheless, not the only ones dealing with health questions as during the nineteenth century some bodies had also been set up at the regional level. Special mention should be made of the four councils, which regu-lated the quarantine procedures in the Mediterranean area,[1] as well as the creation in the Americas at the beginning of the twentieth century, of the Pan American Sanitary Organization, later renamed Pan American Health Organization (PAHO), with an International Sanitary Bureau, which became the Pan American Sanitary Bureau.

1. Constantinople, Tangier, Alexandria, Teheran.

4. It is clear from the above that a number of steps had been undertaken in the field of international public health. But such action was not enough. It had become vital to unify and increase such efforts and activities. The tools were available, the scientific knowledge existed and the political will was undeniable. It was in such a context that the San Francisco Conference opened.

Chapter 2. The Constitution

5. The text of the Constitution is based upon several proposals presented to the Technical Preparatory Committee. The committee devised a formula of compromise between these proposals and submitted a comprehensive text for the conference's approval. The Constitution itself is a document containing nineteen chapters preceded by a preamble in which health is defined as 'a state of complete physical, mental and social well-being and not merely the absence of disease or infirmity'. The text goes on to describe the objective of the Organization and, in a lengthy article containing 22 paragraphs enumerates its functions. These, for the sake of clarity, can be categorized under two main functions: (i) direction and coordination on international health work, including the setting of international norms and standards in different fields of health; and (ii) technical cooperation with members, including research as well as the provision of advice and assistance upon request. The Constitution then regulates the membership, the structure of the Organization, its legal capacity and contains several final provisions. A great number of its articles do not differ fundamentally from those contained in the Constitutions of other agencies belonging to the United Nations system, thus following the classical structure of other international organizations with political, technical and administrative organs. It adopts the traditional voting system of one member, one vote. It emphasizes the importance of the recruitment of staff on as wide a geographical basis as possible. It respects the long-standing, but now much debated, principle of non-interference in the domestic affairs of states. However, in certain respects, the Constitution presents remarkable particularities. It places great emphasis upon the principle of universality of membership. As a corollary to this principle, the Constitution contains no provisions relating either to the withdrawal or the expulsion of a member from the Organization. But the most important particularity of the Constitution is that it adopts the principle of regionalization. The World Health Organization is, indeed, a 'decentralized organization', in which a great part of its power and responsibilities are transferred to a number of regional bodies. Regionalization was one of the questions discussed during the Technical Preparatory Committee as well as during the conference. There were two conflicting views. On the one hand, it was felt that 'a single international health organization'[1] was needed but, on the other hand, it was argued that a regional structure would be more effective in solving local health problems and that existing regional bodies should be protected, in particular those in the American area. It is partly for the latter reason that regionalization was inserted in the Constitution. The conference concluded that 'regional arrangements would at one and the same time assure unity

of action by the central Organization on health matters of world-wide import and allow for adequate flexibility in handling the special needs of regional areas'.[2]

  1. OR 1, p. 31.
  2. OR 2, pp. 24–25.

6.   The text of the Constitution, as adopted, was signed by the representatives of 61 states on 22 July 1946. It entered into force on 7 April 1948 when the number of acceptances required by Article 80 was reached. As provided for by the Constitution,[1] amendments to it were adopted in 1959, 1965, 1967, 1973, 1976, 1978, 1986 and 1998. Five of them entered into force and became integral parts of the constitutional text. In 1995, the Assembly noting the lack of a global review of the Constitution since its entry into force in 1948, called upon the Executive Board to examine whether all of its parts remained appropriate and relevant and, if a review were needed, to consider how this should be done.[2] In response the Board established, in 1996, a special group to undertake this task. The special group held six meetings between 1996 and 1997. It considered WHO's mission and functions and the provisions of the Constitution that might need further examination with a view to possible revision. It also examined questions relating to WHO's regional arrangements within the framework of the existing Constitution, requested by the Board which broadened the mandate of the group.[3] In its report, presented to the Board in 1998,[4] the special group suggested, *inter alia*, enlarging the definition of 'health' contained in the preamble to spiritual well-being. It proposed tightening the sanctions relating to non-payment of financial obligations.[5] It recommended extending the regulatory power of the Assembly[6] to the fields of transplantation and genetic engineering, including cloning. It also suggested modifying the procedure for the acceptance of amendments[7] which would come into force after a specified time unless more than one-third of the members notified their dissent during that period. No action was eventually taken on these proposals. Therefore, apart from the five constitutional amendments entered into force, none of which touches any of the fundamental principles on which the Constitution is based,[8] the text of the Constitution remains substantially that which was adopted in 1946.

  1. Article 73 states: 'Texts of proposed amendments to this Constitution shall be communicated by the Director-General to Members at least six months in advance of their consideration by the Health Assembly. Amendments shall come into force for all Members when adopted by a two-thirds vote of the Health Assembly and accepted by two-thirds of the Members in accordance with their respective constitutional processes'.
  2. Res. WHA48.14, WHA48/1995/REC/1, p. 17.
  3. Res. EB99 R24 and *Dec.EB99(5)*, EB99/1997/REC/1, pp. 24 and 32.
  4. *See* EB 101/1998/REC/1, Annex 3.
  5. Art. 7.
  6. Art. 21.
  7. Art. 73.
  8. All the amendments increased the membership of the Board, except one which set up the biennial budgeting cycle.

7.   However, the Constitution is not the only legal framework upon which the activities of the Organization are based. Other texts, such as the Rules of Procedure adopted by the Governing Bodies, are extremely important. Mention should also be

made of the provisions adopted by the Assembly regulating certain specific areas such as the Financial Regulations, or the Staff Regulations. The decisions and resolutions adopted by the Governing Bodies are also essential and may be considered as the *Corpus Juris* of the Organization. Last but not least, mention has to be made of the 'established practice', whose knowledge is essential to understand the real functioning of the Organization.

Part II. Participation

Chapter 1. Membership

8. Article 3 of the WHO's Constitution provides that membership in the Organization 'shall be open to all States'. This article thus establishes two basic principles: universality of the Organization and statehood as a requirement for admission. With the admission of Timor-Leste on 27 September 2002, WHO's membership stands at 192, i.e., practically universal. A list of WHO Member States is provided in Annex 4.

§1. ADMISSION

9. Putting aside the historical case of the states which sent observers to the International Health Conference,[1] there are two possibilities open to states wishing to join the Organization. Those already members of the United Nations may enter WHO by accepting its Constitution in accordance with their constitutional processes, as provided for in Article 4 of the Constitution, such acceptance being effected by the deposit of a formal instrument with the Secretary-General of the United Nations, the depositary of the WHO Constitution.[2] States that are not members of the United Nations, may become WHO members by submitting an application under Article 6 of the Constitution. Apart from the participants in the International Health Conference, most of the WHO's members have chosen the first option and became members of the United Nations before joining the WHO under the provisions of Article 4. This choice does not create any difficulties within the WHO, all the potential problems having already been dealt under UN auspices. Nevertheless, certain applicants preferred the second option and applied directly for WHO membership. Such a decision may arise from different factors, for example that the applicant does not wish to be a member of the United Nations, as in the case of Switzerland in 1947.

1. *See* Article 5 of the Constitution.
2. *See* Article 81 of the Constitution.

10. Article 6 of the Constitution, however, merely sets out the majority required for the admission to membership of non-UN Members. Other conditions concerning admission are provided by the Rules of Procedure of the World Health Assembly, in particular Rule 115. This lays down that admission involves two different authorities: the Director-General and the World Health Assembly.

11.   In the first instance, applications for admission to membership must be addressed to the Director-General. In accordance with Rule 115 'Applications made by a State . . . shall be transmitted immediately by him to Members . . . [and] placed on the agenda of the next session of the Health Assembly provided the application reaches the Director-General at least thirty days before the opening of such a session'. In addition, it is stipulated in Rule 3 of the same rules that 'the Director-General may invite States having made application for membership . . . to send observers to sessions of the Health Assembly'. The Director-General's responsibilities may appear to be merely procedural. In reality, this is not quite the case. The Director-General's responsibilities are of the essence and it is rather paradoxical that they are fixed, not by the Constitution, but by the Rules of Procedure.

12.   In the second instance, it falls to the Assembly to consider the application and to take whatever decision it deems appropriate. And here appears a particularity of the WHO which, generally, does not exist in the other organizations of the United Nations system.[1] Article 6 expressly stipulates that the applicants will be admitted as members 'when their application has been approved by a simple majority vote of the Health Assembly'. Originally, the constitutional proposal submitted at the International Health Conference was more restrictive regarding the procedural requirement for admission, and a two-thirds majority was foreseen. But, during the debates, it was emphasized that such a requirement would not facilitate accessions and would thus be inconsistent with the proclaimed principle of universality. Consequently, the proposal of the Legal Committee of the Conference was amended to substitute a simple majority for a two-thirds vote. In supporting this amendment, a great number of delegations held the view that membership should be open to all states.[2] This principle was embodied in several provisions of the Constitution.[3] This easy procedural requirement together with the absence of any possibility of a 'veto' as in the UN's Security Council, clearly reveals why WHO has been the first choice of those countries wishing to enter the UN family whose application might be considered controversial or whose international status might be uncertain. To a lesser degree, the fact that the WHO is a technical Organization, as opposed to a political one, is also considered by such applicants as a factor facilitating their admission.

1. Another exception is the International Atomic Energy Agency.
2. Nothing is more significant in this context than the prophetic statement of the then delegate of Canada (who later became the first Director-General of WHO) at the International Health Conference in 1946: 'This is not at all an altruistic gesture but a simple matter of enlightened self-interest. We cannot afford to have gaps in the fence against diseases, and any country, no matter what its political attitudes or affiliations are, can be a serious detriment to the effectiveness of the WHO if it is left outside. It is important that health should be regarded as a worldwide question, quite independent of political attitudes in any country in the world'. Verbatim records, 12th plenary meeting, UN Economic and Social Council, E/H/PV/12 page 13. *See also* summary report on proceedings OR 2, p. 69.
3. *See* for instance Preamble, Articles 1 and 3.

13.   Rule 115 is clearly the keystone in the admission procedure. The word 'state' raises the concept of statehood and sets a dilemma for the Director-General. Should these provisions be interpreted as giving the responsibility to the Director-General of judging whether or not the applicant is a 'state'? Or, conversely, should the Director-General transmit to the members any application sent by any entity claiming statehood? In the former case, such an interpretation would have the effect of transferring to the Director-General a constitutional responsibility belonging to the Assembly. In the latter case, it would contradict the very wording of the Constitution and of the Rules, which expressly make reference to a 'state'. The analysis of precedents may help in providing an answer to this dilemma. In this respect, the case of the then Federal Republic of Germany is particularly significant. In 1951 the Federal Republic of Germany, which was still formally under occupation and whose external relations were being handled by the occupying powers, made an application to become a member of the WHO. This application, although it was presented during a period when restrictions were in place regarding the full exercise of Germany's sovereignty, curiously enough did not create any problem within WHO, either at the level of the Director-General, who circulated the application, transmitted it to the Assembly and invited the Federal Republic of Germany to send observers, or at the level of the Assembly itself[1] which admitted the applicant.[2] The same situation occurred in the case of Japan, which was admitted in the same year.[3] More recently, in 1984, the Cook Islands, whose external relations were conducted by New Zealand on the basis of a Compact of Free Association, were also admitted without problems.[4] It is thus clear that the political will of the Member States remains the key factor for the admission of entities wishing to join the Organization.

1. *See* Resolution WHA 4.43, OR 35, p. 34.
2. At the request of Israel a vote was taken by 'show of hands'.
3. Resolution WHA 4.42, OR 35, p. 34.
4. Resolution WHA 37.1, WHA37/1984/REC/1, p. 3.

14. Conversely, certain applications have been rejected when political will proved insufficient and serious divergences existed amongst members in respect of the statehood of the applicant or its capacity to discharge the obligations and exercise the responsibilities attached to membership. The case of the German Democratic Republic (GDR) is indicative. When, by a letter dated 2 April 1968, the Minister of Foreign Affairs of the German Democratic Republic requested his country's admission, the Director-General took two separate decisions. He circulated the application and placed it on the agenda of the Assembly making formal reference to the pertinent rule of procedure. Nevertheless, to escape from the dilemma mentioned in the previous paragraph, he stated in his circular letter to members that the application was transmitted 'without prejudging in any way the decision the Health Assembly might take as to whether it is receivable'.[1] Regarding the question of inviting the GDR to send observers, the Director-General decided to make use of the option mentioned in Rule 3 and refrained from issuing such an invitation. This resulted in the German Democratic Republic informing the Director-General that it would send observers to the session.[2] The Director-General replied that because no invitation had been sent, it would not be possible to seat the persons whose names appeared in the letter.[3] The application was eventually rejected. No application was submitted in 1969. In 1970 when a similar request was made, the Director-General decided once again to circulate the application and to place it on the agenda of the Assembly but did not include in his circular letter the disclaimer that had appeared in 1968. Nevertheless, as previously, no observers were invited. The same situation arose in 1971. However, the following year, the attitude of the Director-General changed when he again included in his circular letter the disclaimer that had previously been omitted, and, for the first time, invited the German Democratic Republic to send observers. It was clearly stated, however, that these observers should be seated only during the consideration of the item concerning the application. Finally, in 1973, the application was circulated without any disclaimer, and the letter inviting the German Democratic Republic to send observers did not contain any restrictions. The Assembly took the decision to admit the applicant by acclamation.[4]

1. *See* text of the application in the circular letter from the Director-General dated 5 April 1968, ref. C.L. 11.1968.
2. Letter dated 18 April 1968 (unpublished).
3. Letter dated 1 May 1968 (unpublished).
4. Resolution WHA 26.2, OR 209, p. 2.

15. Another case, that of Palestine, differs and reveals particularly interesting elements that emphasize the role of the Director-General and illustrate the difficulties that the Assembly faces when politically sensitive applications have to be considered. On 6 April 1989, the Permanent observer of Palestine, formerly designated as Palestine Liberation Organization (PLO), handed to the Director-General a letter[1] signed by Mr Yasser Arafat, in his capacity as President of the self-proclaimed State of Palestine and as Chairman of the Executive Committee of the PLO, informing the Director-General 'of the desire of the State of Palestine to become a full member of the WHO in accordance with Article 6 of the Constitution'. The letter went on 'to confirm . . . the acceptance of the Constitution . . . by the State . . . its commitment to the Articles of the Constitution, and its undertaking to fulfil all duties and responsibilities arising from the full membership . . . in WHO'.[2] The Director-General was thus confronted with an extremely complex situation. It was decided to circulate the request as a Note Verbale which did not refer to the pertinent Rules of Procedure regarding the application for admission to membership. On receipt of this note, a number of states sent comments, which were also circulated. The question of an invitation to send observers was, in this particular case, not relevant, Palestine being already invited in that capacity.[3] No specific item was placed on the agenda. The application was considered under an existing item 'Admission of new Members and Associate Members (if any)'. It was the subject of an acrimonious debate that focused more on procedural problems than on substance. The few speakers who tackled the substance, mentioned the questions of statehood and recognition. One delegation considered that such a request: 'violates both the Constitution of the Organization and international law and therefore should not have been brought to the Assembly for consideration'.[4] Finally a resolution[5] was adopted by secret ballot under which the Director-General was requested, *inter alia*, 'to pursue his studies on the application . . . [and] to report to the following Health Assembly for its decision'. At the next Assembly a study was presented. However, following protests from countries supporting the application, and which were not satisfied by the contents of the document, it was decided that it should not constitute an official document and therefore not be discussed. The Assembly adopted by consensus a resolution reaffirming the resolution adopted the year before, and requesting the Director-General to pursue his study and to report to the Assembly 'at the appropriate time, taking into consideration any relevant developments'.[6] Since then the question has remained in abeyance.

1. Dated 1 April 1989.
2. Text of the letter in note verbale of 14 April 1989.
3. *See* Resolution WHA 27.37, OR 217, p. 17.
4. WHA42/1989/REC/2, p. 257.
5. Resolution WHA 42.1, WHA42/1989/REC/1, p. 1.
6. Resolution WHA 43.1, WHA43/1990/REC/1, p. 1.

16.   The 'precedents' analyzed above, permit to draw a certain number of observations that clarify the process of admission:

(a) It may be noted that most of the arguments either in favour or against admission presented during the debates rest principally, explicitly or implicitly, on the concept of statehood.

(b) During the discussions relating to the admission of states whose status was uncertain, it was often claimed by certain delegations that the applicant was not 'recognized' by their own government, or at least did not command a sufficient degree of recognition within the international community. Practice, however, shows that this position is inaccurate. The recognition of an entity as a 'state', and the admission of such an entity to membership of the Organization, are two separate questions that are not necessarily linked. The recognition is not a precondition for the admission.[1] In this context a statement by the UN Secretary-General is particularly relevant: 'Since recognition . . . is an individual act, and either admission to membership or acceptance of representation in the Organization are collective acts, it would appear to be legally inadmissible to condition the latter acts by a requirement that they be preceded by individual recognition . . .'.[2] Certainly, recognition of statehood[3] by the highest possible number of members of the Organization greatly facilitates admission by the Assembly.

(c) Besides statehood, another factor is of equal importance for the Assembly in considering applications for membership: the capacity of the applicant to participate fully in the work of the Organization and to exercise the responsibilities deriving from its membership.[4] In the case of the Federal Republic of Germany, its application was accompanied by a declaration of the Allied High Commission according to which the Commission would not exercise any of the powers vested in it under the Occupation Statute in such a way that would prevent or hinder the fulfilment by the Federal Republic of the obligations and responsibilities attaching to membership of the Organization. In the case of Japan, the view was expressed by the United Kingdom delegate that his government took the statement made on behalf of the Supreme Commander for the Allied Powers to mean that the Supreme Commander would not interfere in the international health affairs of Japan and therefore the United Kingdom would support the application.[5] In the case of the Cook Islands the delegate of New Zealand, before the adoption of the resolution admitting the Cook Islands to membership, declared that: 'although New Zealand has certain responsibilities for the defense and external relations of the Cook Islands, it does not have any rights of control . . . in the light of this constitutional relationship, therefore, the application . . . for the full membership is . . . entirely appropriate. For the same reasons, there is no legal impediment to the Cook Islands Government's assuming full responsibility for all the obligations implied by this'.[6]

(d) The above examples show that the Director-General has repeatedly considered that the transmission of an application was an administrative and procedural and not a political act, which, in no way, prejudges the decision of the Assembly. The argument according to which the Director-General would have the duty to exercise a prior judgment on eligibility for membership is not supported by practice.

(e) The concept of statehood has not the same importance and does not carry the same weight depending upon the level at which the application is considered. For instance, the Director-General would presumably not circulate applications presented by entities not having any particular status under international law, but, as far as the applicant possesses sufficient attributes of statehood and is considered as a responsible body able to carry out its obligations, the precedents suggest that the Director-General feels empowered to transmit the application. In other words, the concept of statehood is appreciated by the Director-General, at its minimum level.

(f) The same reasoning is applicable to the corresponding invitation of an observer, which is also considered by the Director-General as an administrative and procedural act. To interpret Rule 3 as vesting a political responsibility in the Director-General would not only contradict the provisions of the Constitution but would also be at variance with WHO's consistent practice.

1. This principle was already acknowledged during the League of Nations.
2. UN Doc. 5/1466; Off. Rec. of the Security Council, 5th year, supp. for Jan.–May 1950, pp. 18–23.
3. It should be recalled that Article I of the 1933 Montevideo Convention lists the following criteria for statehood: 'The state' as a person of international law should possess the following qualifications: (a) a permanent population; (b) a defined territory; (c) government; and (d) capacity to enter into relations with the other states. In D.J. Harris, *Cases and Materials on International Law* (5th Ed., London, Sweet & Maxwell, 1998), pp. 102–104.
4. *See*, in this context Free City of Danzig and International Labour Organization PCIJ, Ser. B, No. 18 (1930) p. 1. Dantzig's foreign relations were conducted by Poland and the Free City was not able to undertake such acts as ratifying international conventions. On the ground that there was no constitutional provision 'which absolves a Member . . . from complying with the obligations of membership' Dantzig was not considered eligible for membership.
5. OR 35, p. 307.
6. *See* WHA37/1984/REC/2.17.

17.   To summarize, one can say that the Director-General possesses a certain margin of discretion in the implementation of the Rules of Procedure, with regard to the circulation of the application, as well as extending an invitation to observers.

§2. INCIDENTS OF MEMBERSHIP

18.   One of the earliest and most well-known incidents relates to the representation of the only country, together with the United Kingdom which, on 22 July

1946, signed the WHO Constitution without reservation as to approval, namely, China.[1] In 1949 the establishment of the People's Republic of China was proclaimed, this regime exercising full control over mainland China. From 1950 until 1953, China did not actively participate in the work of the Organization.[2] The question of China's representation arose at the Sixth Assembly in 1953 when the delegation of the Republic of China presented its credentials. These credentials were accepted after a formal vote had been taken, in which a number of delegations abstained.[3] In all subsequent Assemblies but one,[4] the question of the representation of China was raised in connection with the consideration of the credentials of delegations.[5] However, despite protests regarding the non-representation of the People's Republic of China, no formal proposal was made until 1961 not to seat the delegation of the Republic of China. At the Fourteenth Assembly, a formal proposal having that effect was made for the first time by the delegation of the Union of Soviet Socialist Republics (USSR). From that date onwards several similar attempts were made, all of them unsuccessful. The view taken by the Health Assembly was always consistent with the position adopted by the United Nations General Assembly in its Resolution 396 (V) dated 14 December 1950 which states in part that 'there should be uniformity in the procedure applicable whenever more than one authority claims to be the government entitled to represent a Member State in the United Nations . . . [and] Recommends that the attitude adopted by the General Assembly . . . should be taken into account in . . . the specialized agencies'.

1. In doing so, these two countries became the two first Members of WHO.
2. In 1950 the Republic of China notified the DG of its withdrawal from WHO and in 1953 it resumed its participation, *see* Res. WHA3.90 and OR 28, p. 55.
3. In particular the delegation of UK stated that it could not vote positively in favour because such a vote would imply recognition of the Chinese nationalist authorities as the Government of China. *See* OR 48, p. 347.
4. The Eleventh (1958).
5. *See* for instance statements of Norway, Republic of Korea, Turkey and Yugoslavia at the Ninth Assembly (1956) in OR 71, pp. 59–60.

19. In 1971 the United Nations General Assembly decided to restore its right to the People's Republic of China and to recognize the representatives of its government as the only legitimate representatives of China.[1] The Director-General addressed the Executive Board in January 1972 requesting guidance on two points: the inclusion in the agenda of the Assembly of an item on the representation of China and the addressing of a communication to the People's Republic of China with particular reference to the notice of convocation for the next Assembly. The question of the Board's authority was raised in this connection.[2] However the Board decided to take action based on the position taken by the UN General Assembly and the provisions of Article 28(e) of the WHO Constitution.[3] It therefore decided to include an item on the provisional agenda of the Assembly on the question of the representation of China and also authorized the Director-General to address an invitation to the Government of the People's Republic of China. Furthermore, the Board recommended to the Assembly 'that it recognize the Government of the People's Republic of China as the only Government having the right to represent China in the World Health Organization'.[4] At the following Assembly in May 1972, the Assembly endorsed that recommendation and decided to 'restore

all its rights to the People's Republic of China . . . and to expel forthwith the representatives of Chiang Kai-Shek'.[5]

1. GA Res. 2758 (XXVI).
2. *See* EB49/SR, pp. 224–235.
3. 'The functions of the Board shall be: (e) to submit advice or proposal to the Health Assembly
   on its own initiative . . .'.
4. Res. EB49.R37, OR 198, p. 27.
5. Res. WHA25.1 adopted by 76 votes in favour, 15 against with 27 abstentions, OR 201, p. 1.

20.   More recently, the Organization confronted another problem relating to
changes that had occurred in the constitutional structure of certain of its members.
The USSR, which had been a member of the Organization since 24 March 1948,
ceased to exist on 31 December 1991. This decision was adopted by the former
members of the USSR which had in the meantime gained independence and established a Commonwealth of Independent States. Curiously enough, the newly created Russian Federation simply continued the membership of the former USSR in
all Organizations of the UN system. It was considered as being a member of the
WHO since 1948. The nameplate was simply changed in meetings; the member
of the Executive Board designated in 1990 by the USSR remained in his post and
was considered as having been designated by the Russian Federation from 1992
onwards.[1]

1. The other components of the former USSR had to follow the constitutional process to be admitted
   as new members.

21.   Around the same period, conflicts broke out within the Socialist Federal
Republic of Yugoslavia (SFRY), when some members of the Republic decided to
secede from it. Serbia and Montenegro, previously members of the SFRY, announced
the setting up of the Federal Republic of Yugoslavia (FRY) as the continuation of
the SFRY. Contrary to the decision it had taken concerning the Russian Federation,
the United Nations decided that the FRY could not automatically assume the seat
of the former SFRY and therefore excluded it from the General Assembly.[1] A
similar attitude was adopted by the WHO, in 1993, when the delegation of the FRY
was physically expelled from the plenary meeting and the WHA decided that the
FRY (Serbia and Montenegro) should apply in accordance with the Constitution
should it wish to join the Organization.[2] It was only seven years later that Yugoslavia
became a new member on 28 November 2000, after its admission to the UN.

1. *See* Res. UNGA, Resolution 47/1 of 22 September 1992.
2. Res. WHA46.1, WHA46/1993/REC/1, p. 1.

22.   The Organization has also been confronted with a further problem relating,
this time, not to the continuation of membership but to its termination. It is the
problem of withdrawal and of expulsion. The Constitution does not contain any
provisions relating to withdrawal from membership. From the debates in the Preparatory Committee and in the International Health Conference it is clear that
such a provision was considered inconsistent with the principle of universality.
Nevertheless, it seems that in two cases, such a withdrawal could legitimately be
effected.

23. The first concerns the situation of a member which formally reserved its right to withdraw from the Organization when depositing its instrument of acceptance of the Constitution. At present, this right is enjoyed only by the United States, which, when submitting its instrument of acceptance to the Secretary-General of the United Nations in 1948, formally reserved its right to withdraw from the WHO on a year's notice.[1] In the absence of a specific provision in the WHO Constitution, the UN Secretary-General stated that he was 'not in a position to determine whether the United States has become a party to the Constitution'.[2] It was for the Health Assembly, in accordance with Article 75 of the Constitution, to settle 'any question . . . concerning the interpretation or application of this Constitution . . .'. When the Assembly considered the matter, there were no objections, with several speakers even recommending that the Assembly adopt a liberal interpretation of the Constitution. The Assembly therefore decided to admit the United States as a full member. The Assembly's stance might be considered as an acceptance of the reservation in the meaning of the Vienna Convention of the Law of Treaties.[3] Whether or not another member could claim this right is a question that could be considered. The delegate of India underlined during the first Assembly in 1946 that since no Member State should enjoy a more favoured position than others, the Assembly should lay down as proposition of general application: 'that any Member State may terminate its membership on a year's notice'.[4] No observations having been made on this proposal, the right of withdrawal remained for years an unsettled question.

1. *See* Public law 643, 80th Congress, and also OR 13, p. 383.
2. OR 13, pp. 32 and 382.
3. *See* Art. 20.3.
4. OR 13, pp. 78–80.

24. The second situation where a withdrawal appears possible concerns amendments to the Constitution. The record of the 1946 Conference contains a statement safeguarding the position of any Member State which might find itself unable to accept an amendment to the Constitution duly approved in accordance with Article 73 thereof. During the debates, the delegation of India submitted a text according to which amendments: 'should be binding only upon those Members which subsequently ratified them'. That proposal was later withdrawn on condition that the following declaratory statement be read in plenary session: 'A member is not bound to remain in the Organization if its rights and obligations as such were changed by an amendment of the Constitution in which it has not concurred and which it finds itself unable to accept'.[1] No objections were raised to this formally recorded statement and a valid possibility of withdrawal seems to have been established. However, the fact remains that the Constitution is completely silent regarding the question of withdrawal. It was only in 1949 that the unsettled problem raised above was practically answered. That year, three Members States[2] sent a notice of withdrawal to the Director-General. By telegram, the Director-General replied that he could not consider such a notice as a withdrawal 'because the Constitution of WHO makes no such provision'.[3] He passed the matter on to the Executive Board, which, in turn, referred it to the Assembly. During the resulting debates no mention was made either of the implicit recognition by the previous Assembly of the right of withdrawal claimed by the United States, or to the statement made by India during the debates related to the admission of the USA. The prevailing feeling in the Assembly was that its action should be directed toward obtaining reconsideration of the decision of the Member States concerned and to ignore the constitutional problems arising from such withdrawals.[4] In 1950 and 1951, six other Members States from Eastern Europe[5] plus the Republic of China notified the Director-General of their withdrawal from the Organization.[6] However, all these members later resumed their participation.[7]

1. OR 2, pp. 26 and 74.
2. USSR, Ukrainian SSR and Byelorussia.
3. OR 17, p. 52.
4. *See* debates in OR 21, pp. 304–308.
5. Bulgaria, Romania, Albania, Czechoslovakia, Hungary and Poland.
6. Except China and Poland, all the others members did not used the word 'withdrawal' but stated that 'their States no longer consider themselves Members of the World Health Organization', *see* for instance Res. WHA2.90, OR 21, p. 52 and 3.84, OR 28, p. 52.
7. Ukrainian SSR and Byelorussia rejoined the Organization in 1992 as Belarus and Ukraine.

25.   As previously mentioned, there is no constitutional provision concerning expulsion. Nevertheless, Article 7 might to a certain extent be involved in this connection. This article thus contains two legal bases to sanction a member: non-payment of contributions, and 'exceptional circumstances'. For many years, this article was applied, exclusively in case of arrears of contributions. For the first time, in 1964, it was proposed to use it against South Africa on the basis of 'exceptional circumstances', in this instance the racial policy of apartheid. During the Seventeenth World Health Assembly, the african delegations proposed the adoption of a resolution suspending the voting privileges of South Africa. The Assembly accepted this proposal 'considering that *apartheid* officially raised to the status of a political system by a government represents an exceptional circumstance of failure to adhere to the humanitarian principles governing the World Health Organization, and therefore makes such a government liable to the penalties provided for in the said Article 7 . . . decides to apply to the Republic of South Africa the provisions of Article 7 of the Constitution relating to the voting privileges'.[1] As a consequence South Africa immediately withdrew from the session and was no longer represented at any WHO constitutional meeting. South Africa also informed the Director-General of its withdrawal of cooperation with the Organization and no financial contribution were paid during that period. It was only after the coming into force in South Africa of a new Constitution on 27 April 1994 that the World Health Assembly rescinded Resolution WHA17.50 and decided: 'that all rights and privileges associated with full membership of the World Health Organization be restored with immediate effect to South Africa'.[2]

1. Res. WHA17.50, OR 135, p. 23.
2. *See* Res. WHA47.1, WHA47/1994/REC/1, p. 1.

26.   The potential use of Article 7 against Israel was envisaged in 1971, a process that would doubtless have led to the withdrawal of the member concerned, and possibly to that of the major contributor of the Organization, the United States. A resolution dealing with cooperation with UNRWA was adopted by the Assembly

containing an operative paragraph stating 'that the Organization should consider the application of Article 7' to Israel.[1] However, no practical action was taken. Another resolution adopted by the Assembly some years latter omitted the formal reference to Article 7 and only referred 'to appropriate action to be taken under the Constitution'.[2] This sentence implied the possible use of Article 7 against Israel.

1. Res. WHA24.33 in OR 193, p. 17.
2. Res. WHA30.37 in OR 240, p. 20.

27.   Mention can also be made, in this context, of the case of Portugal. During the 1960s, Portugal declared that it considered its overseas territories as an integral part of its metropolitan territories and this policy had met with strong criticism. In 1966, the Assembly decided to suspend 'the right of Portugal to participate in the Regional Committee for Africa . . . [and] technical assistance to Portugal'.[1] This case is important because it is the only example of suspension of WHO services being enforced under the provision of Article 7.

The following conclusions may be drawn:

(a) The refusal of the Director-General, in the absence of a specific provision in the Constitution, to consider the notifications made in 1949 by certain states as a withdrawal from the Organization was upheld by the Assembly and confirmed by practice. These members having simply resumed their participation at a later date without any formality being requested, it may logically be concluded that they had remained members of WHO during their absence. Accordingly, from a constitutional point of view, the declared withdrawal of a member not having made any reservation at acceptance of the Constitution does not affect its membership.

(b) The Assembly, which had noted 'the resumption of active participation' of four members did not state so again for the remaining others, confirming thus that they had remained members during their absence.

(c) The Assembly devised special financial terms for these states. They were described as 'not actively participating in the work of the Organization',[2] and thus designated as 'inactive Members'. Accordingly they were assessed for token payments during their period of absence.

(d) Consistently, 'inactive Members' were not deprived of the services of the Organization. Replying to a question raised on this subject, the Director-General stated that the Secretariat 'was continuing to furnish documentation, technical publications and services relating to epidemiology'.[3]

(e) However, the suspension of services in the case of Portugal raises an important question of principle: is the suspension of health services to a population truly compatible with the spirit of a Constitution which has as its objective 'the attainment by all people of the highest possible level of health'? In this connection, it should be recalled that the Director-General showed anxiety at the session of the Executive Board over the suspension of services to Portugal, particularly with regard to malaria eradication.[4] Again in 1967, at the session of the Assembly, he expressed his position as follows: 'The Director-General considers that the arrangement [for suspension of technical assistance] are to be subject to the exercise of discretion in the event of any emergency where, in his opinion, there is a serious danger to public health, or where it may be necessary to organize health relief for the victims of a calamity'.[5]

(f) In certain circumstances and depending upon the political context, a provision of the Constitution meant to deprive a Member State of specific rights could be used for the political goal of forcing that Member State to suspend its participation in the Organization.

1. Res. WHA19.31 in OR 151, p. 13.
2. *See* Res. WHA9.9 in OR 71, p. 19.
3. *See* OR 28, p. 364.
4. *See* EB39/min/374.
5. *See* OR 160, p. 100 and OR 161, pp. 515–518. Such an attitude was echoed by succeeding Directors-General of WHO when faced with similar situations.

§3. RIGHTS AND OBLIGATIONS OF MEMBER STATES

28. Membership, besides the right to participate fully in the activities of the Organization and to benefit from its services, also entails the acceptance of the obligations stipulated in the Constitution and the fulfilment of the objective of the Organization. The most important obligation relates to the payment of an equitable share of the Organization's expenses as expressly mentioned in Article 56 of the Constitution. Non-compliance with this constitutional obligation may lead to the enforcement of the sanctions contained in Article 7. There are also some other obligations for a member such as the obligation to implement regulations adopted by the Assembly,[1] as well as the reporting obligations laid out in Articles 61 to 65. These specific requirements are, in fact, part of the overall obligation that each state accepts when it becomes a member of the WHO and which is enshrined in the Preamble to the Constitution which stipulates that: 'Governments have a responsibility for the health of their peoples which can be fulfilled only by the provision of adequate health and social measures'. As it was underlined when the Constitution was drafted, each Member has to be 'able to carry out its obligations'.[2]

1. *See* Articles 21 and 22.
2. OR 2, p. 69.

Chapter 2. Associate Members and Territories

29. Article 8 of the Constitution provides that territories or groups of territories 'which are not responsible for the conduct of their international relations may be admitted as Associate Members by the Assembly upon application made on [their] behalf . . . by the Member or other authority having responsibility for their international relations'. The inclusion of such a provision in the Constitution dates back to the time when some non-self-governing territories were members of the International Office of Public Hygiene (OIHP) and were also parties to the International Sanitary Conventions. It would have been improper not to have permitted such territories to continue their participation in the new Organization. The determination of the nature and extent of the rights and obligations of these associate members was left to the Assembly and was settled at its first and second sessions.[1] They fully participate in the activities of the Organization, but, generally, do not enjoy the right to vote. No application for associate membership was made until 1950. The first admitted, as associate member was Southern Rhodesia at the request of the United Kingdom. Further applications followed.[2]

1. Res. WHA2.103, OR 21, p. 55.
2. For instance Morocco, Tunisia, Sudan, Gold Coast, Sierra Leone, Mauritius, Qatar and Papua New Guinea. Most of them became members at their independance. At present there are only two associate members: Puerto Rico and Tokelau.

30. Territories or groups of territories which are not associate members may also become involved in the work of the Organization. Article 47 of the Constitution provides that they 'shall have the right to be represented and to participate in regional committees' with the exception that they will have no vote in plenary meetings.[1] These rights and obligations are subject to consultations between the members in the region concerned and the authority having responsibility for the international relations of these territories. For years, the participation of these territories took place through the member responsible for their international relations. It is only in 1989, that, for the first time, the Governments of the United Kingdom and China made simultaneous declarations permitting Hong Kong to be represented and to participate in its own name in the Regional Committee for the Western Pacific.[2] Soon after, the same procedure was undertaken with respect to Macao. After the transfer of these territories to China, they continue to enjoy separate representation at the regional level. It should also be noted that, on the same basis, Palestine participates in the Regional Committee for the Eastern Mediterranean.[3]

1. *See* Res. WHA2.103, *supra*.
2. Declarations contained in letters dated 16 August 1989 from the two permanent missions addressed to the Director-General (unpublished). This privilege was 'noted' by the Regional Committee of the Western Pacific in September 1989.
3. *See* Res. EM/RC40/R2.

Part III. Structure

Chapter 1. The World Health Assembly

31. Chapter V of the Constitution deals with the Assembly. It contains fourteen articles, which cover three main questions.

§1. Composition

32. The Constitution provides that the Assembly 'shall be composed of delegates representing Members'.[1] However, these delegates are not the only component of the Assembly, which also includes representatives and observers.

  1. Article 10.

I. Delegates

33. Each member is entitled to send a delegation to attend sessions of the Assembly. A delegation is composed of delegates properly so-called, whose number is limited by the Constitution to three. They may be accompanied by an unlimited number of alternates and advisors, which results in certain delegations being extremely large, some exceeding 30 persons, while others may consist of a single delegate.

34. Because of the technical nature of the work of the Organization, the Constitution requires that delegates be 'chosen from amongst persons most qualified by their technical competence in the field of health, preferably representing the national health administration of the Member'.[1] No rigid interpretation of this requirement has been applied over the years, and, in particular, it has not been thought necessary that a delegate should be a medical doctor. Moreover, this constitutional requirement applies only to delegates and not to alternates and advisors. In general, delegations are either designated by Ministries of Health or by Ministries of Foreign Affairs to ensure that their members have the knowledge necessary to cover all the items discussed during the session, some of which fall outside the field of health.

  1. Article 11.

II. Representatives

35.   Under that qualification different categories of persons are subsumed. In accordance with Article 8 of the Constitution, associate members are entitled to appoint representatives to attend the Assembly. As in the case of delegates, these representatives 'should be qualified by their technical competence in the field of health' but, in addition, they 'should be chosen from the native population'.[1] The Executive Board also sends representatives to participate in the work of the Assembly as provided for in the WHA Rules of Procedure.[2] At present, four such persons represent the Executive Board at the Assembly; its Chairman is designated *ex officio* together with three others members of the Board.[3] Representatives of the United Nations and of other intergovernmental and non-governmental organizations admitted into relationship with the Organization[4] also participate in the work of the Assembly.

1. Article 8.
2. WHA Rule 44.
3. Res. EB59.R7, OR 238, p. 5.
4. *See* Rule 19 of the WHA Rules of procedure. About 70 NGOs attend the Assembly.

III. Observers

36.   Unlike delegates and representatives, observers are not mentioned in the Constitution. Reference is made to them, however, in specific cases, in the Rules of Procedure. But it is mainly the practice that has created and developed the concept of observers. Two categories of observers may be identified: the observers invited for a limited period, on the one hand and the 'quasi-permanent observers' on the other.

37.   The first category relates to potential members of the WHO. Initially, only the states which had signed but not accepted the Constitution could be invited as observers. In 1952, upon proposal of the Secretariat, it was extended by the Assembly to the states which had submitted an application for membership (Rule 3 of the WHA Rules). It was felt that the presence of such an observer during the discussion on its country's admission would not only be a timely gesture towards the applicant, but would also facilitate representation of the new member following admission and indeed, the practice confirms that former observers take on the role of delegates once their countries become members of the Organization. As a general principle, except in the case of those whose international status was controversial, all the applicants have been invited to attend the Assembly by the Director-General, on the basis of Rule 3.

In the same category are observers representing 'non-Member States' mentioned in WHA Rules 19 and 47.

38.   Besides these observers, who are supposed to be invited for a brief period of time, also so-called 'quasi-permanent observers' exist, that is, certain bodies which are regularly invited to all sessions of the Assembly. This practice is now well established and has given rise to a new category of observers not provided for in texts. At present, five observers are regularly invited by the Director-General to attend sessions of the Assembly: the Holy See, the Order of Malta, the International Committee of the Red Cross, the International Federation of Red Cross and Red Crescent Societies, and Palestine. A subtle distinction is made between these observers which becomes apparent in the list of participants where the Holy See appears under 'Observer for a non-Member State', the three following observers under 'Observers' and the last one, Palestine, under 'Observers invited in accordance with Resolution WHA27.37'.

39.　The Holy See was invited for the first time in 1949, to participate in the Second Session of the Assembly. The fact that this Assembly had been convened in Rome is perhaps related to the issue of such an invitation. Indeed, the Holy See was not invited to another session until 1953. Since then it has been invited to every session of the Assembly.

40.　The situation is, however, clear in the case of the Order of Malta, which appears under the heading 'Observer'. In a letter dated 19 December 1962 addressed to the Director-General the Order requested to be invited to all meetings of the governing bodies of the Organization.[1] This request raised complex problems. In what capacity should the Order be invited? As an observer of a non-Member State? As a representative of an international organization? As a representative of a non-governmental organization? None of these options were acceptable either to the Director-General or to the Order. An *ad hoc* solution had to be found. On his own initiative the Director-General decided to invite the Order subject to two restrictions: invitations would be limited exclusively to meetings of the Assembly; and only for items dealing with 'matters of particular concern' to the Order. Today only the former restriction is in force and the Order has been invited since 1963 to send observers to sessions of the Assembly.

> 1. This request was not the first one. Between 1950 and 1952 the Order had made several attempts to join the Organization.

41.　A slightly different situation existed concerning the two other observers, the ICRC and the International Federation, both of which had been admitted 'into official relations with WHO'[1] as non-governmental organizations (NGOs) and, as such, were each invited to send a representative to sessions of the Assembly. Their representatives were seated alongside those of other NGOs. The ICRC, having obtained the status of observer at the United Nations in 1990 approached the Director-General and expressed the wish to be transferred into the category of 'Observer'. In 1995, the Director-General assented to that request. Three years later, the same decision was taken concerning the International Federation of Red Cross and Red Crescent Societies.

> 1. This type of relation will be described later *infra*.

42.　In the light of this practice the following conclusions may be drawn regarding these 'quasi-permanent observers', the case of Palestine being put aside for the time being.

(a) Except in the case of the 'Observer for a non-Member State', i.e., the Holy See, for which a legal basis might be found in the Rules of Procedure, there is no clear legal instrument confirming the right of the other three observers to attend sessions of the Assembly. The situation is purely based on practice.

(b) The Director-General always considered that, by analogy with the provision of Rule 3, he was vested with a discretionary-power[1] to issue an invitation and to include limitations therein.

(c) In all of these examples, the Director-General did not consult the Assembly but decided on his own.

(d) It is extremely significant that the Director-General, when issuing invitations, has deliberately avoided making any reference to 'observers status'. These observers are invited on a regular basis, but *de jure* the status of permanent observer has never existed in the WHO, this status existing only *de facto*.

1. The fact that the Holy See was not invited between 1950 and 1952 confirms that assumption.

43.   The case of Palestine is an entirely different matter. In 1974, on the basis of UN General Assembly Resolution 3118 (XXVIII), the Assembly adopted a resolution requesting the Director-General 'to take the necessary steps to invite the representatives of the national liberation movements recognized by the Organization of African Unity or by the League of Arab States to attend the meetings of WHO in an observer capacity'.[1] The Director-General complied with that request and invited a number of liberation movements to the following session of the Assembly, five of which attended. However, over the years, their number decreased, and since 1994 only the PLO, referred to as 'Palestine' since 1989 was invited on that basis. This example is particularly instructive for a number of reasons. It constitutes the only case, within the WHO, of the Assembly intervening in the creation of a category of observers. In this specific case, the Director-General is not vested with a discretionary-power as he is for the other observers, but has to comply with the request of the sovereign body. Moreover, such a precedent suggests that when political issues arise in connection with the granting of the status of 'quasi-permanent observer', such a matter will not be dealt with by the Director-General alone but will be dealt with by the Assembly as indeed was the case in the situation related below.

1. Res. WHA27.37, *supra*.

44.   In 1997, three Governments, by letters addressed to the Director-General, requested the inclusion of a supplementary item to the Assembly's agenda entitled: 'To invite the Republic of China (Taiwan) to participate in the World Health Assembly as an Observer'.[1] These proposals were submitted to the General Committee of the Assembly for its consideration. It decided, by consensus, to recommend to the Assembly not to include such an item in its agenda. After an acrimonious debate, the Assembly decided to follow this recommendation. The following year, a similar request was presented by five governments.[2] The General Committee formulated the same recommendation, which was likewise approved by the Assembly. A similar process was repeated the following years with the same result.[3] In January 2002, a proposal was presented to the Board, responsible as explained later for the preparation of the provisional agenda of the Assembly, to include such an item in the WHA provisional agenda. The Board decided that this proposal should not be considered.[4]

1. Honduras, Nicaragua and Senegal. *See* Doc. A50/GC/2.
2. *See* Doc. A51/GC/2.
3. For the year 2001 *see* Doc. A54/GC/2.
4. *See* debates in EB109/SR/1 and EB109/SR/10.

§2. OPERATION

45. According to the Constitution, the Assembly 'shall meet in regular annual session'.[1] Since 1950 and mainly for financial reasons, a number of attempts have been made to introduce biennial Assemblies rather than annual sessions. These proposals have, so far, not been retained and, since the first Assembly convened in 1948 a regular yearly session has been held. At each annual session the Assembly, in accordance with the Constitution,[2] selects the country or the region in which the next session shall be held, the Board subsequently fixing the place. In the first years of the Organization's existence, the opinion was frequently expressed that its Assemblies should be held in different parts of the world so as to permit members to gain knowledge and experience of various health conditions. A proposal was even submitted by the delegation of India to the Assembly in 1951 recommending 'that the Director-General arrange to have alternate meetings of the Health Assembly at Geneva and at suitable places in different countries respectively'.[3] This proposal was transmitted to the Board for further study. The Board recommended that 'in view of the present financial situation, no action should be taken at the present time . . .'.[4] Nevertheless, the desirability of occasionally holding meetings of the Assembly at places other than Headquarters was reiterated and despite the reluctance of some members, the Assembly occasionally accepted invitations to meet outside Geneva.[5]

1. Art. 13. This article provides also that special sessions shall be convened at the request of the Board or of a majority of the members. So far, no special session have been requested or convened.
2. *See* Articles 14 and 15.
3. OR 35, p. 275.
4. Res. EB8.R25, OR 36, p. 7.
5. It met in Rome in 1949, in Mexico City in 1955, in Minneapolis in 1958, in New Delhi in 1961 and in Boston in 1969.

46. At its Thirty-first Session in 1963, the Board discussed the principles that should govern the holding of sessions away from Headquarters and adopted a resolution which, although reiterating this desirability, recommended that host countries should meet the total additional costs involved and that at least two successive Assemblies be held at Headquarters following any Assembly held elsewhere.[1] Following an invitation made in 1983 by the Government of Cuba, which was later withdrawn, the Board reconsidered this question. Following upon its recommendations the Assembly concluded that it was in the interests of all members to maintain the practice of holding Assemblies at the site of the Head-quarters, which it believed to be beneficial in terms of efficiency and effectiveness.[2]

1. Res. EB31.R40, OR 124, p. 22.
2. Res. WHA38.14, WHA38/1985/REC/1, p. 95.

47. In line with the Constitution, the Board determines the opening date of the session. In 1977, the Assembly decided that the Board would also fix the duration of each session.[1] During the first 30 years, the average duration of the Assembly has been seventeen days. However, with the introduction of biennial budgeting,[2] the Assembly decided to limit the duration of its sessions in even-numbered years, when there is not a proposed programme budget to consider, to two weeks, and, in odd-numbered years, to as near to two weeks as is consistent with the efficient and effective conduct of business. In practice, the duration of the Assembly has gradu-ally been reduced.

1. *Dec. WHA 30 (xvi)*, OR 240, p. 38.
2. The amendments to the Constitution introducing biennial budgeting adopted in 1973, entered into force in 1977.

48. After consideration of the proposals submitted by the Director-General, the Board prepares the Assembly's provisional agenda during its January session. The Board is the master of this preparation, but its freedom is limited by Rule 5 of the WHA Rules of Procedure which mentions a number of items that the Board, *inter alia*, shall include, such as the annual report of the Director-General, all items that the Assembly has ordered to be included, or any item proposed by a member or by an associate member.[1] Supplementary items may be added to the agenda during the session if the Assembly so decides. Although on several occasions supplementary items have been included,[2] experience has shown that the Assembly does not favour the inclusion of supplementary items and tries to limit it as far as possible, in particular when they raise sensitive issues. One of the ways to avoid the addition of an item is to consider the question under existing items. A number of examples of such a method is provided by the practice.[3] A more drastic alter-native is for the Assembly to decide not to include the item on its agenda. The most recent examples are the refusals by several consecutive Assemblies to add a sup-plementary item inviting Taiwan as an observer.[4]

1. It has to be noted however that at its 109th Session in January 2002, the Board decided not to consider a proposal submitted by five Member States to include in the provisional agenda of the Assembly an item entitled 'Inviting the Republic of China (Taiwan) to participate in the World Health Assembly as an observer'. *See* EB109/SR/1 and EB109/SR/10.
2. *See* for instance WHA37/1984/REC/2.184 or WHA39/1986/REC/2.10.
3. *See* for instance WHA34/1981/REC/3.5; WHA36/1983/REC/2.46.
4. *See* Doc. A51/GC/2.

49. At the beginning of each session, the Assembly appoints a Committee on Credentials of twelve members on the proposal of the President of the Assembly.[1] In practice, the Director-General suggests to the President a list of countries taking into account an equitable geographical distribution, i.e., selecting for each of the regions of the Organization a number of members proportionate to the number of countries included in the region. From amongst its members, this committee elects its bureau, i.e., chair, vice-chair and rapporteur. It has a duty to examine, during a private meeting, the credentials of delegates of members and representatives of associate members and to report to the Assembly thereon without delay. Credentials may be issued by the Head of State or by the Minister for Foreign Affairs or by the Minister of Health or by any other appropriate authority such as Ambassadors or Permanent Representatives. In the past it was thought that the Committee should meet at the very beginning of the session, to permit the delegates to enjoy, as soon as possible, their full rights. Unfortunately, it happened frequently that not all credentials were received by the Secretariat at the opening of the session. For that reason, the practice had to be changed and at present the committee meets on the second day. This change has resulted in fewer provisional credentials issue, credentials submitted by fax, telegrams, electronic mail or signed by the delegate himself than before and with most of the formal documents being provided in time. It had been the practice that when formal credentials replacing provisional ones finally arrived the entire committee was obliged to meet to present a new report to the Assembly. This system has also been changed and the Bureau of the Committee is empowered to recommend to the Assembly the acceptance of the formal credentials' of delegates who have previously submitted 'provisional credentials'.[2] It is not exceptional that, during the meeting of the committee difficult questions may be raised, with delegations not recognizing the credentials of some members, challenging the legitimacy of their government or expressing reservations on their participation. As a general rule, all the sensitive problems involving representation are raised at the committee level and, for instance, up until 1971, the question of China's representation had been brought before the Committee on Credentials.[3] The practice of the committee has been to note these reservations in its report to the Assembly.[4] On very rare occasions, the Assembly itself has approved credentials directly, without a committee's report. This has been the case when an important vote was imminent and the late submission of credentials left no time for the committee to consider them in the usual way.[5]

1. WHA Rules 22 and 23.
2. It is not exceptional that provisional credentials be never replaced by formal ones.
3. The position of the Committee has generally been to recall Resolution 396 (V) of the UN General Assembly previously mentioned.
4. *See* for instance WHA42/1989/REC/2.320; WHA50/1997/REC/3.233; WHA51/1998/REC/3.155.
5. *See* WHA41/1988/REC/2.71. The matter concerned was the appointment of the Director-General.

50.   Immediately after the appointment of the Committee on Credentials, during the opening meeting, the outgoing President submits to the Assembly a list consisting of 25 members to comprise with the President, *ex officio*, the Committee on Nominations. The Director-General, having regard to an equitable geographical distribution, in fact upon the informal suggestions made by the regions, generally prepares this list. As provided for in Rule 25, the role of this committee, again having regard to an equitable geographical distribution, is to propose to the Assembly nominations for the offices of President and five vice-presidents,[1] the chairman of each of the two main committees and the seventeen elected members of the General Committee. It has also to propose to each of the two main committees, nominations for the posts of the two vice-chairmen and rapporteur. It is the custom to present the Assembly with a single name per post, but it has to be noted that the text of Rule 25 is somewhat ambiguous, as 'nominations' (plural) could be read in either sense. In addition to the principle of equitable geographical distribution, a well-established practice of regional rotation exists regarding the Office of President. This principle has become a non-written rule for the last 30 years to which the attention of delegates is drawn in the first report of the committee. However, this principle, so far, does not extend to the posts of chairmen of the main committees. This question was raised at the Assembly and the Director-General underlined that there was no written agreement regarding rotation for the main committees. On his own initiative, nevertheless, he decided to ask the Executive Board to clarify the issue.[2] In the opinion of the Board it appeared that there was no practice of regional rotation regarding chairmen of the main committees, but following a review of elections to the chairmanship and vice-chairmanships reasonable geographical distribution appeared to have been respected.[3]

1. Called the 'Officers of the Assembly'.
2. WHA40/1987/REC/2.7.
3. EB81/1988/REC2.64–67.

51.   Another organ that plays a prominent part in the Assembly is the General Committee.[1] It consists of 25 members, namely, the President of the Assembly, who chairs the committee, the five vice-presidents, the chairmen of the two main committees and seventeen other members elected by the Assembly. The meetings of the General Committee are held in private unless it decides otherwise, and in this respect it is specified that only one member of delegations not represented in the committee will be authorized to attend. The General Committee is the steering committee of the Assembly. It exercises its responsibilities either in formulating recommendations or in taking decisions. Among the first type of responsibilities is the important role played by the committee relating to the agenda. It is the General Committee, in the first instance, which examines the provisional agenda prepared by the Executive Board together with any requests for the inclusion of supplementary items and formulates the appropriate recommendations to the Assembly. It also proposes to the Assembly the initial allocation to the two main committees of items of the Agenda and, if appropriate, the deferment of any item to a future Assembly. The committee is one of the key elements in the process of the election of members entitled to designate persons to serve on the Executive Board. Further to these issues for which the committee formulates recommendations, it has the authority to make independent decisions in a number of matters. It is the General Committee, for example, which may transfer items from one committee to another, which decides on the programme of work, and which, within the limits of the duration fixed by the Executive Board, decides the date of adjournment of the session. In addition to these specific functions, Rule 33(h) stipulates that the committee shall 'otherwise facilitate the orderly dispatch of the business of the session'. Practice has shown that this provision has served as a legal basis permitting the committee to deal with matters perhaps not initially provided for within the text. For instance, the committee has in the past discussed the question and subsequently proposed a resolution to the Assembly concerning the withdrawal of certain members from the

Organization.[2] It was likewise consulted when these 'inactive Members' resumed their participation.[3] It was also involved when the question of the representation of China was raised. More recently, the committee was asked by the chairman of one of the main committees to give its opinion as to whether or not the Secretariat should distribute a draft resolution, reference being made to Rule 33(h).[4]

1. A number of provision mention the General Committee mainly Rules 31, 32, 33 and also Rules 101 and 102.
2. OR 21, p. 138.
3. OR 71, p. 143.
4. WHA37/1984/REC3.9.

52. The Plenary decides on certain important items such as the admission of new members, the appointment of the Director-General, the election to the Executive Board, and considers the reports of the main committees to which, as a general principle, most of the agenda items are allocated. There are two main committees of the whole, Committee A and Committee B. The former deals predominantly with programme and budget matters, the latter with administrative, financial and legal matters. The activities of these two committees are far more important than they may appear and it is through them that most of the work of the Assembly is conducted. In addition to these two bodies, the Assembly may establish such other committees, as it may consider necessary. In turn the main committees may also set up sub-committees or other subdivisions under their own auspices.

53. The conduct of business at plenary and in committee meetings is laid down in various provisions of the Rules of Procedure. Most of them are similar to those applicable in other comparable organs within the UN system. However, certain features are distinctive to WHO and should be mentioned. At plenary meetings, a majority of the members represented at the session constitutes a quorum. In committees, the presence of only one-third of members is required to start the discussions, but the presence of a majority of delegates is necessary for voting.

54. The WHA Rules provide that, when two or more proposals are moved, the Assembly shall first vote on the one deemed by the chair to be furthest removed in substance from the proposal first presented and then on the proposal next removed there from and so on.[1] This rule, which is different from the Rules of the UN General Assembly and the comparable rules of other agencies, which call for voting in the chronological order of presentation, requires the determination of the proposal 'first presented', not an easy task for the Chair and the Secretariat.[2]

1. WHA Rule 68.
2. An application for membership has been so considered as the 'first presented' proposal in the meaning of the Rules.

55. Provision is also made for the Assembly to vote on any matter by secret ballot.[1] Such a vote has to be requested by a delegation and the decision to vote by secret ballot has to be adopted by a show of hands. If so adopted, no other mode of voting may be requested or decided upon. There is no definite pattern in the use of the secret ballot on questions other than elections. Practice shows that secret ballot is requested for 'sensitive questions' such as admission to membership of a contested applicant[2] or similar matters of a political nature.[3] Normally, a simple majority is required for the adoption of a decision. Exceptionally a two-thirds majority is required for questions considered as important either by the Constitution itself (adoption of conventions or agreements, approval of agreements bringing the Organization into relation with the UN and inter-governmental organizations and agencies, amendments to the Constitution),[4] or by the Rules of Procedure (decisions on the amount of the effective working budget, suspension of the voting privileges and services under Article 7 of the Constitution).[5]

1. Except on budgetary questions *see* Rule 78.
2. OR 210, p. 243.
3. OR 234.574. Also WHA32/1979/REC/3.337; WHA35/1982/REC/3.234; WHA42/1989/REC/2.226.
4. Article 60.
5. Rule 72.

§3. ROLE

56. Broadly speaking, one can say that, within the frame of the Constitution, the Assembly has the power to do whatever it deems appropriate to achieve the objectives of the Organization. Article 18 of the Constitution enumerates thirteen functions, some of which are redundant. The Assembly's main responsibility which contains all the others, is 'to determine the policies of the Organization'. Apart from this overriding purpose, it is important to mention that the Assembly possesses important elective functions. It appoints the Director-General and designates the members entitled to send a person to serve on the Executive Board. Another extremely important responsibility is its supervision of the Organization's financial policies, which includes the power to review and approve the general programme of work and the proposed programme budget. The Constitution offers the Assembly several means through which it can fulfil its role. Most, not to say the quasi-totality of the decisions of the Assembly, are taken under Article 23 of the Constitution which gives it the 'authority to make recommendations to Members', such recommendations taking generally the form of 'resolutions', but may also appear under the name 'decisions' when they relate to the adoption of certain reports, appointments and procedural matters.[1] But, by whichever name they are known, decisions, recommendations, resolutions, are, from a constitutional perspective, 'recommendations' under Article 23 of the Constitution. These 'recommendations', in spite of the fact that they are not legally binding, play an important role in the Organization's functioning and have, over time, undergone a remarkable development. Besides these 'recommendations', the Assembly has two other methods at its disposal, both of which, opposite to the previous one, are of a binding nature. Under Article 19 of the Constitution the Assembly has the authority to adopt conventions or agreements on health matters. The other method is provided for in Article 21 of the Constitution, empowering the Assembly to adopt regulations in certain specific fields. The normative functions of the Assembly will be reviewed in Part VI.

1. *See* Res. WHA30.50, OR 240, p. 30.

Chapter 2. The Executive Board

§1. COMPOSITION

57. The Board is composed of 32 persons who may be accompanied by alternates and advisers. It initially consisted of eighteen persons, its size having progressively increased. During the drafting of the Constitution it was suggested that the size of the Board should not be too great, in order to ensure its efficient working while realizing the 'equitable geographical distribution' stipulated in Article 24. The selection of the members of the Board is rather peculiar. The Assembly first elects the members 'entitled to designate a person to serve on the Board', and those members, in turn, appoint to the Board 'a person'. The first stage in this process, the election of a 'Member', confirms that the Assembly takes into account regional criteria and elects, for each region, a number of states more or less proportional to the total numbers of members included in the region.[1] In the second stage of this process, the appointment of a 'person' by the member elected, the Constitution requires that the person appointed be 'technically qualified in the field of health'. The practice shows that this requirement is generally complied with in the case of the member of the Board. It is more flexible regarding the alternates and advisors.[2] These members are elected for three years, partial renewal being made every year to ensure a staggering. This process of selection has historical origins. The drafters of the Constitution did not want the members of the Board to exercise their powers 'as representatives of their respective governments' but wished them to serve in their personal capacities.[3] In this regard, the very language of Article 24 which designates by the name of 'persons' who are members of the Board, compared with the language of Article 10 which designates by the name of 'delegates' who are members of the Assembly is particularly significant.[4] This clearly recognized the fundamental principle which remained untouched for years and an attempt was made to amend Article 24 in giving the members of the Board the status of 'government representatives' which was flatly rejected by the Assembly[5] thus confirming the personal nature of Board membership. In fact, this 'dogma' was found difficult to apply and a number of situations were not entirely consistent with the personal capacity of Board members. The fact that the five permanent members of the UN Security Council were quasi-permanent members of the Board was not in line with the demand that the Board members serve in their personal capacities. The *de facto* rotation between the regions which had been followed over the last twenty years with regard to the post of Chairman of the Board is also not really compatible with this demand. But the determinant factor was the transformation that occurred in the very nature of the Board. It was becoming obvious that a large number of Board members did in fact act as government representatives and therefore the principle was no longer being respected. A radical change occurred in 1998 when the Assembly decided that members of the Board should, from then on, act 'as government representatives'.[6] How did such a change come into force and what were the legal techniques employed to bring it about? In theory the simplest way to change the status of the Board's members would be to amend the Constitution, but such an option was not realistic. Experience has shown that the entry into force of an amendment requires several years. Obviously, it was necessary to find a faster way. Most opportunely, it was noted that a discrepancy existed between the English and the French versions of the second sentence of Article 24 of the Constitution, the former using the word 'person', the latter, the word 'délégué'. Article 24 thus required clarification and it fell to the Assembly, under Article 75, to provide interpretation which it did by deciding that members of the Board would act as government representatives.[7]

1. Current distribution: Africa 7; Americas 6; South-East Asia 3; Europe 7; Eastern Mediterranean 5; and Western Pacific 4.
2. Nevertheless, the validity of the appointment of a non-technical alternate has been questioned, *see* EB38/Min.4.
3. *See* OR 1, p. 72.
4. In this respect, *see also* Articles 18(b) and 67(b).
5. *See* OR 28, p. 165.
6. Res. WHA51.26, WHA51/1998/REC/1, p. 29.
7. The only known scholarly contribution on the question of the status of EB members is C.H. Vignes, 'mythe et réalité: le statut des membres du conseil exécutif de l'organisation mondiale de la santé', in 103 *Revue Générale de Droit International Public*, No. 3, 1999, pp. 685–696.

§2. OPERATION

58.   The principles governing the operation of the Board are found partly in the Constitution but mainly in the Rules of Procedure of the Board. Normally, the Board meets twice a year, once in January for about ten days, and again, for less than two days, immediately after the Assembly.[1] Its agenda is drawn up by the Director-General in consultation with the Chairman and contains a certain number of items ordered by the Assembly or the Board itself, or proposed *inter alia* by a member of the Board, by a Member State or by the Director-General. The meetings are public unless the Board decides otherwise. The Board elects its officers, namely a Chairman and three Vice-Chairmen from among its members each year at the session after the Assembly. The regional rotation principle applicable to the President of the Assembly does not officially apply to the Chairman of the Board[2] but current practice shows that such a rotation, while not systematic, in practice takes place. The Board may establish such committees as it may deem necessary. Thus, the Board has created three main committees: one dealing with the programmatic matters (the Programme Development Committee), the other dealing with administrative and financial matters (the Administration, Budget and Finance Committee), and the third aimed at improving financial oversight (the Audit Committee), each of which are convened just before the January session of the Board. In addition to these main committees, the Board frequently convenes temporary working or drafting groups during its sessions.

1. Special sessions may also be convened.
2. *See* EB80/1987/REC/1, p. 41.

59. The rules followed by the Board concerning the conduct of its business and for voting are similar to those used at the Assembly, with some differences such as the quorum, which demands the presence of two-thirds of its members. As in the Assembly, the Board adopts decisions and resolutions most often by consensus. However, there are two particularities peculiar to the Board regarding participation. The Director-General invites the members of the Board, and sends also invitations to the members, associate members and to the intergovernmental organizations usually invited to the Assembly, but he does not invite the 'quasi-permanent observers' whose mention was previously made. Moreover, Rule 3 provides that 'If any matter of particular concern to a State Member or an Associate Member or to a non-Member State is to discussed at any meeting of the Board, the Director-General shall give adequate notice thereof to the State or Associate Member concerned so as to enable that State or Associate Member, if it so desires, to designate a representative who shall have the right to participate without vote in the deliberations thereon . . .'. This rule is frequently applied. In general practice, the notion of 'particular concern' has been interpreted as applying to questions directly affecting the member concerned in its individual relations with the Organization which, for example, may include its financial contributions,[1] invitations to hold a session of the Assembly away from Headquarters,[2] questions relating to the sitting of a regional office or its transfer from one country to another,[3] or discussions relating to the Tchernobyl incident[4] to mention only a few examples. Certain Member States have expressed dissatisfaction with the limits imposed by the Rules to participation of Member States not represented on the Board. Acknowledging this concern, the Assembly, during its 54th Session in May 2001, included a supplementary item on its agenda and adopted a resolution requesting the Board 'to conduct a review of its working methods and those of its subsidiary bodies in order to ensure that they are effective, efficient and transparent, and to ensure improved participation of Members States in its proceedings, including working groups and drafting committees'.[5] In response to this request, the Board, at its 109th Session in January 2002, established an open-ended working group to review its working methods and make recommendations to the Board.

1. Chile was invited when its assessment was reviewed. *See* EB/41/SR/3.
2. *See* for instance EB25/Min/8 Rev.1 Invitation to hold the Assembly in New Delhi, India was invited.
3. For instance for the Regional Office for the Eastern Mediterranean EB64/1979/REC/1.75.
4. *See* EB87/1991/REC/2.5 and 186.
5. Res. WHA54.22, WHA54/2001/REC/1, p. 35.

§3. ROLE

60. Article 28 of the Constitution lists a number of the Board's functions which are complemented by several rules and provisions from other sources. From the reading of Article 28, the role of the Board appears to be mainly of a technical nature. It prepares the work of the Assembly and gives effect to the decisions and policies of the Assembly. As a preparatory organ, the Board not only prepares the provisional agenda of the Assembly, but also considers proposals for Assembly

resolutions on technical matters.[1] This role is particularly important in respect of
the budgetary process and the general programme of work. It also has to submit
a nomination for the post of Director-General to the Assembly. As an executive
organ, the Board is responsible for implementing the Assembly's decisions. In
addition to these powers, it may on its own initiative submit advice or proposals
to the Assembly and has the specific competence to take emergency measures in
order to deal with events requiring immediate action such as epidemics and health
relief to victims of calamities. Over the years, in addition to the technical aspects
of its work the Board has become more and more political in nature. Today it is
impossible to ignore the importance of its role in the adoption of the Organization's
budget. How to disregard the political responsibility of the Board when preparing
the agenda of the Assembly given that the inclusion or non-inclusion of an item and
the title given to it may be of the essence, particularly when 'sensitive' questions
are at issue? And finally, how would it be possible to ignore the political role of
an organ that is undoubtedly the determining factor governing the choice of the
Director-General of the Organization? It is appropriate to examine the process of
the nomination of the Director-General at this stage.

1. Res. WHA44.30, WHA44/1991/REC/1, p. 26.

61. The pertinent provisions concerning the nomination of the Director-
General are to be found in the Constitution,[1] in the Rules of Procedure of the
Board[2] and the Assembly[3] and in several resolutions and decisions of both organs.
Until 1953, there was no precise directive fixing the modalities of the nomination
of the Director-General by the Board except the succinct sentence contained in
Article 31 of the Constitution. In 1953 it was decided that the Board during its
meeting should establish a list of candidates from amongst which a name would
be selected.[4] However a number of Member States were not satisfied with this
system and in 1974, the rules were amended to improve the process, in particular
in requesting that each candidature should be accompanied by a *curriculum vitae*
which would be distributed to Board members on the opening day of the session,
the nomination itself taking place some days later. But again, this system was considered as unsatisfactory, none of the EB members knew the name of the potential
candidates for the post of the Director-General until the meeting of the Board. More
precise and coherent procedures were needed extending the range of sources for
nomination for the post and establishing more detailed rules on the nomination
process within the Board. Accordingly, in 1996, the procedure was again modified.
It may be summarized as follows. Six months before the session at which the
nomination takes place, all Member States and the members of the Board are
invited to send candidatures and *curriculum vitae* to the Chairman of the Board,
which must be received at least two months before the opening of the session.
These candidatures and attached documents are circulated amongst the Board
members one month before the opening. So, it is expected that each Board member
be duly informed before the opening of the session. During the session, and in the
light of the practice provided by the only precedent of 1998, the nomination process
can be divided into three main phases, each of them taking place during a private
meeting. The first meeting consists of an initial screening of the proposals and the

drawing-up of a short list limited to five candidates.[5] During the second phase, the Board interviews each of the candidates on the short list. Each interview, limited to 60 minutes, is equally divided between an oral presentation and a question-and-answer period. The third phase is the nomination of a candidate by secret ballot from amongst the candidates on the short list. The changes which have been highlighted, related particularly to the capacity of the members and the political responsibilities of the Board, demonstrate a considerable increase in its role, increase which, most probably, will not stop at this stage.

1. Art. 18, 31.
2. Rule 52.
3. Rules 108 to 114.
4. Res. EB11.RA47, OR 46, p. 18.
5. *Dec. EB100 (7)*, EB100/1997/REC/1, p. 8.

Chapter 3. The Secretariat

§1. THE DIRECTOR-GENERAL

62. The appointment process has already been described in detail. What we have to consider now are the profile and calibre that the incumbent of the post is expected to possess and the duties that the Director-General has to accomplish. In 1996, the Board decided that any candidate for the post should fulfil a number of criteria: qualification and experience in international public health and organizational management, proven leadership, good physical condition and sufficient skill in at least one of the official and working languages.[1] Suggestions had been made to fix an age limit for the candidates, but this attempt was unsuccessful.[2] Since its establishment, five persons have occupied the post.[3] All of them have been initially granted a five year term, but until recently there was no limitation related to the number of successive terms. It was only in 1996 that the Assembly decided to amend its Rules of Procedure to specify that the term of office shall be five years renewable once only.[4]

1. Res. EB97.R10, EB97/1996/REC/1, p. 10.
2. Such a limitation does not exist in any of the organizations in the UN system.
3. Dr. Brock Chisholm (Canada) 1948–1953; Dr. Marcolino Gomes Candau (Brazil) 1953–1973; Dr. Halfdan T. Mahler (Denmark) 1973–1988; Dr. Hiroshi Nakajima (Japan) 1988–1998; Dr. Gro Harlem Brundtland (Norway) 1998–2003; Dr. Jong-Wook Lee (Republic of Korea) 2003–.
4. WHA Rule 108.

63. The Constitution stipulates that the Director-General is 'the chief technical and administrative officer of the Organization'. Broadly speaking all the administrative decisions are taken by the Director-General. Functions of an administrative nature may be delegated, and most of the time they are not exercised personally by the Director-General, but on his behalf. In addition, the Director-General represents the Organization and is the person to whom all business concerning it should be addressed. The Director-General is also vested with responsibilities of a political nature which, unlike his administrative duties, may demand direct action by him. The Director-General's competence extends far beyond what is laid down in official texts. He exerts remarkable influence and the Organization's prestige rests to a great extent upon his personality and charisma. The position occupied by the Director-General is somewhat unique. He must understand the workings of the Organization inside out, be in constant liaison with its various constituents including in particular governmental representatives, and act as the 'go-between' when disputes arise, while at the same time maintaining a strictly neutral role. The

Director-General also has an important influence in relation with the meetings of the constitutional bodies of the Organization. His role concerning the preparation and the participation in the meetings has already been mentioned. But during the meetings themselves his weight is essential. He may 'at any time'[1] make an oral statement[2] which made at an opportune time may change the conduct of the debates and have an important effect on the attitude of the delegations. The Director-General's influence has been especially marked in debates concerning the budget of the Organization when he used the 'supreme weapon', his own political responsibility, for the purpose of obtaining a favourable vote.[3] This political responsibility cannot be found in any written text but devolves from the way the Director-General carries out his duties. Depending upon the calibre of the highest figure in the Organization, this political role may be huge, but it may also be modest.

1. WHA Rule 56; EB Rule 19.
2. It happened once that the Chair following a proposal for the closure of the debate deprived the Director-General and the Legal Counsel, on behalf of the Director-General, of this right. In response to further request for a statement, the Chair reiterated the ruling WHA33/1980/REC/ 3.258. Such an interpretation of the rules appears inconsistent with the right to make a statement 'at any time'.
3. *See* for instance OR 161, p. 417.

§2. THE STAFF

64. The entire staff of the Organization under the authority of the Director-General constitutes the Secretariat which is the third organ of the Organization within the meaning of Article 9 of the Constitution.

65. In 2001, the Secretariat comprised around 3,500 staff members holding fixed term appointments of one year or more. More than one-third were in the professional category and the remainder in the general services. In addition, there is a large number of staff holding short-term contracts or other categories including consultants and professional and general services staff. The Organization remains committed to achieving the goal of gender parity within the next decade. The proportion of women in the professional category has increased from 20 per cent in 1990 to more than 30 per cent.[1] Using the formula adopted by the Assembly,[2] the recruitment of professional staff normally applies the principle of geographical distribution, keeping in mind nevertheless that, under Article 35 of the Constitution 'The paramount consideration in the employment of the staff shall be to assure that the efficiency, integrity and internationally representative character of the Secretariat shall be maintained at the highest level'.

1. The proportion varies from approx. 37 per cent in the Americas to approx. 22 per cent in Africa.
2. Res. WHA50.15, WHA50/1997/REC/1, p. 12.

66. The functions of the Secretariat may be considered from two different perspectives. Some of them appear as autonomous activities. The Secretariat is in charge of the management of the Organization. The task may not always appear to be of great importance but it is indispensable. More than 2,000 new files are registered annually and more than 35,000 letters a year reach the Organization. The correspondence and files are dealt with by the Secretariat. The Secretariat centralizes the notifications and information related to diseases in the frame of its surveillance programme and of the international health regulations and circulates this information. Further autonomous activities will be discussed in due course. The Secretariat also has functions related to the activities of the constitutional bodies, mainly the Assembly and the Board but also conferences convened by the Organization. Within that framework, the Secretariat prepares the meetings, sends invitations, drafts the documents, circulates them, and prepares the 'briefings'[1] which will be used during the meetings. It is in charge of the logistics of the meetings, seating, interpretation, and material arrangements. Besides this visible role, certain members of the Secretariat have an underground activity before and during the meetings. They may have a certain influence in the selection of the officers, in the preparation of the draft resolutions and in the manner the business is carried out. The Secretariat is responsible for the records of the meetings, verbatim for the plenary, summary for the committees. The Secretariat is in charge of the execution of the decisions taken by the constitutional bodies. After the meetings, it dispatches the final version of the documents adopted by the meeting, and of course, takes the appropriate measures to implement those decisions. All the elements which have been provided show that the nature of the Secretariat has evolved considerably since the creation of the international organizations and that at present, the Secretariat is certainly no longer the 'understrapper' which certain diplomats considered it was during the League of Nations period. Undoubtedly, the quality of the Secretariat, which in turn is directly related to the quality of its leader, is a key factor on which the performances and the success of the Organization depend.

1. In the jargon of the Secretariat, a briefing is an internal document that contains the possible scenario of the meeting, including the various options that may exist.

Chapter 4. Regional Arrangements

67.   As has been already explained the regionalization has a historical origin. An entire chapter of the Constitution is devoted to the subject. The first article in this chapter[1] gives the Assembly the responsibility to define 'geographical areas' in which a 'regional organization' is to be established.

    1. Article 44(a).

§1. GEOGRAPHICAL AREAS

68.   The Constitution is rather concise regarding the conditions under which these geographical areas may be defined and one of the main tasks of the first Assembly was to clarify them. The first problem was to delineate the areas. It was not an easy task in the absence of any pertinent directives regarding the number of areas to be established as well as the group of countries that should be included in each area. On what basis should these areas be delineated? As a result of an inquiry made with governments, it appeared that, in addition to the continental groupings which were generally mentioned, a number of other factors should be retained such as the standard of health of the countries to be included, the epidemiological situation in the area and the existence of permanent foci of epidemics. In the light of these suggestions and using a document prepared by the Secretariat,[1] the Assembly delimited six geographical areas: Africa, the Americas, South-East Asia, Europe, Eastern Mediterranean and Western Pacific. The delineation did not follow a strict rule. For the Americas, it was the entire continent. The European area included the whole of Europe. The African area included all areas of Africa south of the 20 degree N. parallel of latitude. Other areas were simply defined by the countries they contained. A quick look at these regions shows that they differ as to their surface, population, prevalent health problems, economic development and number of countries included in each region. Nevertheless, in spite of this pragmatic approach, and except for some changes in individual assignments of countries to regions, there has been no fundamental revision of the geographic areas as defined by the first Assembly. However, that possibility could not be disregarded as the Board recalled in a study made several years ago. The Board stated that 'the present six regions . . . are not necessarily permanent', and in particular that 'the present geographical areas of WHO could be altered if this would lead to better local and regional coordination'.[2]

    1. OR 5, p. 75.
    2. OR 46, pp. 160–172.

69.   After the original delineation of geographical areas, another problem was to assign the different countries to the regions so defined. Successive Assemblies carried out this task. Once again there was no guiding principle. The Assembly recognized 'the necessity of determining rules and criteria which permit the assignment of Members States, Associate Members and territories or groups of territories to the geographical areas determined . . .'. It is for this reason that the Assembly requested the Board, in close collaboration with the Director-General, to undertake a thorough study of that matter.[1]

The Board proposed two different options to the Assembly. Both of these options took into account similar factors such as the wishes of the state, its geographical position, the similarity of health problems, economic aspects, administrative consideration and arrangements made by other international organizations. However, in the first case, it was stated that the wishes of the state 'shall be paramount', in the second that they 'be considered'.[2] In the presence of these contradictory proposals, the Assembly ruled not to decide and stated, in a rather peculiar manner, that the establishment of rules and criteria 'shall be deferred . . . [and] that, in the meantime, the assignment . . . shall be decided upon by the . . . Assembly on the lines hitherto adopted'.[3] In practice the deciding factor is the wish of the country concerned as is demonstrated by the examples of initial assignment to, or subsequent transfers from, a region. In 1949, Greece, though it had been initially included in the Eastern Mediterranean area, expressed the wish to join Europe, and so this was done.[4] Indonesia, originally listed in the Western Pacific area was included in the South-East Asia area, upon its request.[5] Bangladesh, which as part of Pakistan was included in the Eastern Mediterranean Region, was assigned after its independence to the Region of South-East Asia.[6] More recently, Ethiopia left the Eastern Mediterranean for the African Region,[7] Algeria was transferred to the African Region,[8] Israel was transferred from the Eastern Mediterranean Region to Europe, Morocco was transferred in the opposite direction, and Mongolia was transferred from South-East Asia to the Western Pacific.[9] In order for a transfer to take place, a request must be addressed to the Director-General by the member concerned. After consultations with the regional committees concerned, a specific item is included on the agenda of the Assembly and the Assembly adopts a resolution resolving that the country 'shall form part' of the region.[10] Even though the final authority rests with the Assembly, practice shows that the latter has never hindered a country in transferring from one region to another. This system led to some peculiar situations. For example the inclusion of the Democratic People's Republic of Korea (North) in South-East Asia and of the Republic of Korea (south) in the Western Pacific, the inclusion of Algeria in Africa and Morocco in Eastern Mediterranean, of Syria in the latter region and Israel in Europe. It seems clear that in certain situations, the determining factor may be of a political nature.

1. Res. WHA5.43, OR 42, p. 31.
2. Res. EB11.R51, OR 46, p. 21.
3. Res. WHA6.45, OR 48, p. 34.
4. Res. WHA2.96, OR 21, p. 53.
5. Res. WHA3.118, OR 28, p. 71.
6. Res. WHA25.22, OR 201, p. 10.
7. Res. WHA30.35, OR 240, p. 19.

8. Res. WHA37.12, WHA37/1984/REC/1, p. 6.
9. Res. WHA38.1 and 39.1. The transfer of Israel to Europe is the final result of a complex situation that began in 1950 when Israel could not, in fact, participate in the Regional Committee for the Eastern Mediterranean as its presence would have led to the refusal of the other members to participate.
10. Res. WHA49.6, WHA49/1996/REC/1, p. 6.

§2. REGIONAL ORGANIZATIONS

70.   Article 44(b) states that 'The Assembly may, with the consent of a majority of the Members situated within each area so defined, establish a regional organization to meet the special needs of such area'. For the sake of rationalization and efficiency, the Constitution specifies that there shall be no more than one regional organization in each area. The Assembly instructed the Board to establish regional organizations in accordance with the delineation decided upon within each of the six regions,[1] which was carried out between 1949 and 1952. Apart from the Americas which will be examined separately, all the regions are organized in a similar manner. Each regional organization consists of a regional committee and a regional office.

1. Res. WHA1.72, OR 13, p. 330.

I. Regional Committees

71.   The Regional Committee is composed of representatives of the members and associate members 'in the region concerned'. A complex problem of interpretation occurred regarding the meaning of these words during the first years of the Organization as a result of the presence of numerous colonial territories in most regions. The countries exercising responsibility for those territories considered that, in accordance with Article 47, they should be recognized as members 'in the region concerned'.[1] An opposite view, expressed in particular by the USA, was to consider that only the countries having their seat of government in the region should be entitled to participate in the regional committee. Eventually a compromise was reached and the Assembly adopted a resolution according to which 'for the purposes of Article 47 of the Constitution, States Members in a region shall be deemed to be those States Members having their seat of government within the region', it being understood that 'those Members not having their seat of government within the region, which (a) either by reason of their Constitution consider certain territories . . . in the region as part of their national territory, or (b) are responsible for the conduct of the international relations of territories . . . within the region, shall participate as Members of the regional committee . . . with only one vote for all the territories . . .'.[2] In addition to these representatives, territories or groups of territories within the region that are not responsible for the conduct of their international relations and are not associate members shall have the right to be represented and to participate in regional committees within the terms of Article 47 of the Constitution. As already explained, it is under this provision that Hong Kong and Macao participate in the Regional Committee for Western Pacific, and Palestine enjoys the same privilege in the Regional Committee of the Eastern Mediterranean.

1. *See* OR 21, Annex 24.
2. Res. WHA2.103, *supra*. It has to be noted that these provisions were not applicable in the region of the Americas.

72.   The regional committees usually meet once a year, generally in the autumn. They have their own rules of procedure that are similar and contain the same basic elements as the Rules of Procedure of the Assembly. The functions of the regional committees are specified in Article 50 of the Constitution. Beyond these constitutional powers, the regional committees play an important consultative role regarding the budgetary process as will be related in more detail further on. It is also during the regional committee that informal discussions take place to select the officers of the next Assembly, who are chosen on a regional basis as already mentioned. Moreover, it is at the regional level that the countries 'entitled to designate a person to serve on the Board' are chosen in practice. Accordingly the importance of the regional committees and, more generally of the regions, should not be underestimated as it is at the regional level and in the field that the essential part of the activities of the Organization is conducted.

II. Regional Offices

73.   The second organ of the region is the regional office. Unlike the location of the Headquarters of the Organization which, under Article 43 of the Constitution, is determined by the Assembly, there is no specific provision regarding the site of the regional office. It may be recalled nevertheless, that the first Assembly resolved that the Board should be instructed to carry out the establishment of regional organizations. On the basis of these provisions, the initial sites of the six regional offices have been fixed by resolutions of the Executive Board,[1] following the recommendation of the Regional Committee concerned. To facilitate coordination within the UN system, and in accordance with Article XI of the Agreement between the United Nations and WHO, the selection of the site has been made following consultation with the UN. For years, and with the exception of the reassignments mentioned above, the regions remained practically unchanged. In particular the location of the regional offices was not questioned with the exception of that for the Eastern Mediterranean (*see infra*).

1. *See* Res. EB9.R37 (Brazzaville); EB7.R48 (Washington); EB2.R29 (New Delhi); EB14.R17 (Copenhagen); EB3.R30 (Alexandria now Cairo); EB8.R8 (Manila).

74.   The regional office is led by the Regional Director. As part of the staff of the Organization, the staff of the regional office do not present specific characteristics and are submitted to the rules and regulations normally applicable. Article 52 of the Constitution deals with the appointment of the Regional Director. An earlier version of this article stated that 'the appointment of the Regional Directors would be made by the Regional Committee, with the approval of the Board'.[1] After

lengthy discussions, the initial text was replaced by the present text which reads as follows: 'The head of the regional office shall be the Regional Director appointed by the Board in agreement with the regional committee'. In the earlier version the main responsibility belonged to the regional committee. In the present one, the main responsibility rests with the Board. This deliberate change was made to accentuate the role of the Board in the selection process. However, in reality the selection process is carried out exclusively at the level of the regional committee. Since the beginning of the Organization, without any exception, the candidate presented by the regional committee has always been appointed by the Board. Nevertheless, this practice has been questioned on occasion. In 1956, it was suggested that the regional committee should submit all the candidatures for the post to the Board. When consulted by the Director-General, four regional committees expressed themselves against such a proposal and two reached no clear conclusion. Consequently the Board, decided that it was 'not necessary to make any changes in the practice followed so far'.[2] In 1962, the Regional Committee for Europe suggested a procedure by which there would be advance nomination of candidates, thus granting the representatives an opportunity to assess their qualifications in advance. It was also suggested that more than one candidate should be presented to the Board. In a report submitted in 1964 to the Board, the Director-General stated that: 'Since it appears from the text of Article 52 . . . that its framers intended the major responsibility for decision to rest with the Executive Board, it would appear reasonable that the Board request Regional Committees normally to submit the names of more than one candidate . . . so as to permit the Board to exercise its responsibilities of making the appointment'.[3] In its resolution[4] the Board requested the regional committees 'to consider the suggestions contained therein'. Only one of them, the Regional Committee for Western Pacific, decided to modify the process accordingly. The change was only temporary and in 1979, the committee returned to the previous system. In 1987, the matter was brought up again at the Board and was discussed throughout 1987 and 1988 in the regional committees, in the Board and in the Assembly. The proposal was made to give the Director-General a more important role in establishing criteria for the post of Regional Director and to create a search committee to assist the regional committees in their selection. The Regional Committee for Europe, which amended its rules of procedures in 1990, as well as that for Africa, accepted those proposals. The practice of presenting a single name to the Board remains unchanged and in the selection process the role of the Board is only to appoint the candidate presented by the regional committee.

1. OR 2, p. 63.
2. Res. EB23.51. OR 91, p. 24.
3. OR 88, Annex 5.
4. Res. EB33.R42, OR 132, p. 23.

III. The Advisory Opinion of 22 December 1980

75.   In this regional context, it is appropriate to examine a serious crisis within the Organization, which was raised by the request to transfer the Regional Office

for the Eastern Mediterranean. In May 1979, due to political problems within the region increased by the signing by Egypt and Israel of the Camp David Agreements, a majority of members of the Eastern Mediterranean Region expressed the wish that the regional office be transferred from Alexandria to another state in the region. Meanwhile, the question had also been placed on the agenda of the Assembly during its annual session. The question was referred to Committee B, which considered that such a decision needed studying and recommended that the Executive Board undertake the study. The Assembly adopted the recommendation of the committee. In compliance with the request of the Assembly, the Board in turn appointed a working group for the purpose of reporting to the next session of the Board.[1] The report of the working group covered all aspects of the matter including the question of the Host Agreement with Egypt and more particularly the applicability of Section 37 related to the revision of the Agreement, and considered that it was not in a position to make a decision on that point. The report stated that 'the final position of the Organization on the possible discrepancies of views will have to be decided upon by the Health Assembly'. Accordingly, the Board transmitted the working group's report to the Assembly for consideration and decision.[2] The Assembly considered the question in May 1980.

1. EB65/1980/REC2.254.
2. *Dec. EB65(10)*, EB65/1980/REC/1, p. 24.

76.   The resolution eventually decided, pursuant to Article 76 of the Constitution, to submit to the International Court of Justice for its Advisory Opinion the following two questions: '1) Are the negotiation and notice provisions of Section 37 of the Agreement of 25 March 1951 between the World Health Organization and Egypt applicable in the event that either party to the Agreement wishes to have the Regional Office transferred from the territory of Egypt? 2) If so, what would be the legal responsibilities of both the World Health Organization and Egypt, with regard to the Regional Office in Alexandria, during the two-year period between notice and termination of the Agreement?'.[1]

1. Res. WHA33.16, WHA33/1980/REC/1, p. 13.

77.   On 22 December 1980, the Court delivered its Advisory Opinion.[1] After having described the factual and legal background to the submission of the request and recognized its competence to deliver the opinion, the Court considered the meaning and implications of the questions on which it was asked to advise. One of the points was whether a transfer of the seat of the regional office was covered or not by the provisions of the 1951 Agreement which to a large extent deals with privileges, immunities and facilities. Another was to determine whether the provisions of Section 37 relate only to the case of a request by one or other party for revision of provisions of the Agreement or are also apt to cover its total revision or outright denunciation.[2] Having regard to the differing views expressed in the Assembly, it appeared to the Court that the true legal question submitted to it was not the one formulated by the Assembly, but the following: 'What are the legal principles and rules applicable to the question under what conditions and in accordance with what modalities a transfer of the Regional Office from Egypt may be

effected?' In answering the question, the Court first noted that the right of an international organization to choose the location of its headquarters or its regional office is not contested. Whatever view may be held on the relevance and the applicability of the 1951 Agreement, the Court found that certain legal principles and rules were applicable in the case of such a transfer. By the mutual understandings reached between Egypt and the WHO from 1949 to 1951, a contractual legal régime was created between the two parties that remains the basis of their legal relations (on the modalities of the conclusion of such a regime, *see infra* Part IV, paragraph 106). The very fact of Egypt's membership in the Organization entailed certain mutual obligations. Egypt offered to become host to the regional office and the Organization accepted that offer. Egypt agreed to provide the privileges, immunities and facilities necessary for the independence and effectiveness of the office. As a result, the legal relationship was that between a host state and an international organization, the very essence of which is a body of mutual obligations of co-operation and good faith. What are these mutual obligations? They consist of: a) consultation in good faith as to the question under what conditions and in accordance with what modalities a transfer may be effected; b) if a transfer is decided upon, consultation and negotiation regarding the arrangements needed to effect the transfer in an orderly manner and with a minimum of prejudice to the work of the Organization and the interests of Egypt; c) the giving of reasonable notice by the party wishing the transfer. It follows from the foregoing that the Court's reply to the second question was that the legal responsibilities of the two parties during the transitional period would be to fulfil in good faith the mutual obligations which the Court had set out.

1. *Interpretation of the Agreement of 25 March 1951 between the WHO and Egypt, Advisory Opinion, ICJ: Reports 1980*, p. 73.
2. Section 37 reads as follows: The present Agreement may be revised at the request of either party. In this event, the two parties shall consult each other concerning the modifications to be made in its provisions. If the negotiations do not result in an understanding within one year, the present Agreement may be denounced by either party giving two years' notice.

78. During its next session, in 1981, the Assembly considered the Advisory Opinion. After lengthy debates, it was decided to request the Director-General to initiate discussions with the Government of Egypt.[1] The Personal Representative of the Director-General conducted negotiations in November 1981 and in March 1982. A report was presented to the Board and then to the Assembly requesting the Director-General and Egypt to continue their consultations. The Assembly adopted identical resolutions during its sessions in 1983 and 1984. Following this session, the item was removed from the agenda.

1. Res. WHA34.11, WHA34/1981/REC/1, p. 9.

IV. The Special Arrangements (PAHO)

79. The regional arrangements are normally similar in all the regions of the Organization. However, certain particularities exist which result from the presence of pre-existing regional structures at the time the Constitution was drafted. These

peculiarities have to be examined in this regional context. Two regional health agencies were concerned when, in 1946, the WHO was established: the Pan Arab Regional Health Bureau at Alexandria, which was the far-off successor of the Egyptian Quarantine Board, and the Pan American Sanitary Organization, renamed later Pan American Health Organization (PAHO). It was essential to determine what the relations would be between these regional mechanisms and the newly established WHO. The Technical Preparatory Committee had not been able to resolve the problem. For this reason it proposed to the Health Conference two alternatives: the first favoured a system whereby the regional bodies would be absorbed and would form an integral part of the Organization, so bringing about the 'integration' of these bodies within a single administrative structure – the second was in favour of a flexible attitude allowing the conclusion of special arrangements with the regional structures 'with a view to their facilities and services being utilized to the fullest possible extent as regional office of the Organization'.[1] The situation of the Bureau in Alexandria did not raise any problems and it was ultimately integrated within the regional organization of WHO for the Eastern Mediterranean Region.[2]

1. OR 1, p. 73.
2. Res. EB3.R30, OR 17, p. 16.

80. The real difficulty was over the Pan American Sanitary Organization, and the question of the relationship between the two organizations was a difficult issue that the Health Conference had to settle after lengthy debates. With a view to devising a formula generally acceptable, a special committee of sixteen members was established which proposed a compromise solution. This was finally adopted by the Conference and became Article 54 of the Constitution, whose pertinent part reads as follows: 'The Pan American Sanitary Organization represented by the Pan American Sanitary Bureau and the Pan American Sanitary Conferences . . . shall in due course be integrated with the Organization. This integration shall be effected as soon as practicable through common action based on mutual consent of the competent authorities expressed through the organizations concerned'. On the base of this provision, an agreement was negotiated and concluded between WHO and PAHO in May 1949. According to the agreement, the Pan American Sanitary Conference, through the Directing Council of PAHO and the Pan American Sanitary Bureau, shall serve respectively as the Regional Committee and the Regional Office of WHO for the Americas. The Director of PAHO assumes the post of Regional Director of WHO for the Americas. Some other peculiarities should be noted. The budget of PAHO contains two components, the most important one provided by PAHO and the other by WHO. The staff also have a double origin: there are PAHO staff and WHO staff. It should be noted that until some years ago, the membership of PAHO was not identical to that of the WHO Region for the Americas[1] (AMRO). Taking into account these differences, one might wonder whether or not the 'integration' referred to in the article has been fully implemented. In this respect, the views which were expressed when Article 54 was discussed are extremely relevant. In particular, the delegate of Canada (who later became the first Director-General of WHO) said: 'The real point . . . lay in the definition of the word "integrate", and he thought that it should be clear in the record that the meaning of the word was the first dictionary meaning of "making it whole" or "entirely becoming part of a single organization" '.[2] The official records go on in mentioning that the delegation of Canada took the position that, in the absence of a clear understanding on this point, it could not sign the Constitution.[3] The official records mention in conclusion of the debates on that Article: 'There being no objection to the definition of "integrate" given by the delegate of Canada, the Chairman put Article . . . to the meeting, and declared it unanimously approved'.[4] Would it not be possible to conclude that the Conference has endorsed the definition of 'integration' given by Canada? Whatever the answer to this question may be, it must be noted that the question remained unclear, at least in the minds of a number of people. The problem of integration was again raised after the adoption of the Agreement with PASB (PAHO). The Board considered that the conclusion of the Agreement did not yet constitute 'integration' in accordance with the Constitution of WHO[5] and a statement to this effect was made by the Director-General in his letter of 24 May 1949 to the Director of PASB. The Director-General stated that: 'the adoption of this initial Agreement, although representing a further step in the implementation of Article 54 . . . does not yet constitute "integration" in accordance with the Constitution'.[6] In the light of these elements it seems reasonable to consider that in spite of the fact that a great number of steps have been taken under Article 54 of the WHO Constitution towards integration, the full integration has not yet been totally realized. That situation was elucidated by the Legal Counsel of the Organization in his oral arguments before the International Court of Justice in the case concerning Interpretation of the Agreement between the WHO and Egypt.[7] It is a similar position that the special group established by the Board to review the Constitution adopted when it observed: 'that integration between the two organizations had not proceeded to the extent that WHO and PAHO constituted a single entity. Nevertheless . . . WHO and PAHO were to a large extent functionally integrated'.[8]

1. Indeed Canada was a member of AMRO, and not a member of PAHO.
2. OR 2, p. 60.
3. *Ibid.*
4. *Ibid.*
5. OR 14, p. 12.
6. OR 21, pp. 308 and 383, Annex 12, Appendix 2. On that question *see also* WHO OR 248, p. 580; EB/1981/REC/2.361–363 and EB101/1998/REC/2.68.
7. *ICJ Pleadings, Interpretation of the Agreement of 25 March 1951 between the WHO and Egypt*, pp. 278 *et seq.*
8. Doc. EB/Constitution/4/5 §10. *See also* EB/101/1998/REC/2.68.

Chapter 5. Non-statutory Bodies

81. All the organs which have been reviewed so far were foreseen in the Constitution. The presentation of the Organization would, however, remain incomplete if no mention was made of a peculiar subsidiary body which has been created within the framework of the competence of the Health Assembly but for which provision was not initially made in the Constitution, namely, the International Agency for Research on Cancer (IARC).

82. The origin of IARC lies in the growing interest by a number of French scientists who rallied the support of the French President, Charles de Gaulle. He rallied in turn the support of the *Union internationale contre le cancer* (UICC) and WHO in the early to mid 1960s to promote research and training in carcinogenesis and cancer control. Five countries, namely, France, Germany, Italy, the United Kingdom and the United States, discussed, at a number of meetings held between 1963 and 1965, the prospects and modalities for creating a forum for international cooperation on cancer research. The main alternatives appeared to be either the creation of a research programme within WHO or the establishment of a dedicated international organization. Both alternatives, however, presented a number of disadvantages if seen in isolation, especially since just a few developed countries were actively interested in the issue. In particular, integration with WHO risked hampering a strong research programme by 'diluting' it within a more diversified organization, while the idea of an entirely new organization seemed excessive in comparison with the scope of the activities envisaged.[1]

1. The policy considerations underlying the establishment of IARC are reviewed in C.H. Vignes, 'Le centre international de recherche sur le cancer', XIII *Annuaire Français de droit international*, 1967, pp. 531–544.

83. Consequently, the sponsoring states, after consulting with the Director-General, proposed to the Eighteenth World Health Assembly a draft statute which struck a compromise between the aforementioned alternatives. The Statute of IARC was unanimously adopted on 20 May 1965 by Resolution WHA18.44 and entered into force on 15 September 1965 in accordance with its Article XI, upon notification to the Director-General by the five founding countries of their undertaking to observe and apply the provision of the Statute.[1]

1. The Statute is annexed to Resolution WHA18.44, in OR 143, p. 26.

84. The agency was established pursuant to Article 18(l) of the Constitution – recalled in the preamble of Resolution WHA18.44 – which empowers the Health

Assembly 'to establish such other institutions as it may consider desirable'. It is, consequently, a subsidiary institution of WHO and, as such, under its overall authority and deriving its international legal status from that of its parent organization. At the same time, the Health Assembly purposely granted to IARC a remarkable degree of independence in view of its nature as a scientific research institution. It is thus a hybrid institution, in which the links with WHO and the latter's power of control are counterbalanced by a certain autonomy in order to safeguard its independence and objectivity as a scientific research agency. These elements also characterize the modalities of its establishment, through a statute sharing some of the characteristics of an international treaty and at the same time those of a constitutive resolution of the Health Assembly.[1] It should also be stressed that the delegation of authority[2] which WHO has made in favour of the agency has to be seen, and finds its general limits, within the context of WHO's Constitution and competence. In other words, IARC cannot do more than WHO, otherwise the Health Assembly would have, by creating the agency, amended the Constitution without respecting Article 73 thereof.

1. *See* C.H. Vignes, *supra* 533.
2. The Health Assembly has tacitly delegated to IARC, in the area of cancer, the functions that the Organization can carry out under Article 2(n) of the Constitution.

85.   IARC is open to participation (the statute purposely avoids the term 'membership') of all WHO Member States which notify the Director-General accordingly. Such a notification is subject to a decision by the Governing Council that the candidate is able to contribute to the work of the agency. No deposit of a formal instrument is required. Also in this case, therefore, the procedure is in part similar to that of admission to a separate organization and in part to that of admission to a subsidiary organ of an existing organization. As of September 2002, IARC had sixteen Participating States.[1] Participating States may withdraw, pursuant to Article XIII of the statute, through a simple notification to the Director-General. Argentina and Brazil had joined the Agency in 1998 but withdrew at the end of 2000 due to financial difficulties. Also Israel, admitted in 1966, withdrew in 1971. The withdrawal of Argentina and Brazil raised the question of the disposition of their unpaid contributions, and whether they would still be responsible for them should they wish to join IARC again.

1. Australia, Belgium, Canada, Denmark, Finland, France, Germany, Italy, Japan, the Netherlands, Norway, the Russian Federation, Sweden, Switzerland, the United Kingdom and the United States.

86.   The choice of Lyon, France, as the Agency's headquarters stems from the French origin of the initiative, and also from the fact that Lyon was close to Geneva and easily accessible by public transport. The agency currently employs around 270 staff from 39 countries.[1] The status of the agency in France is regulated by a host-country agreement and a related exchange of notes concluded between that country and WHO, endorsed by IARC's Governing Council and approved by the Health Assembly in 1967.[2] Under the agreement, France undertakes to grant IARC most of the customary facilities, privileges and immunities enjoyed by organizations of the UN system. WHO thus remains, in principle, responsible for the international

legal relations of IARC. This consideration is strengthened by the fact that, under Article XVIII of the Agreement, the Director-General has primary authority for waiving the immunities of IARC's staff, and that disputes arising from IARC's activities will be settled by WHO and France under Article XXI.

1. Information about IARC, its activities and publications are available on its web site at: <www.iarc.fr>.
2. Resolution WHA20.25, in OR 160, p. 15. The agreement is reproduced in *ibidem*, p. 88.

87. IARC's structure comprises a Governing Council, a Scientific Council and a Secretariat. The Governing Council is the policy-making body of the agency. Its membership includes all Participating States as well as, *ex officio*, the Director-General. The inclusion of the Director-General as representative of the parent organization stresses the hybrid character of IARC. The Director-General has full rights of participation, except for decisions of a financial nature, on the admission of new Participating States, and on the amendment of the Statute which are for obvious reasons reserved to states. The Governing Council, *inter alia*, approves the programmes of the agency, adopts the budget and exercises financial oversight, selects the Director and decides on the size of the Secretariat. It is, consequently, a fully-fledged governing body with authority that largely transcends that of a subsidiary organ of an international agency.

88. The Scientific Council is IARC's expert body and focuses its functions on the evaluation of its scientific programmes and projects and on proposing new activities, for approval by the Governing Council. It is composed of independent experts, appointed by the Governing Council upon proposal by the Director-General, who serve for a non-renewable four-year term. Article VI of the statute foresees a membership of up to twenty, and to date, the Governing Council has followed the practice of appointing one expert from each Participating State.

89. The status and management of IARC's Secretariat also reflect the hybrid nature of the agency. Article VII of the Statute envisages a director, as executive head with broad technical and administrative responsibilities, as well as technical and administrative staff. The appointment of the director of the agency is in part election and in part nomination, since he/she is selected by the Governing Council and appointed by the Director-General who, as a member of the Council, also participates in his or her selection. At the same time, it is the Governing Council and not the Director-General that sets the terms for the director's tenure. Article VII provides that IARC's staff shall be appointed in a manner to be agreed upon between the director and the Director-General. In practice, both the director and the members of the secretariat are WHO staff, subject to the WHO Staff Regulations and Rules even though the staff report to the director as administrative authority.

90. As indicated in Article I of the Statute, IARC's objective is to promote international collaboration in cancer research. As such, IARC arguably represents the main activity by WHO in the area of research. Article II of the Statute spells out this objective into three main functions: (i) the collection and dissemination of information on cancer epidemiology and research as well as on the causation and prevention of cancer; (ii) support of cancer research projects; and (iii) education and training of personnel for cancer research. The activities of the agency, as required by the Statute, include a programme of permanent activities, financed from the regular budget, as well as special projects which are financed from other sources, mainly from donations, grants and contracts as well as from a special fund established by the Governing Council.

91. The main source of financing for the agency and its programme of permanent activities consists of contributions assessed annually from Participating States. The agency operates on a biennial budget basis; the budget for 2002–2003, approved in May 2001, is at the level of around USD34 million.[1] Unlike WHO which follows a scale of assessments similar to that of the United Nations, IARC's budget is financed as follows: 70 per cent is financed by equal contributions of each Participating State. The remaining 30 per cent is paid through a system of units based on a scale depending on the percentage of the WHO's budget contributed by each Participating State. Thus, the share of the budget for each Participating State will be between 5.31 per cent and 9.88 per cent for 2002–2003. This system aims at striking a compromise between an emphasis on equality among its members and the consideration of their financial capabilities, particularly with a view to attracting new Participating States. Pursuant to Article VIII.5 of the Statute, a Participating State in arrears for an amount exceeding its assessed contribution for the preceding financial year loses its vote in the Governing Council.

1. Governing Council Resolution GC/42/R9, unpublished.

92. In this connection, the Council has adopted an exceptional course of action concerning the Russian Federation, affected in recent years by financial difficulties. Faced with growing arrears and no realistic prospects of regular payments, the Governing Council first offered the Russian Federation the possibility of paying its arrears accrued until 1998 in a number of instalments, while at the same time waiving the loss of right to vote.[1] Since this offer did not prove acceptable to the Russian Federation, the Council, in order to avoid the withdrawal of such an important country, agreed on an exceptional basis to suspend temporarily its 'active participation', as a consequence of which that country would not participate in the work of the agency but would also not be assessed annual contributions.[2] This decision was based on the precedent of the suspension of participation in WHO by the Soviet Union, Belarus and Ukraine.[3] Although the Russian Federation does not participate in the meetings of the governing bodies, and therefore cannot influence the programme of activities or the budget, some of its institutions continue to participate in IARC's scientific programmes.

1. Resolution GC/39/R13 of May 1998, in *Handbook of Resolutions of the Governing Council of the International Agency for Research on Cancer* (16th edition, Lyon, IARC, 2001), p. 129.
2. Resolution GC/40/R3, May 1999, in *ibidem*.
3. *See supra*, Chapter 2.

93. IARC also relies heavily on various sources of voluntary contributions, including donations from individuals, as well on financing from outside sources in the form of grants and collaborative contracts. The Governing Council, moreover, has established a Governing Council Special Fund, financed in part through voluntary contributions by Participating States. Through this fund, the Council finances short-term projects, in particular feasibility studies for long-term projects to be financed from the regular budget, as well as other items such as upgraded instrumentation for the Agency's laboratories.

94.   The funds and assets of the Agency are deposited with WHO and treated as trust funds under its Financial Regulations. At the same time, pursuant to Article VII of the Statute, IARC has authority to administer them pursuant to financial regulations adopted by the Governing Council. The Financial Regulations provide that the corresponding WHO regulations shall by default govern the financial policies, practices and administration of the Agency except as provided in the Statute and in IARC's Financial Regulations. Such a cross-reference raises delicate issues in case WHO's Financial Regulations are substantially amended in areas not covered by IARC's Statute or Financial Regulations. This could result in the application to the Agency of aspects of financial management which are not considered relevant or appropriate. In such a case, the Governing Council may have to amend its Regulations.

Part IV. Relations of WHO

Chapter 1. Relations with States

95. WHO's relations with states are partly structured around the obligations deriving for the latter from their membership in the Organization, and partly from a web of agreements. These agreements define and regulate the status of WHO in the jurisdiction of the states concerned, with particular regard to its privileges and immunities, and/or are concerned with the activities of the Organization in those countries. The two areas may be combined in a single agreement, for example those concluded with the host country of a project office. The present Chapter will focus on those agreements that regulate the status of the Organization, in particular the Convention on the Privileges and Immunities of the Specialized Agencies, the host-country agreements concluded by WHO, as well as the so-called 'basic agreements'.

96. The WHO Constitution, like most constitutive instruments of comparable international organizations, only contains in Articles 66 to 68 very general provisions on the status of the Organization. Article 67, in particular, echoes the long-standing principle of functional necessity, by linking the privileges and immunities to be enjoyed by the Organization and individuals connected with it to what is necessary 'for the fulfilment of its objective' or 'for the independent exercise of their functions'.

97. Besides the Constitution, the Convention on the Privileges and Immunities of the Specialized Agencies (hereafter the General Convention)[1] is the main multilateral instrument regulating the status of WHO *vis-à-vis* its Member States. While a commentary of the provisions of the General Convention is beyond the scope of the present essay, it should be noted that the Health Assembly, pursuant to Section 36 of the Convention, adopted at its first session Annex VII modifying the standard clauses of the Convention with respect to WHO.[2] The Annex was revised three times between 1950 and 1958[3] to extend its scope to persons serving on expert advisory panels and to the high officials listed in its paragraph 4.[4]

---

1. Adopted by the UN General Assembly on 21 November 1947 (Resolution 179 (II)) and by the First World Health Assembly on 17 July 1948. UNTS, Vol. 33, p. 261.
2. OR, 13, p. 332.
3. By Resolutions WHA3.102, WHA10.26 and WHA11.30, respectively.
4. For the text of the Annex, *see infra*, Annex 2.

98.   As of July 2002, 107 Member States have acceded to the General Convention with respect to WHO, and have thus accepted Annex VII either in its original form or as revised. Several states filed reservations at the time of accession. Many reservations concern the granting to the specialized agencies, pursuant to Section 11 of the Convention, of treatment not less favourable than that accorded to governments for their official communications. Part of the difficulties encountered by states parties in complying with these obligations derive, curiously, from the position adopted by the International Telecommunication Union, which has expressed its opposition to privileged treatment for specialized agencies in matters of communications.

99.   A special mention should be made of the case of France. The proximity of the Headquarters of WHO to the Swiss-French border have led many WHO officials (as well as those of the other organizations headquartered in Geneva) to establish their residence in France. At the same time, France has not concluded any host-country agreements with the agencies concerned and neither was it, for a long time, a party to the General Convention, to which it acceded only on 2 August 2000. Consequently, besides the broad provisions of Article 67 of the WHO Constitution and the corresponding articles of the constitutions of the other Geneva-based agencies of which it is a member, until recently France had accepted no general conventional obligations concerning the treatment of those specialized agencies and its officials. Notwithstanding this apparent legal vacuum, France treated WHO officials resident on its territory roughly in accordance with the provisions of the General Convention; in particular, it did not levy income taxes on salaries and emoluments paid by WHO, allowed the purchase by officials enjoying diplomatic status in Switzerland of duty-free cars to be issued with a special series of licence plates, and issued residence permits.

100.   However, around 1993, some officials of specialized agencies residing in France started receiving requests from French tax authorities for the payment of income taxes on the salaries paid by their organizations. This request obviously raised concern among Geneva-based organizations, which took a number of steps with the French Ministry of Foreign Affairs and obtained a suspension of the procedure instituted by the tax authorities pending consultations. The request was based on the consideration that there was no applicable international agreement justifying a tax exemption for the officials of specialized agencies, thus making them fall under the general regime applicable to French residents. In October, France announced that it would have acceded to the General Convention with a number of reservations. Prominent among them would have been a reservation under which France would have taxed the 'international' income of officials, while at the same time granting them a tax credit equivalent to the amount paid by them to their organizations under the staff assessment system. Through this device, there would have been no tax exemption for staff of specialized agencies, but at least double taxation would have been partially avoided.[1] The agencies concerned, including WHO, noted that such measures would have been inconsistent with the generally accepted principles on the privileges and immunities of international organizations, as reflected in the relevant provisions of their constitutions. Furthermore, that reservation would have introduced an inequality of treatment between staff of the specialized agencies and those of the United Nations, in view of the fact that France had acceded to the Convention on the Privileges and Immunities of the United Nations without reservations. Such inequality of treatment would have been at variance with the concept of the UN common system and was expressly excluded under Article VI, Section 19(a) of the UN General Convention. The agencies cast doubts on the compatibility of the planned reservation with the object of the General Convention and, consequently, on the acceptability of France's plan.[2]

1. The French position is described in WHO Doc. EB95/INF.DOC/19, 26 January 1995.
2. *Ibidem.*

101. On 2 August 2000, France deposited an instrument of accession to the General Convention. That instrument was accompanied by five reservations and an interpretative declaration, as follows:

'Only property, funds and assets belonging to agencies, administered by them and earmarked for the functions assigned to them under the agreements by which they were established, and to which France has acceded, shall enjoy the privileges and immunities provided for in the Convention.

When an official of the agencies who does not have the same status as a member of the diplomatic staff under the Convention commits a traffic violation or causes a road accident, the privileges and immunities shall not apply.

The provisions of Section 11 concerning facilities in respect of communications shall not apply to the specialized agencies.

Officials employed abroad and resident in France shall be subject to the provisions of the law applicable in France with respect to entry and stay in the national territory.

The privileges and immunities, exemptions and facilities accorded to the executive head of each agency in reference to diplomatic envoys shall not be extended to any other official, except one acting on the former's behalf during his absence from duty.

The privileges and immunities of experts sent on mission to the specialized agencies shall not exceed those accorded to officials of the specialized agencies.

France shall not be bound by the provisions of Section 32 concerning the International Court of Justice, except where a prior attempt to settle the difference amicably has failed.

Interpretative Declaration (Translation) (Original: French)

In the event of a conflict between the provisions of the Convention and the provisions of the individual agreements concluded between the specialized agencies and France, the provisions of these agreements shall have precedence.'[1]

1. The text of the depositary notification is available on-line at <http://untreaty.un.org/English/CNs/701_800.asp>.

102. The reservation concerning income taxation was eventually not filed by France. At the same time, the competent French customs office has notified the agencies that, in view of the reservation limiting the granting of diplomatic status to the sole executive heads and the official acting on their behalf during their absences, France will no longer allow the other officials enjoying diplomatic status in Switzerland to purchase duty-free cars and to register them with the corresponding series of licence plates.

103. The second category of agreement regulating the status of WHO are the so-called 'host-country agreements' concluded by the Organization with countries hosting its Headquarters or regional offices. The agreement concerning the legal status of WHO in Switzerland ('Headquarters Agreement') was concluded with the Swiss Federal Council in 1948 and supplemented by an arrangement for execution and an exchange of notes. It was considered as concluded on 21 August 1948, the date of its approval by the Swiss Federal Council, but entered into force retroactively as of 17 July 1948.[1] Even though Switzerland is not a party to the General Convention, several provisions of the Headquarters Agreement reproduce verbatim its corresponding provisions.

> 1. Agreement concerning the legal status of the World Health Organization and Arrangement for the execution of the said Agreement, approved by the First World Health Assembly on 17 July 1948 and by the Swiss Federal Council on 21 August 1948, and an Exchange of Notes relating to the entry into force of the Agreement and Arrangement. Berne, 23 December 1948, and Geneva, 12 January 1949, UNTS, Vol. 26, p. 333.

104. The Headquarters Agreement is supplemented by Swiss federal and cantonal legislation and regulations, as well as by a large number of instructions and circulars clarifying or modifying particular aspects of the legal regime concerning WHO. The Swiss Government bases the treatment of the international organizations present on its territory, thus including WHO, on a number of fundamental principles. For example, Switzerland extends to the organizations and certain defined categories of senior officials the regime contained in the 1961 Vienna Convention on Diplomatic Relations. At the same time, unlike other host countries, it does not apply the restrictive doctrine of jurisdictional immunities based on the distinction between acts *jure imperii* and *jure gestionis*, which is arguably inappropriate for functional entities such as international organizations. Moreover, Switzerland applies the so-called 'most favoured organization' principle, whereby it extends to all organizations benefits granted to one of them. This device helps ensuring uniformity of treatment among organizations hosted by the same country.

105. WHO has also concluded host-country agreements for its regional offices as well as for certain representative or liaison offices, such as the Liaison Office to the European Union in Brussels.[1] These agreements were largely based on a model host-country agreement developed by the Secretariat in the late 1940s, which mostly drew on the standard provisions of the General Convention. It should be noted that neither PAHO in its own right nor WHO on its behalf have concluded a host agreement with the United States. The legal status of PAHO/AMRO is thus based on the applicable US legislation and on the rules of general international law recalled by the latter.

> 1. WHO has concluded, in particular, the following agreements related to its regional offices: Agreement between WHO and the Government of India, signed at New Delhi, on 9 November

1949. Came into force on 22 September 1949, by an exchange of notes, in accordance with Section 33. Agreement between WHO and the Government of Egypt, signed on 25 March 1951, supplemented by an exchange of notes of same date. Came into force on 8 August 1951. Agreement between WHO and the Government of the Republic of the Philippines, signed on 22 July 1951, entered into force on 29 September 1952. Agreement between the Government of the French Republic and the World Health Organization, related to the seat of the Regional Office for Africa in Brazzaville. Signed on 23 July 1952, entered into force on 29 September 1952. OR 46, Annex 4. The Congo continued the agreement after its accession to independence. Agreement between the World Health Organization and the Government of Denmark, signed at Geneva on 29 June 1955, and at Copenhagen, on 7 July 1955 Came into force on 29 June 1956.

106.   The events that led to the 1980 ICJ advisory opinion on the interpretation of the host-country agreement with Egypt, and the contents of the opinion itself, have been dealt with *supra* (Part III, paragraph 77) and will not be repeated here. A point, however, that should be mentioned here and that was raised during the written and oral pleadings concerns the conclusion and effects of the 1951 agreement on the status of the regional office. The sequence of actions and negotiations which took place at the central and regional levels of WHO between 1947 and 1951, led to the establishment and start of operation of the Regional Office in Alexandria on 1 July 1949, whereas the agreement concerning the privileges and immunities of the Organization in Egypt was only concluded on 25 March 1951 and approved by the Fourth World Health Assembly in May of the same year. This circumstance led some states to construe the 1951 agreement as extraneous to the legal establishment of the regional office, which had been completed in 1949 through an offer by Egypt and its acceptance by WHO. Consequently, the agreement would be a separate transaction concluded after the establishment of the office to provide for the privileges and immunities of WHO in Egypt. As such, the agreement would have been immaterial for the presence of the regional office in Egypt, and its removal would not have required its denunciation or entailed its termination. This view was supported by Judge Manfred Lachs in his separate opinion.[1] Proponents of the opposing view maintained that the transfer of the Alexandria Bureau to WHO and the factual establishment of the office were only a step in a complex process which was only completed with the conclusion of the 1951 agreement. The removal of the office would then have entailed the termination of the agreement, and this led to the controversial question whether Article 37 thereof provided for a right of termination. The Court was eventually able to evade this issue by reformulating the question posed by the WHA and focusing on the essence of the legal relationship established between WHO and Egypt.

1. *See* ICJ Reports, 1980, *supra*, p. 109.

107.   Finally, mention must be made of the so-called 'Basic Agreements' for the establishment by WHO of technical cooperation with its Member States, in particular with developing countries. These agreements have been concluded, since the early 1950s, on the basis of a model agreement developed by the Secretariat, while those concluded by PAHO/AMRO with countries in the American continent have followed a different model and tend to be less standardized. The model text is fairly short and streamlined. It covers the main principles concerning the establishment of technical cooperation as well as the main activities expected to be carried out by WHO; the respective obligations of the government and WHO; and the applicability of the appropriate provisions of the General Convention, including the granting of diplomatic status to the head of the WHO country office. WHO has concluded basic agreements with more than 150 Member States.

108.   The continuing utilization of a model going back to the early days of WHO, notwithstanding the many changes in the general philosophy of the Organization concerning technical cooperation, has led to a relative inadequacy and obsolescence of the model basic agreement. The most significant example is that most states simply do not provide WHO and its country offices with the services and facilities which they are in principle bound to furnish under Article IV of the agreement.[1] Another gap is that the agreement regulates in detail neither the establishment of a WHO country office nor its functions or status. Article V, moreover, states that the 'WHO Programme Coordinator/Representative' in a country should be afforded diplomatic treatment. The issue has thus arisen whether the 'liaison offices' established by WHO in several countries are 'WHO offices' and their heads 'WHO representatives' within the scope of the basic agreement. The practice of establishing liaison rather than representative offices is primarily based on financial considerations. Consequently, several liaison offices have experienced difficulties in obtaining recognition as 'WHO offices' from their respective host countries as well as in securing the application of the relevant privileges and immunities. Finally, the agreements are essentially structured around the idea that WHO's technical cooperation with Member States aims at contributing to national or local health programmes. However, it has become more visible in recent times that WHO may engage in technical cooperation programmes with governments which have a global scope and purpose, e.g., clinical trials or product development. These types of activities might not be seen as falling within the scope of the current model basic agreement and could thus run the risk of falling into a legal grey zone.

> 1. Pursuant to Article IV, for example, the host government should pay for or provide office space, equipment and supplies; transportation services within the country; and postage and telecommunications.

109.   For these and other reasons, at the request of the first meeting of WHO country representatives held in February 1999, the Secretariat is in the process of revising the model basic agreement along the lines of corresponding agreements of a number of UN programmes and funds, so as to make it more responsive to realities in the field and the changing structure of WHO's country activities.

Chapter 2. Relations with Intergovernmental Organizations

§1. GENERAL CONSIDERATIONS

110. The constitutional basis for WHO's relations with other intergovernmental organizations can be found in Articles 69, 70 and 72 of the Constitution. The proceedings of the International Health Conference do not shed much light on these provisions, besides pointing out that the Organization had been established as a specialized agency of the United Nations and that its mandate could not be pursued in isolation from other organizations which dealt with complementary or overlapping issues. Article 72 is obviously related to the question of WHO's relations with PAHO as well as the pre-existence of several international agencies, such as the International Office of Public Health, the UN Relief and Rehabilitation Administration, and the Health Organization of the League of Nations, whose functions were taken over by WHO.

111. The development of the UN system has resulted in the progressive establishment of a decentralized system resisting strong leadership or coordination on the part of the United Nations. WHO became formally a specialized agency with the conclusion in 1948 of a relationship agreement with the United Nations.[1] The agreement largely follows the pattern of relationship agreements concluded by other specialized agencies with the UN.

1. Adopted by the First World Health Assembly on 10 July 1948, OR 13, pp. 81, 321.

112. WHO has concluded formal agreements approved by the Health Assembly under Article 70 of the Constitution with some sixteen organizations besides the United Nations.[1] These organizations are mostly within the UN system, but also include the African Development Bank, the League of Arab States and PAHO. The agreements concluded with a number of specialized agencies follow a rather standardized pattern and constitute general frameworks for cooperation and to avoid overlaps or duplications. They provide the basis for the subsequent conclusion of specific and more informal arrangements, for example with regard to joint projects, and usually contain the following elements:

– A statement of mutual recognition of the respective mandates, in particular to avoid conflicts of competence;
– A commitment to consult and co-operate in matters of common interest;
– A provision on reciprocal representation, in some cases accompanied by the right to propose items for the agenda of meetings of the other organization;

– Exchange of information and documents, without prejudice to the safeguarding of confidential material;
– The establishment of joint committees to deal with questions of common interest;
– A number of provisions to avoid duplications or competitive situations, for example, in the areas of personnel and statistical and administrative services.

> 1. The texts of some of them are reproduced in *Basic Documents* (43rd edition, Geneva, World Health Organization, 2001) pp. 50–76.

113.   Besides formal agreements approved by the Health Assembly, the practice has developed for the WHO Secretariat to conclude more informal arrangements, usually in the form of memoranda of understanding or exchanges of letters. These arrangements, which are not submitted to the Assembly for approval, may constitute umbrella arrangements not unlike those just examined, for example in the case of the exchange of letters of December 2000 with the European Community.[1] In other cases, however, such arrangements regulate specific technical areas or activities and do not imply a broader co-operation.

> 1. Text reproduced in *Official Journal of the European Communities*, 4 January 2001, C 1/7–10.

114.   At a policy-making level, WHO participates in the work of ECOSOC, especially on thematic issues such as HIV-AIDS and tobacco control. In order to advocate effectively on health as the centre of poverty reduction and development, WHO has also been an active participant in the cycle of conferences convened by the General Assembly during the 1990s and the beginning of the present decade. Recent examples are the Third United Nations Conference on Least Developed Countries (Brussels, May 2001) and the special session of the General Assembly on HIV/AIDS (New York, June 2001). Within the United Nations system, WHO is also the Chair of the *Ad Hoc* Inter-Agency Task Force on Tobacco Control. The Task Force was established in 1998 by the Secretary-General to appropriately reflect both the predominant health dimension of tobacco control and the crucial importance of an inter-sectoral approach. Participants in the Task Force include UN programmes and agencies and, pointedly, the international financial institutions and the World Trade Organization.

§2. Relations with UNDP

115.   WHO has, since its inception, been an active participant in the UN system of technical assistance and cooperation to development, and its relationship with UNDP has logically been one of the linchpins of this participation. Historically, as soon as the UN Expanded Programme of Technical Assistance (EPTA) was set up, the Health Assembly authorized the Director-General to accept funds drawn from the Special Account established by the Technical Assistance Conference, subject to any conditions established by the Executive Board or the World Health Assembly.

116.   The relationship between WHO and EPTA, and subsequently UNDP, has been characterized by the search for a balance between on the one hand assertion of independence from attempts by the UN to 'dominate' and centralize the system of technical cooperation around the lead of the resident coordinator, and on the other hand an effort to cooperate with UNDP for the integration of health programmes in development activities. In this connection, the Board and the Assembly have consistently indicated that cohesiveness at the UN system level could not jeopardize WHO's privileged access to national health authorities, and that the unique regional structure of the Organization could not be sacrificed to adapt it to UNDP's structure in developing countries. An interesting example of this attitude consists in the adoption on 20 December 1977 by the General Assembly of resolution 32/197 on the restructuring of the economic and social sectors of the United Nations. The resolution established the post of Director-General for Development and International Economic Cooperation, *inter alia*, to ensure leadership to the various components of the United Nations system and to exercise overall coordination. In response to that resolution, the Executive Board at its 61st Session in January 1978 adopted Resolution EB61.R19, by which, *inter alia*, it affirmed that Resolution 32/197 implicitly recognized the constitutional responsibilities of WHO with respect to operational activities; and reaffirmed that WHO's technical cooperation with governments represent an integrated approach to the achievement of its constitutional objectives. Subsequently, by Resolution EB87.R20, the Board requested the Director-General to maintain WHO's direct and privileged access to national health authorities, as well as to reinforce WHO's cooperation with governments in the formulation and execution of national health plans and activities. It only requested the Director-General to ensure continued 'collaboration' at country level between the WHO representatives and other field representatives of the United Nations system, particularly the United Nations resident co-ordinator.[1]

1. The evolution of WHO's relationship with EPTA and UNDP is reviewed in Y. Beigbeder, *The World Health Organization*, (Dordrecht, Nijhoff, 1998), pp. 106–111 and 174–176.

117. While the percentage of UNDP funds used by WHO as executing agency has been historically limited, UNDP participates in a number of large and long-term programmes, such as the Special Programme for Research and Training in Tropical Diseases, the Cosponsored Programme on Research, Development and Research Training in Human Reproduction, and the Joint United Nations Programme on HIV-AIDS, which are reviewed below.[1]

1. *See ibidem*, p. 111.

118. The last few years have been characterized by a broad reform process within the United Nations system, largely spurred by the initiatives taken by the Secretary-General.[1] One of the central decisions in the field of cooperation for development has been the establishment of the United Nations Development Group (UNDG) as a decisive step towards overcoming the traditional fragmentation of United Nations cooperation activities while preserving the mandates of existing development actors. The grouping of United Nations programmes, funds and agencies engaged in development assistance and related activities into the UNDG, chaired by the Administrator of the United Nations Development Programme (UNDP), is meant to provide a framework for greater coherence and cooperation in United

Nations development operations. The UNDG is led by an Executive Committee chaired by the Administrator of UNDP. While only a limited number of UN programmes and funds enjoys permanent membership in the Executive Committee, other agencies may participate on a case-by-case basis as need arises. This has been the case of WHO, which joined the UNDG in July 1999 and participates in the work of the Executive Committee when the nature of the discussions warrants its presence. At the local level, WHO had participated as a member of UN teams in common country assessments – the main instrument to ensure cohesiveness at the implementation level – in a number of countries. By December 2000, WHO had participated in 110 common country assessments (CCAs) and 44 United Nations Development Assistance Frameworks (UNDAFs), and over 40 country teams had undergone joint training.

    1. *See* UN Doc. A/51/950, 14 July 1997.

§3. RELATIONS WITH UNICEF

119.   The international body with which WHO has had the closest links since its inception is undoubtedly UNICEF. The potential for both overlap and synergy between the two bodies is evident, in view of UNICEF's emphasis on maternal and child health and nutrition. As Yves Beigbeder has remarked: 'Most [of UNICEF's] programmes overlap with WHO's in the specific area of public health: fighting against diseases through immunization, assistance to maternal and child health centres, improving environmental health, family planning, applied nutrition programmes, emergency relief'.[1] The history of the relationship between the two thus alternates between fruitful cooperation and occasional rivalries.

    1. Beigbeder, *supra*, p. 176.

120.   The Health Assembly at its Third Session in 1951, spelled out, in Resolution WHA3.46, the principles guiding WHO-UNICEF's cooperation in terms that remain relevant to date: UNICEF would furnish supplies and services to governments while WHO would provide expertise both to governments and to UNICEF.[1] This division of labour has remained by and large relevant: UNICEF has, unlike WHO, developed into an operational agency with a strong fund-raising capacity, which gives it more leverage for running the more capital-intensive components of cooperation programmes.

    1. It should be recalled that, initially, WHO had the authority to approve health-related projects to be then implemented by UNICEF, in order to ensure their compliance with existing international sanitary standards.

121.   The first World Health Assembly and the Executive Board of UNICEF also established a Joint Committee on Health Policy (JCHP), composed of members of WHO's Executive Board and UNICEF's governing body, initially to co-ordinate the transfer of UNICEF's programmes to WHO in view of its intended termination. Subsequently, it became the principal mechanism to ensure coordination between the health activities of the two bodies and to determine the principles that would govern the division of labour between them. The JCHP is probably the longest-standing inter-agency committee in the UN system, with a membership elected by each governing body for an equal number of members. The terms of reference of the JCHP were revised by the Executive Board in January 1960 to reflect the positive evolution of WHO/UNICEF cooperation.[1] The Health Assembly and Executive Board have continued to review such cooperation on a biennial basis until the 1990 World Summit for Children, and annually therafter, and give directions for its development. The JCHP has been credited for steering effectively WHO-UNICEF cooperation and having been particularly influential in the development of their child immunization policy. In 1996/1997, the Executive Board of the United Nations Fund for Population Activities (UNFPA) requested the Executive Boards of UNICEF and WHO to expand the JCHP to it, since the latter's mandate covered a good part of the follow-up to the 1994 United Nations International Conference on Population and Development.[2] After a relatively prolonged negotiation of its terms of reference, the WHO/UNICEF/UNFPA Coordinating Committee on Health formally came into existence in 1999. Its membership has been expanded to sixteen members selected by the respective executive boards. WHO continues to provide the Secretariat of the Committee.[3]

1. EB Resolution EB25.R30 of 25 January 1960, in OR 99, p. 15.
2. *See* EB document EB99/22 Add.1. The Conference had given UNFPA guidance on health-related issues such as reproductive rights, gender equality and male responsibility in family-planning.
3. The chronology of the establishment of the CCH and its terms of reference are provided in EB document EB103.22.

122.   Whereas UNICEF has developed and adapted its basic philosophy to encompass 'the whole child' as the target of its action – with an emphasis on areas such as education, training and home economics and an increasing multidisciplinary coordination at the national and international levels – a relative majority of its resources have consistently been devoted to child and maternal health. While this ensures a constant synergy with WHO, it has also evidenced some problems deriving from differences in structure, budgeting and programming methods. One example during the 1960s was UNICEF's reluctance, in a number of instances, to maintain assistance to disease control programmes as complementary to the development of basic health services; another example is the different concept of regionalization between the two bodies, including the delineation of the respective regions and the more intense decentralization of programmatic authority in the case of WHO. This has on occasion lengthened negotiations between governments, WHO and UNICEF as regards the approval of plans of operation.[1] It has also been stated that WHO, usually confined to a role of expert and adviser, did not always appreciate some of UNICEF's initiatives, which normally benefit from higher media visibility than WHO's.[2]

1. *See Organizational Study on Co-ordination with the United Nations and the Specialized Agencies* (Geneva, WHO, 1987), pp. 39–41.
2. Beigbeder, *supra*, p. 179.

123.   Subject to the overall coordination of the JCHP and with the support of WHO's governing bodies, the first joint programmes of WHO and UNICEF concerned the eradication of a number of diseases, such as yaws, tubercolosis and malaria.[1] However, cooperation has gone much beyond disease-specific activities and addressed health policy-making in some fundamental areas. Possibly the most important example of such cooperation was the launching of the strategy of Health for All by the year 2000 and the emphasis on primary health care as the key to attaining that goal. The 1978 Alma Ata International Conference on Primary Health Care was in fact jointly organized by the two organizations. Both the UN General Assembly and the Health Assembly recognized that WHO and UNICEF shared the major responsibility at the international level to follow-up on the findings and recommendations of the conference. Just a few years later, the 33rd World Health Assembly endorsed the recommendations of a joint WHO/UNICEF Meeting on Infant and Young Child Feeding held in October 1979 and, *inter alia*, requested the Director-General to prepare an international code of marketing of breastmilk substitutes.[2] The code was adopted in 1981 by the 34th Health Assembly as a recommendation under Article 23 of the Constitution.[3] WHO and UNICEF have also been, together with UNDP, the World Bank and the Rockfeller Foundation, the sponsors of the Children's Vaccine Initiative (CVI), launched at the World Summit for Children in 1990. CVI was meant not as a new institution but rather a network and global think tank for vaccines and immunization for the improvement of the global supply and quality of existing vaccines.[4] The findings and priorities identified through CVI have led to the establishment in 1994 by WHO of the Global Programme for Vaccines and Immunization (GPV). UNICEF has been particularly successful in mobilizing political and financial support and has greatly contributed to the immunization programme by providing low-cost vaccines and materials for the cold chain.[5]

1. *The World Health Report 1995 – Bridging the Gap* (Geneva, World Health Organization, 1995), p. 87.
2. Resolution WHA33.32 of 23 May 1980, in WHA33/1980/REC/1, p. 32. On the code, *see infra* Part VI.
3. Resolution WHA34.22 of 21 May 1981, in WHA34/1981/REC/1, p. 32.
4. Beigbeder, *supra*, pp. 138–139.
5. *Ibidem.*

§4. Co-sponsored Programmes

124.   While the examples and instances of WHO's interaction with intergovernmental organizations are too numerous and diverse to be summarized here, mention should be made of a number of important long-term programmes co-sponsored by WHO together with other UN bodies and agencies. Such joint or co-sponsored programmes have their own system of governance and funding, and exercise programmatic authority by taking decisions which are then implemented by the WHO Secretariat based on its consent to act as executing agency. In other cases, they establish separate secretariats. They have thus raised a number of legal questions as far as WHO is concerned, especially on the authority of the Secretariat to join and implement such programmes and the need for explicit approval by the Health Assembly. Arguably, the programmes in question have a direct impact on the programme of work of WHO, and require the Secretariat to implement decisions partly taken by outside entities. They would, therefore, appear to require endorsement by the governing body with programmatic and financial authority, namely, the Health Assembly. The practice of WHO in this sense is, however, not entirely consistent.

125.   Among the most important and best-known examples of such co-sponsored programmes are the Special Programme for Research and Training in Tropical Diseases (TDR), the Special Programme of Research, Development and Research Training in Human Reproduction (HRP), the Joint United Nations Programme on HIV/AIDS (UNAIDS), the FAO-WHO Codex Alimentarius Commission and the co-sponsored programmes of *onchocerciasis* which will be reviewed in Part VI.

I. HRP and TDR

126.   These programmes share the same basic institutional philosophy and structure, even though they were established for rather different reasons. In both cases, it was felt that the need to tackle effectively the many unsolved issues in human reproduction research in developing countries and, respectively, the growing health impact of the major tropical diseases made it necessary to pool expertise, political will of the states most concerned, and financial resources of institutional donors. On this basis, the arrangement found most suitable was in the form of a programme co-sponsored and executed by WHO, governed by a steering body and almost entirely financed by extra-budgetary contributions.

127.   TDR was established in the 1970s as a result of the growing awareness that, on the one hand, the progress in biomedical sciences facilitated research in the prevention and treatment of the major tropical diseases, while on the other hand the pharmaceutical industry was not interested in investing in research on typical 'diseases of the poor'. It should be added that a number of technical problems rendered research and development activities more difficult and costly – in particular, the growing resistance of vectors and parasites to traditional treatment lines or the lack of effective and safe drugs. The Board and the Assembly had endorsed since 1975 the steps taken by the Director-General to develop the special programme. An MOU concluded in 1978 established the co-sponsored programme and defined its structure as follows:

– Cooperating parties, defined as the governments contributing to the special programme, those whose countries were most affected by the diseases in question, as well as organizations contributing to the special programme. The co-sponsors of the programme are UNDP, the World Bank and WHO, which also serves as executing agency;
– A 30-member Joint Coordinating Board (JCB), acting as the governing body of the programme. The JCB decides upon the planning and execution of the programme, approves the plan of action and the budget and exercises financial and programmatic oversight. The membership of the JCB reflects the diversity of the parties involved in the programme: major contributors, affected countries selected by the regional committees, and the three co-sponsors;

– A Standing Committee, composed of the co-sponsoring agencies, reviews plans of actions and budgets for submission to the JCB, allocates resources between programme areas, and reports to the JCB on a number of matters affecting the programme;
– A Scientific and Technical Advisory Committee (STAC), composed of fifteen to eighteen experts selected by WHO, reviews the overall programme from a scientific and technical standpoint and recommends priorities within it.

128.   In the case of TDR, the Health Assembly was kept informed by the Director-General of the development of the programme and the negotiation of the MOU, but did not expressly approve the co-sponsored nature of the programme or the MOU. As noted, the 28th Health Assembly approved 'the Executive Board's endorsement of the steps taken or envisaged to develop the special programme . . .',[1] while the 29th Assembly approved '. . . the development so far of the special programme'.

1. Resolution WHA28.71 of 29 May 1975, in OR 226, p. 39.

129.   HRP was established as a WHO programme in 1965. The Eighteenth Health Assembly considered that, while it was not the responsibility of WHO to endorse or promote any particular population policy, the changes in the size and structure of the population had repercussions on health conditions and justified the participation by WHO in an inter-agency programme to promote research and training in the field of fertility regulation and human reproduction.[1] The special programme was established in 1972 but became a co-sponsored programme jointly with UNDP, UNFPA and the World Bank only in 1988. The structure of the programme is essentially the same as that of TDR, whose MOU was used as a basis for HRP's. The main structural differences are that the governing body is called Policy and Coordination Committee (PCC) and the expert body Scientific and Technical Advisory Group (STAG). By decision probably unprecedented within the UN system at that time, an NGO – the International Planned Parenthood Federation – was designated as a permanent member of the PCC. In addition, the following expert bodies have been established but are not envisaged in the MOU: Scientific and Ethical Review Group (SERG), a senior peer review body for research proposals within the programme; Gender Advisory Panel (GAP), which reviews the work from a gender and reproductive rights perspective; and Regional Advisory Panels (RAPS), which continually monitor and evaluate the work in their respective geographic regions. In the case of HRP, the 41st Health Assembly explicitly approved 'the co-sponsorship of the Programme', even though it did not approve the MOU as such.[2]

1. Resolution WHA18.49 of 21 May 1965, in OR 143, p. 35.
2. Resolution WHA41.9 of 11 May 1988, in WHA41/1988/REC/1, p. 6.

II. Codex Alimentarius

130.   A major example of a structurally and procedurally complex co-sponsored programme is the Joint FAO/WHO Food Standards Programme and its executive organ, the Codex Alimentarius Commission. The establishment of the Commission marked the culmination of a historical process of codification of food standards with the aim of protecting consumers and public health and enhancing compatibility between standards and criteria adopted at the national and regional levels. In response to a decision adopted by the 11th Session of the FAO Conference in 1961, the 16th World Health Assembly in 1963 adopted Resolution WHA16.42 by which it approved 'the establishment of a joint FAO/WHO programme on food standards whose principal organ will be the Codex Alimentarius Commission', and adopted the statutes of the Commission.[1]

> 1. The Statutes and Rules of Procedure of the Commission, as well as the General Principles of the Codex Alimentarius, the procedures for the elaboration of Codex standards and a number of other regulatory texts are reproduced in *Codex Alimentarius Commission – Procedural Manual*, (12th edition, Rome, FAO/WHO, 2002).

131.   The statutes, which were revised in 1966, entrust the Codex Alimentarius Commission with the responsibility of making proposals to, and be consulted by, FAO and WHO on all matters pertaining to the implementation of the Joint Food Standards Programme. The primary purpose of the programme is described in Article 1 as 'protecting the health of the consumers and ensuring fair practices in the food trade'.

132.   The Commission first met in 1963 and currently meets every other year, alternatively in Rome and Geneva. The statutes also establish an Executive Committee, which meets on an annual basis and is chaired by the chairperson of the commission. Participation, under Article 2 of the statutes, is open to all members and associate members of FAO and WHO. There is no admission procedure and membership, which currently stands at 168, is established upon a simple notification to the Directors-General of the two organizations. Pursuant to the link between membership in FAO and in the Codex Commission, the European Community has indicated its interest in becoming a member of the Commission on the basis of its membership in FAO. In fact, Article 2 of the FAO Constitution contains a so-called 'assimilation clause', whereby references to 'Member Nations' in the Constitution would normally also include the EC. In view of the particular status of the Community and the rules governing the alternative exercise of membership rights between it and its Member States, discussions are continuing on the implications of the Community's participation in Codex and the specific conditions thereof. There seems to be general agreement, in particular, that the Rules of Procedure will have to be amended along the lines of FAO's General Rules of the Organization.[1]

> 1. *See* Docs. ALINORM 01/33A, Report of the Sixteenth Session of the Codex Committee on General Principles, pp. 19–20; and ALINORM 03/33, Report of the Seventeenth Session of the Codex Committee on General Principles, pp. 18–20.

133.   The function of the Commission is the adoption of food standards and their publication in the series of volumes constituting the Codex Alimentarius. The Codex Procedural Manual defines the sequence of steps for the proposal, elaboration and adoption of standards.[1] This is an elaborate process which can take several years to complete and can be slowed down by the consistent attempt to reach consensus on standards without resorting to a vote. The Commission may adopt commodity standards or general standards. The former relate to a specific foodstuff, while the latter have across-the-board application to all foods and are not product-specific. Examples of general standards include food labelling, food additives, methods of analysis, food hygiene and pesticide residues. The term 'standard' in Codex practice also includes guidelines, codes of practice and other texts of an advisory nature. The standard-setting work is carried out by a network of committees and task forces which are established by the Commission and which draft standards for the latter's final adoption.[2] A feature of this system is that, with few exceptions, each committee is hosted by a member country, which is chiefly responsible for the cost of the committee's maintenance and administration and for providing its chairperson.

1. The procedure, which can either be regular or accelerated and consist of either five or eight steps, is described in the *Procedural Manual, supra*, pp. 19–30.
2. There are currently approximately twenty active committees and task forces, not including regional coordinating committees. A list of subsidiary bodies and their terms of reference is provided in *ibidem*, pp. 103–138.

134.   The work of the Codex Alimentarius Commission used to be familiar and well-known only to a relatively limited group of food regulators in its Member States. However, its importance and the economic significance of its decisions have dramatically increased since the entry into force of the Marrakesh Agreement establishing the World Trade Organization (WTO) and the set of multilateral trade agreements related thereto. Two such agreements explicitly or implicitly refer to the use of Codex standards and recommendations by states parties as justifying non-discriminatory barriers to trade, namely, the Agreement on the Application of Sanitary and Phytosanitary Measures (SPS)[1] and the Agreement on Technical Barriers to Trade (TBT).[2] In particular, Article 2 of the SPS requires that any sanitary and phytosanitary measures be only applied to the extent necessary to protect human, animal or plant life or health and be based on scientific principles. Article 3 adds that 'Members shall base their sanitary or phytosanitary measures on international standards, guidelines and recommendations . . .'. In its pursuance of harmonization of trade practices, with regard to food safety, Annex A to the SPS Agreement refers to Codex standards, guidelines and recommendations for food additives, veterinary drugs and pesticide residues, contaminants, methods of analysis and sampling, and codes and guidelines of hygienic practice. This means that Codex standards are considered scientifically justified and are accepted as benchmarks against which trade-restrictive national measures are evaluated.

1. The text is reproduced in *The Legal Texts – The Results of the Uruguay Round of Multilateral Trade Negotiations* (Cambridge, Cambridge University Press, 1998), pp. 59–72.
2. *Ibidem*, pp. 121–142.

135.   Article 2 of the TBT Agreement contains a general reference to 'relevant international standards' to ensure that technical regulations and standards at the national level, including those concerning packaging, marking and labelling requirements, and analytical procedures for assessing conformity with technical regulations and standards do not create unnecessary obstacles to trade. As far as food is concerned, the relevant internationally accepted standards on matters such as labelling and analytical procedures are undeniably Codex standards. Article 2.6 moreover requires states to play a full part 'in the preparation by appropriate international standardizing bodies of international standards . . .'.

136. The importance of WTO agreements on global trade, and the need to balance national health-protecting measures against possible challenges by trade partners affected by such measures, has led to a greatly increased interest in the work of the Codex Commission and its network of committees and task forces. At the same time, in the view of WHO, the linkage between Codex standards and WTO risks diverting the focus of the Commission from health to trade considerations. The composition of national delegations in Codex meetings increasingly reflects the commercial importance of Codex decisions, as does the increasing difficulty in the negotiation of general principles for the elaboration of standards.

137. Even though the statutes emphasize the advisory nature of the commission's work *vis-à-vis* the co-sponsoring organizations, this link has progressively become more tenuous with the passage of time. The submission of reports to the governing bodies of FAO and WHO for example, required under Article 5 of the statutes, does not actually take place. The Codex Alimentarius, as a collection of food standards and related documents recommended for adoption by national governments, has assumed an independent relevance and status, which has recently assume renewed importance in view of the reference made to them by WTO's trade agreements. Still, the joint nature of the programme determines a number of linkages between the commission and its parent organizations, as well as a situation of subsidiarity in several respects. To begin with, the commission and its subsidiary bodies are serviced by a joint Secretariat, stationed at FAO Headquarters, whose staff have the status of FAO officials but are accountable to both Organizations. Expenses incurred in Codex activities, which are not defrayed by host countries of committees, are financed by the two organizations with a ratio of approximately 75 per cent for FAO and 25 per cent for WHO. FAO and WHO exercise a form of control over Codex activities through, for example, the need for their approval to bring amendments to the rules of procedure into force, and their authority to admit NGOs into observer status with the commission. More significantly, the Codex Commission is not an operational but a normative organ. Still, its standards necessitate an adequate technical and administrative infrastructure to be adopted by governmental agencies and effectively incorporated into national systems. FAO and WHO thus play a complementary role by supporting developing countries to this end. Such support takes the form, for example, of the review of national food legislation, organizing scientific and training events, strengthening laboratory and food inspection capabilities and helping with the establishment and strengthening of food control agencies.

138. Most importantly, WHO and FAO provide Codex with scientific data and expert advice in the areas of pesticide residues, veterinary drugs and other food additives, of fundamental importance for the latter's standard-setting activities. More recently, the microbiological and the biotechnology areas have been included in specific FAO/WHO activities to provide Codex with scientific data and expert advice. In the chemical area, input is provided by two joint bodies: the joint FAO/WHO Meeting on Pesticide Residues (JMPR), established in 1963, and the joint FAO/WHO Expert Committee on Food Additives (JECFA), established in 1955. Both are expert bodies, whose members are individual scientists selected by either organization and participating in their personal capacity. JMPR cooperates with the Codex Committee on Pesticide Residues (CCPR). CCPR identifies pesticides requiring priority evaluation, JMPR performs the evaluations and recommends maximum residue limits (MRLs) which are then considered by CCPR and forwarded to the Codex Commission for adoption as Codex MRLs. A similar interaction takes place between JECFA and the Codex Committees on Food Additives and Contaminants and on Residues of Veterinary Drugs, respectively. In the microbiological area, a new joint and rather informal body has been established, namely the Joint FAO/WHO Expert Meeting on Microbiological Risk Assessment. Similarly, a series of FAO/WHO expert meetings on foods derived from biotechnology has provided input to the *ad hoc* Codex Intergovernmental Task Force on Foods Derived from Biotechnology.

III. UNAIDS

139.   The origins of UNAIDS are linked to the realization within the UN system in the early 1990s that the growing HIV/AIDS pandemic presented the international community with a increasingly complex and cross-sectoral challenge which required a coordinated action. WHO responded to the pandemic with the establishment in 1987 of the Global Programme on AIDS, initially headed by Dr. Jonathan Mann.[1] At the same time, the first attempts to coordinate the actions of the various agencies started with the establishment of an Inter-Agency Advisory Group on AIDS and of a WHO-UNDP Alliance to Combat AIDS. Still, both the major donors and countries deeply affected by the pandemic (e.g., Uganda) were showing increasing frustration at the lack of effective coordination among UN bodies and agencies both at global and country levels, the provision of sometimes conflicting advice, and the competition for financial resources.

1. For a review of WHO's activities predating the establishment of UNAIDS, *see* Beigbeder, *supra*, pp. 140–144.

140.   Based on these considerations, with a view to changing the international approach to the epidemic while retaining WHO's coordinating role on a major public health problem, the Forty-sixth World Health Assembly in 1993 requested the Director-General to consider the benefits of a joint inter-agency programme in consultation with UNDP, UNICEF, UNFPA, UNESCO and the World Bank.[1] These will remain the initial six co-sponsors of UNAIDS. The Director-General, on the basis of sometimes challenging consultations with the organizations in question, submitted a report to the 93rd Session of the Executive Board in January 1994.[2] He presented three possible options to implement the principle of co-sponsorship and joint ownership of the programme, with the preferred one presented as a 'consensus option'. The consensus option foresaw the establishment of a unified secretariat administered by WHO, headed by a director selected by the co-sponsors and appointed by the UN Secretary-General. Governance of the programme at the global level would be ensured by a programme coordinating board. At country level, the programme would rely on the coordination mandate of the UN Resident Coordinator and on the establishment of theme groups composed of the cosponsors and other organizations.

1. Resolution WHA46.37 of 14 May 1993, in WHA46/1993/REC/1, p. 40.
2. Doc. EB93/27, in EB93/1994/REC/1, Annex 3, pp. 163–167.

141. The Executive Board, by Resolution EB93.R5, requested the Director-General to pursue the further development of the consensus option and to bring the resolution to the attention of the co-sponsors with a view to obtaining the endorsement of the concept of co-sponsorship by their governing bodies. While negotiations on the establishment of the programme were being pursued by the six co-sponsors, ECOSOC became involved in the matter and began exercising increasing authority over the governance, operational and structural aspects of UNAIDS and its establishment by the co-sponsoring agencies.[1] In particular, by Resolution 1994/24 of 26 July 1994, ECOSOC endorsed the establishment of the Joint Programme along the lines of the consensus option, and requested the six co-sponsors to take a number of steps such as to constitute a Committee of Co-sponsoring Organizations, to submit to the Secretary-General a candidate for appointment as executive director; and to submit to the 1995 session of ECOSOC a detailed report on the organizational, programmatic and financial aspects of the programme, including a legal instrument to be concluded among the cosponsors 'to establish the programme formally'. At the same time, the Council requested its President to pursue informal consultations for the purpose of deciding the composition of the Programme Coordinating Board (PCB). The six co-sponsors and the President of ECOSOC complied with those requests and submitted their reports to the 1995 session of the Council.[2] Based on those reports, the Council adopted Resolution 1995/2, by which it formally established the PCB, approved its terms of reference and membership and adopted arrangements for the participation of five NGOs in its work. Moreover, the Council proceeded to elect the initial members of PCB, which held its first meeting on 13 and 14 July 1995.

1. The six co-sponsors had initially involved ECOSOC to help find a formula for the election of the members of the Programme Coordinating Board.
2. UN Doc. E/1995/60 contains the report of the President of the 1994 session; UN Doc. E/1995/71 contains the report of the co-sponsors.

142. The Health Assembly, by Resolution WHA48.30 of 12 May 1995, took note of ECOSOC Resolution 1994/24 and 'endorsed establishment [of UNAIDS], to which WHO will provide the administrative framework'. By Resolution WHA49.27 of 25 May 1996, the Assembly 'endorsed' the formula drawn up by ECOSOC for the membership of PCB as well as its functions as decided, for all intents and purposes, by ECOSOC. The governing bodies of the other co-sponsors took similar decisions between 1994 and 1995, by and large endorsing the establishment of the programme and the actions of ECOSOC.[1] Finally, the executive

heads of the co-sponsors signed at the end of 1995 a Memorandum of Understanding which reads as follows in its initial provision: 'There is hereby established a
joint and co-sponsored United Nations programme on HIV/AIDS'.[2]

1. Beigbeder, *supra*, p. 145.
2. The text is reproduced in UN Doc. E/1996/42, Appendix.

143.   The foregoing account shows that, for a number of political reasons and
the need to urgently set up an international mechanism to address the global spread
of the epidemic, the establishment of UNAIDS has left certain grey areas from a
legal point of view. Indeed, the main question is: who established UNAIDS, and
thus what is its legal status *vis-à-vis* its creators? Whereas ECOSOC decided on the
terms of reference and membership of the PCB and elected its members, it has no
direct decision-making authority with regard to separate agencies such as WHO or
the World Bank and could only make recommendations to them. At the same time,
the governing bodies of the co-sponsors did not purport to immediately establish the
new programme through their own decisions, but limited themselves to endorsing
its establishment, i.e., with reference to separate acts of establishment. Finally, as
noted in the previous paragraph, the language used in the 1995 MOU suggests that
the executive heads of the co-sponsors intended to establish the programme under
their own authority. Probably the most plausible explanation is that UNAIDS was
established progressively and conjointly by ECOSOC and by separate actions of
the co-sponsoring organizations, both through governing body endorsement and
through the conclusion of the MOU by their executive heads. The co-sponsors also
accepted *ex post facto* the actions taken by ECOSOC, which continues to elect the
members of the PCB notwithstanding the initially declared intention to reconsider
the election mechanism.

144.   The modalities of the establishment of UNAIDS are thus rather unusual,
and without a direct precedent within the UN system. They bear witness to the
determination by the UN and its agencies to find innovative structure and mechanisms to tackle together the HIV/AIDS epidemic. However, whereas the joint nature
of the programme strengthens its co-ownership by the co-sponsors, it also raises
legal issues about its status and its structural relationship with them. It seems
evident, in this respect, that UNAIDS is not a separate legal entity. It can be
actually questioned whether the co-sponsors and ECOSOC had the authority to co-
establish a new and separate subject of international law, and this intention is in any
case never expressed in the various resolutions. The closest organizational links of
UNAIDS are arguably those with the UN and WHO. On the one hand, ECOSOC
elects the PCB and the UN Secretary-General appoints the Executive Director (the
appointment is actually implemented by the WHO Director-General). On the other
hand, as expressed in the consensus option and ECOSOC Resolution 1994/24, and
enshrined in Article XI of the MOU, WHO provides administration of UNAIDS,
which is subject to WHO's Regulations and Rules. UNAIDS officials for example,
albeit recruited for service with UNAIDS only, are subject to WHO's Staff Regulations and Rules and are thus protected by the privileges and immunities enjoyed by
WHO staff under the relevant international instruments. It can thus be argued that

UNAIDS derives its legal personality from that of WHO, a position shared by Switzerland in its practice as host country.

145. The structure of UNAIDS at the global level, as emerging from the ECOSOC resolutions and the MOU, consists of the PCB, the Committee of Co-sponsoring Organizations (CCO) and a Secretariat. The PCB is the governing body of the Programme. It is composed of 22 states elected by ECOSOC on a regional basis. The cosponsors also participate without the right to vote. Moreover, in another interesting break from UN practice, five NGOs participate as non-voting members.[1] This decision was taken and spelled out in detail by ECOSOC in Resolution 1995/2. NGOs coordinate their candidatures among themselves, which are then approved by the PCB for terms of three years. Even though Resolution 1995/2 makes it clear that NGOs do not have a negotiating role and cannot participate in decision-making, their preparation and activism ensures their influence on the decisions adopted by the Board. The PCB acts as the governing body of UNAIDS on all programmatic issues concerning policy, strategy, finance, monitoring and evaluation of the programme. It is responsible for establishing the policies and priorities and deciding on the planning and execution of the programme. The Board approves the budget and exercises general financial authority over the programme, and makes recommendations to the cosponsors regarding their activities. The PCB holds an annual session devoted to the general programme of work of UNAIDS, but has also held *ad hoc* thematic sessions on specific issues.

1. As noted *supra*, one NGO is a full member of the Policy and Coordination Committee of HRP.

146. The CCO serves as the standing committee of the PCB and is the forum through which the co-sponsors implement their joint ownership of UNAIDS and provide input into its policies and strategies. It should, in practice, exercise the collective control of the sponsoring organizations over the activities and decisions of the Secretariat, in view of the joint nature of the programme. In its capacity as PCB's standing committee, it reports to it on the cosponsors' activities in support of the programme; it also reviews or prepares work plans, the draft programme budget, financial statements and technical reports, for the Board's consideration. The CCO meets twice a year, once at the executive head level and once at the focal point level. Its chairmanship rotates among the co-sponsors on an annual basis. Besides the six original co-sponsors, the United Nations Drug Control Programme became the seventh co-sponsor in March 1999, and ILO the eighth in October 2001.

147. The programme is managed by a Secretariat located in Geneva, headed by an Executive Director appointed by the UN Secretary-General upon the proposal of the cosponsors. His position corresponds to that of an Under-Secretary-General of the United Nations.[1] Although UNAIDS staff are subject to WHO's Staff Regulations and Rules, the Executive Director holds responsibility for the selection, supervision and termination of UNAIDS staff, while WHO implements those decisions from an administrative point of view. WHO also holds in trust and disburses, in conformity with its Financial Regulations and Rules, financial contributions to UNAIDS and, more generally provides the administration of the programme. At the same time, unlike WHO, UNAIDS was conceived as an operational body, whose rules and practices may have to be adapted to this purpose. For this reason, the MOU foresees the possibility of agreed special arrangements to take into accounts UNAIDS's operational needs, which could deviate from WHO's rules and practices.

1. The current Executive Director is Dr. Peter Piot, a Belgian medical doctor. The structure of the Secretariat can be browsed at <http://www.unaids.org/about/staff/index.html> (visited on 20 May 2002).

148. In developing countries, UNAIDS operates mainly through the country-based staff of its co-sponsors. Meeting as the United Nations Theme Group on HIV/AIDS, representatives of the co-sponsoring organizations share information, plan and monitor coordinated action between themselves and with other partners, and decide on joint financing of major AIDS activities in support of the country's government and other national partners. The principal objective of the Theme Group is to support the host country's efforts to mount an effective and comprehensive response to HIV/AIDS. In most cases, the host government is invited to be part of the Theme Group. Increasingly, other partners such as representatives of other United Nations agencies and bilateral organizations working in the country are also included. In priority countries the Theme Group has the support of a UNAIDS staff member, called a Country Programme Adviser. Elsewhere, a staff member of one of the seven co-sponsors serves as the UNAIDS focal point for the country. In addition to supporting the UN system, these staff endeavour to build national commitment to AIDS action and provide information and guidance to a range of host country partners, including government departments and groups and organizations from civil society, such as people living with HIV/AIDS. For their day-to-day operations, most Theme Groups have set up special working groups that involve donors, NGOs and groups of people living with HIV/AIDS.[1]

1. *See* <http://www.unaids.org/about/what.asp#country> (visited on 20 May 2002).

Chapter 3. Relations with Non-governmental Organizations

149. The importance of securing cooperation from non-governmental organizations (what today would be referred to as 'civil society organizations') in pursuing social and humanitarian goals was very apparent at the time of the establishment of the UN system. Such awareness was also reflected in Article 71 of the WHO Constitution. Article 71 has to be seen in the context of Article 2 paragraphs (b) and (j) of the Constitution, which lists among WHO's functions collaboration with 'professional groups and such other organizations as may be deemed appropriate' and the promotion of 'co-operation among scientific and professional groups which contribute to the advancement of health'.

150. WHO's interaction with a broad range of mostly international NGOs has been and continues to be one of the most active and vibrant instruments through which the Organization pursues its mandate. After all, for a normative and coordinating agency acting in a complex and constantly changing field, consultations and cooperation with professional, scientific and grass-roots organizations is obviously of primary importance. The same can be said about NGOs active or interested in public health, for which interaction with WHO represents a unique platform to have their voice heard at an intergovernmental level and to try to influence and shape international health policy. The sheer number of NGOs admitted in official relations testifies of the mutual importance of this relationship: from 26 in 1951 to 68 in 1966, 184 in 1996 and more than 190 at the beginning of 2002.[1]

1. A list of NGOs in official relations, offering a description of the structure and mission of each organization, is provided at the following web address: <http://www.who.int/ina-ngo> (visited on 1 June 2002).

151. The Health Assembly has formalized, through the adoption of a set of principles, the system of relations between WHO and NGOs around the concepts of working relations and official relations.[1] In so doing, especially through its last revision of the principles, it has consciously deviated from the concept and modalities of the consultative status which NGOs may enjoy with ECOSOC. This difference reflects the fact that the United Nations is an organization of a parliamentary nature, where the focus of cooperation with NGOs lies in their participation in meetings and debates. WHO is instead an organization engaged in scientific and technical work, thus emphasis is placed on cooperation in technical and operational activities.

1. 'Principles Governing Relations between the World Health Organization and Nongovernmental Organizations', annexed to WHA Resolution WHA40.25 which replaced the principles adopted by the First and Third World Health Assemblies; *Basic Documents, supra*, pp. 77–82.

152. The principles recognize only one type of formal relations, known as 'official relations', the establishment of which is subject to a decision by the Executive Board. Any other relation is of an informal character. The principles describe step-by-step the normal evolution of contacts and relations between WHO and NGOs. The main points to note are the following:

(1) Admission into official relations is the culmination of a process, which may last several years (but at least, normally, two years), of bilateral contacts, exchange of information, technical collaboration, planning and implementation of joint activities, which is defined as 'working relations'. Only at the end of this period, and after a positive joint assessment of the outcome of the collaboration, the NGO may apply, or be invited to apply, for official relations;
(2) NGOs must normally be international in character and have a well-established and representative structure. This includes NGOs of a federal nature, which have actually proliferated in recent times with the growth in number of national and regional organizations. Their main area of competence must fall within the purview of WHO, which would normally exclude non-health-related organizations;
(3) National organizations may only be considered in exceptional circumstances, in consultation with the 'Member State concerned', and then normally only for working or official relations at the regional level;
(4) The applications of NGOs for admission into official relations are considered by a committee of the EB on non-governmental organizations which, based on presentations made by the Secretariat, may recommend to the Board for approval the admission of the NGOs concerned or else the postponement or rejection of their application;
(5) The Committee and the Board are also responsible for reviewing each year a third of the NGOs already in official relations, with a view to continuing or terminating relations. The Board may also, regardless of its annual review, suspend or discontinue official relations in the light of changing circumstances or if the organization no longer meets WHO's criteria;
(6) The admission into official relations mainly confers the privilege of participating in the meeting of WHO's governing or other bodies, if foreseen by the applicable rules of procedure. NGOs may make statements at the invitation of the presiding officer, receive sessional documents and submit memoranda to the Director-General for appropriate circulation.

153. NGOs in official relations form a diverse group, which comprises professional and scientific associations, advocacy organizations, several humanitarian organizations, patient organizations, women and youth organizations and federations of private companies. The Secretariat, in a report submitted to the 101st Session of the Executive Board,[1] has exemplified the main forms of WHO-NGO collaboration as follows:

Advisory. An international coordinating group advised WHO on the best means of allocating a limited number of doses of a meningitis vaccine in Africa;
Advocacy. The International Council of Women contributes to the dissemination of WHO health education information to national NGOs dealing with women's issues;

Coordination and service provision. Illustrated by the cooperation between WHO and a group of NGOs concerned with blindness;

Data collection and health information management. The International Association of Cancer Registries has provided data for use in a number of WHO world health reports;

Financial. Rotary International helped fund operation MECACAR, an initiative that supported coordinated national immunization days in a number of developing countries;

Human resources development. WHO collaborates with such NGOs as the World Federation for Medical Education in the development and implementation of WHO's policy on changes in medical education and medical practice;

Participation in NGO meetings. Among the many possible instances, WHO participates in the meetings of the International Planned Parenthood Federation's International Medical Advisory Panel, whose recommendations are applied by family planning programmes throughout the world;

Publication. The *Manual of Diagnostic Ultrasound*, for example, is a joint publication with the World Federation for Ultrasound in Medicine and Biology;

Scientific review and clinical support. On the basis of the pioneering work undertaken by the International Union Against Tuberculosis and Lung Disease, the 'directly observed treatment, short course' (DOTS) strategy was developed to control and cure tuberculosis;

Standard-setting and development of nomenclature. The International Council of Societies of Pathology contributed to WHO activities relating to the international histological classification of tumours.

1. EB101/33 of 8 December 1997.

154.   Moreover, since WHO is not primarily an operational agency, its collaboration with, and reliance on, non-governmental partners for its emergency and humanitarian action is of crucial importance. Such interaction takes place both at a central planning and coordination level, through WHO's participation in the Inter-Agency Standing Committee on Humanitarian Questions as well as regarding its activities in specific emergencies, be they natural, man-made or complex emergencies. Major partners in this context are the International Committee of the Red Cross (ICRC), the International Federation of Red Cross and Red Crescent Societies (IFRC), Care International, Caritas, Oxfam and the World Council of Churches.[1]

1. Beigbeder, *supra*, pp. 180–183.

155.   While collaboration with NGOs active in the medical and health-related field are widespread, WHO has traditionally expressed reservations about expanding its network of contacts and cooperation with NGOs active in other fields. Whereas a few non-health-related organizations have been admitted into official relations,[1] the Director-General, in the aforementioned report submitted to the 101st session of the Executive Board, recommended that further contacts with other similarly placed organizations be in principle maintained at an informal level. The lack of the necessary programme framework, the lack of expertise within WHO, and the risk of an undesirable shift away from the health sector militated for limiting official relations to health-related NGOs.[2] The Board requested the Director-General to initiate a consultation process on official relations, including NGOs whose main area of competence lies outside the health and related field, while at the same time encouraging increased informal contacts (as opposed to official relations) with such organizations.[3]

1. Examples include the Inter-parliamentary Union, the International Air Transport Association (IATA), the International Organization for Standardization (ISO), and the International Union of Architects.
2. EB101/33, *supra*.
3. EB Decision EB101(16), in EB/101/1998/REC/1, p. 39.

156. The system of working and official relations, reflects WHO's nature as a technical agency. As noted above, participation in the work of the governing bodies is the culmination of a process of interaction and collaboration. However, this system revealed its limits with regard to the first long-term multilateral negotiation carried out by WHO, i.e., the negotiation of a framework convention on tobacco control (FCTC). While the substance and the process of negotiation will be reviewed *infra*, suffice it to note at this stage that the Health Assembly established, by Resolution WHA52.18, an Intergovernmental Negotiating Body (INB) to negotiate the framework convention. The INB is a subsidiary of the Health Assembly and the latter's rules are, in principle, applicable to it, including the Principles on Collaboration with NGOs.

157. In a multilateral diplomatic process such as the negotiation of the FCTC, 'participation' for NGOs obviously means attending meetings of the INB. The existing system, however, would not have given interested NGOs not in official relations enough time to be accredited during the negotiations, since these are scheduled to be completed by 2003. This would have penalized several NGOs, active on tobacco control issues, which were in working relations with the WHO Secretariat but not yet in official relations. The rights of participation granted to NGOs by the principles, moreover, seemed too limited to some Member States for a process in which civil society was expected to ensure the preeminence of public health considerations.

158. For these and other reasons, Resolution WHA53.16 requested the INB to examine the question of an extended participation of NGOs in its work. The INB at its first session in October 2000 established an open-ended working group to consider the question. The agreement eventually reached by the INB reconfirms the applicability of the existing principles and practices but encourages the Executive Board to 'expedite review' of pending applications by NGOs.[1]

1. WHO doc. A/FCTC/INB1/PL/SR/9, p. 6.

159. The Executive Board, at its 107th Session held in January 2001, responded by adapting its procedures while remaining within the scope of the principles, so as to allow NGOs to be provisionally admitted into official relations for the exclusive or main purpose of attending meetings of the INB.[1] Under that decision, the Chairperson of the EB, acting jointly with the Chairperson of the Standing Committee on NGOs, were authorized to admit into provisional official relations NGOs already in working relations and whose mandate was relevant to the work of the INB. Such admission could take place between Board sessions, and would be reviewed by the Board at its subsequent January session so that approximately two years of working relations would have elapsed by the time the Board conducted this formal review. While not departing from the existing rules, the decision of the Board has accelerated and simplified the admission of NGOs already 'in the pipeline'.

1. Decision EB107(2), in EB107/2001/REC/1, p. 20.

Chapter 4. Relations with the Private Sector and 'Partnerships'

160. Relations with commercial companies have become an increasingly important aspect of WHO's efforts to engage a broad range of actors crucial to the pursuit of its public health agenda. The Constitution, unsurprisingly, does not deal with the issue which was also largely ignored during the preparatory works. The only relevant provision to this effect is Article 57, whereby the Assembly or the Board may accept gifts and bequests provided that the conditions attached thereto are acceptable to the governing bodies and are consistent with the objective and policies of the Organization. This provision has consistently been interpreted by the WHO Secretariat as allowing the acceptance of donations by private companies, provided they do not generate conflicts of interests or are subject to unacceptable conditions.

161. When WHO was established, commercial companies were not universally recognized as potential important contributors to international public health. Even though their role in the discovery, production and delivery of health-related products and technologies is evident, the emphasis in WHO's policies was for a long time on the primary role of the public sector[1] as the only legitimate partner for an intergovernmental organization. The relationship between WHO and the commercial private sector developed in the course of time in two complementary directions: on the one hand, the Organization realized the increasingly important role which the private sector, especially pharmaceutical companies, may play in the pursuit of public health goals which appeared unattainable if reliance was placed only on governments or non-profit research institutions. On the other hand, as a normative and scientific agency, WHO has developed an ingrained caution in dealing with powerful economic actors, which led to the elaboration of safeguards for the protection of WHO's image against conflicts of interests. From the latter point of view, it is evident that WHO may affect the commercial sector in a variety of ways 'through for example, its public health guidance, its recommendations on regulatory standards, or other work that might influence products costs, market demand, or profitability of specific goods and services'.[2] It is thus equally evident that the commercial sector may have (or may be perceived as having) an interest in influencing the outcome of WHO's activities, and that the perception by the public of an undue influence on WHO by corporate interests may tarnish its credibility as an international public health agency.

1. With the partial exception of NGOs, which were considered suitable partners from the beginning of the Organization.
2. WHO Doc. EB107/20, Annex, p. 2.

94

162. WHO may interact with commercial companies in a variety of ways, such as:

- The establishment of alliances – sometimes jointly with other public or private entities – to address specific health issues, subject to a number of procedural requirements;
- Consultations, participation in meetings and exchange of information;
- Research and development of health-related products;
- Generation of cash and in-kind donations to WHO; and
- Advocacy on specific health issues.

163. An important facet of the relations between WHO and the private sector concerns the collaboration with pharmaceutical companies in the research and development of new drugs and vaccines, in particular with a view to promoting their availability at affordable prices to the public sector of developing countries. This is of particular importance for diseases which are mainly prevalent in developing countries and which would normally not attract the interest of the pharmaceutical industry in view of the relatively low return that addressing them may offer. WHO has been working in various ways with the pharmaceutical industry to support and encourage the development of safe and affordable drugs to treat 'forgotten diseases' or 'diseases of the poor' such as leishmaniasis, Chagas disease, trypanosomiasis and dengue fever.[1]

> 1. More information on tropical diseases and on-going research and treatment efforts can be found in the WHO's web site: <http://www.who.int/tdr/topics/default.htm> (visited on 15 June 2002).

164. In this connection, WHO has established as a policy since the early 1980s to use intellectual property rights in appropriate circumstances, as a device to cooperate with the pharmaceutical industry to foster the discovery, production and commercialization of new drugs. The patent policy of WHO is embodied in Health Assembly Resolution WHA35.14 of 12 May 1982 which states that:

> 'it shall be the policy of WHO to obtain patents, inventors' certificates or interests in patents on patentable health technologies developed through projects supported by WHO, where such rights and interests are necessary to ensure development of the new technology; the Organization shall use its patent rights, and any financial or other benefits associated therewith, to promote the development, production and wide availability of health technology in the public interest.'

165. The rationale and implementation of WHO's patent policy is functional to the achievement of public health goals rather than to obtaining revenues or other benefits through a proprietary control over products or processes. The comparison of the costs involved in the establishment and maintenance of intellectual property rights against potential revenues is thus in principle not one of the considerations in deciding whether or not WHO should file patents or similar instruments.

166. It should be noted that the traditional approach for public sector agencies funding research work (by institutions such as hospitals, laboratories, research centres or universities) is normally to place the results of the work in the public domain through public disclosure, to avoid that the acquisition of exclusive rights becomes an obstacle to the availability of such results. However, whether this approach is in the public interest depends on the circumstances. In particular, certain products or technologies require an investment of such magnitude that companies would be unwilling to invest in their development without a period of exclusivity in the marketing of the product. Public disclosure in these cases could actually discourage the development of the work concerned. In such cases, WHO acknowledges the importance of obtaining appropriate intellectual property rights in the results of research work. The Organization then negotiates with interested companies on a licence to the intellectual property concerned.

167. The patents and other similar rights that WHO sometimes holds are usually acquired in research work performed by institutions and funded by WHO through a grant. The contract governing the grant allocates rights to the invention and its exploitation either to the researcher, with WHO retaining a licence to use the invention, or to the Organization itself. WHO increasingly organizes a series of individual research projects that form part of a larger research and development programme (such as, for example, those conducted by TDR on malaria). In order to permit the coordinated application of the results of the projects and to be able to conclude an agreement with a company for the development of those results into a final product, WHO needs to hold certain rights in them, usually in the form of a non-exclusive licence.

168. In addition to funding research projects carried out by research institutions, WHO has a significant amount of collaboration directly with industry for the development of new products. WHO may, for example, arrange and fund studies, trials and other developmental work or provide technical expertise with regard to the proprietary compound of a commercial company. WHO may also license to a company intellectual property rights on a compound patented by WHO for the further development of a product, possibly in combination with the provision of technical and financial support. When WHO funds studies and trials on a proprietary compound, it agrees that the rights to the results of the collaborative work between the parties will vest in the company. In return, WHO seeks to ensure that its objectives are achieved by requiring that the final product will be made generally available to the public, either by the company itself, or in the case the company would decide to abandon the project, through a licence to WHO. In addition, WHO generally requires that the product will be made available to the public sector of developing countries at a preferential price, i.e., preferential if compared to that under which it is marketed for private sector use. Particularly in cases where the product in question has potential for both public and private sector use – one can think, for example, of drugs against malaria and their attractiveness for the market of travellers to malarial areas – a collaborative arrangement will serve both the public health objectives of WHO as well as the corporate interest of the company.

169.   To give a concrete example, reference may be made to the drug Miltefosine, originally developed as an anti-cancer agent by the company ASTA Medica, and later by the biotech company Zentaris. While its use in cancer treatment was discontinued, it was found to be effective against leishmaniasis. Zentaris thus concluded an agreement with WHO for the clinical development of Miltefosine for the treatment of visceral leishmaniasis. A task force of independent scientists was established by TDR to supervise a clinical development programme in India; WHO and Zentaris cooperated in the implementation and monitoring of the studies. The product in question was quickly approved for use against visceral leishmaniasis in India. As a spin-off of the collaboration, Zentaris supplied the drug free of charge for treatment of patients with HIV and leishmaniasis co-infection.[1]

   1. reported at <http://www.who.int/tdr/publications/tdrnews/news68/miltefosine-zentaris.htm> (visited on 15 June 2002).

170.   In the area of tropical diseases – the quintessential 'forgotten diseases' – TDR has reported that, of the thirteen new drugs registered between 1975 and 1997, six were developed with its support, while a further seven chemical entities or drug combinations have been registered or recommended for use with input from the programme. Among the main examples offered are those of Artemether, registered in 30 endemic countries for the treatment of severe malaria; Eflornithine, licensed in several countries for use in sleeping sickness; and Ivermectin, the major tool for the treatment and control of onchocerciasis.[1]

   1. <http://www.who.int/tdr/about/products/registration.htm> (visited on 15 June 2002).

171.   Besides collaborative relations for the development of new drugs, WHO has sometimes served as a conduit and a catalyst for the donation by private companies of either cash or drugs destined for developing countries, especially if those donations are part of a more complex and coordinated programme for research, control and treatment of certain diseases. In these cases, WHO maintains its role as the lead international health agency by, for example, arranging for the distribution of the drugs, monitoring their use, and carrying out broader disease management and control activities, as well as research and development. Reference may be made, for example, to the donation in 2001 by Aventis Pharma of three drugs – Pentamidine, Melarsoprol and Eflornithine – for five years for the treatment of trypanosomiasis (sleeping sickness).[1] WHO is responsible for providing the company with biannual reviews of amounts needed and for approving requests for the drugs from endemic countries, based upon the recommendations of a group of experts. WHO also coordinates the shipping and distribution of the drugs through the NGO 'Médecins sans Frontières'. In addition to this donation in kind, Aventis has pledged under the same cooperation programme a donation of funds to strengthen WHO's surveillance and control activities in trypanosomiasis-endemic countries in Africa. Other examples of successful private in-kind drug donations reported by the Director-General to the Executive Board in 1999 include those by Merck to the Onchocerciasis Control Programme in West Africa; by SmithKline Beecham for the elimination of lymphatic filariasis; and by Pasteur Mérieux Connaught to the Global Polio Eradication Initiative.[2]

1. *See* press release WHO/23 of 3 May 2001.
2. WHO Doc. EB105/8, p. 2.

172. Large-scale donations of pharmaceuticals by companies are subject to a number of criteria set up by the Secretariat to assess their acceptability, such as:

– Requirements as to the safety and efficacy of the drug and its approval in the recipient countries;
– The availability of a secure supply system in the recipient countries;
– The donation should not create a demand for the drug which is not sustainable once the donation has ended;
– A system for monitoring adverse drug reactions, with the cooperation of the company.[1]

1. WHO Doc. EB107/20, *supra*, Annex, p. 7.

173. As noted above, the intensification and broadening of collaboration with the private sector, while opening new avenues for WHO to deal with growing challenges on its agenda, has rendered more acute concerns about safeguarding the reputation of the Organization as an impartial, credible and objective technical and policy-making agency from undue influence by corporate interests. Contradictory pressures have been recently increasing in this connection. Some critics accuse the Organization of courting too deliberately corporate contributions while compromising the integrity of its policies, while other actors, including several Member States, argue in favour of an expansion of WHO's partnerships with a variety of stakeholders, including the private sector.[1]

1. *See* e.g., Bosley, S., 'Unhealthy Influence' (*The Guardian*, on-line edition, browsed on 7 February 2002 at <http://www.guardian.co.uk/print>). *See also* the divergent positions sometimes expressed by Members of the Executive Board at its 107th Session, in WHO Doc. EB107/2001/REC/2, pp. 155–158.

174. To guide WHO staff in assessing the acceptability of specific relations with the private sector, the Secretariat has elaborated a set of internal general guidelines. The 'Guidelines on interaction with commercial enterprises to achieve health outcomes', although they did not purport to represent a policy statement on the Organization's relations with 'commercial enterprises', were sent to Member States and a variety of other partners for comments, and a revised version was submitted to the Executive Board at its 107th Session in January 2001.[1]

1. WHO Doc. EB107/20, *supra*.

175. The guidelines attempt to strike a balance between the need to protect the Organization from undue commercial influence and conflicts of interest, on the one hand, and the equally relevant need not to hamper the exploration and development of interaction with the private sector. In addition to setting out a number of general criteria by which the Secretariat should assess the suitability of specific commercial companies, the guidelines identify the main forms of collaboration and provide guidance as to whether and in what form they may be acceptable. At the same time, the implementation of the guidelines by WHO's technical units is based on the case-by-case advice from the Office of the Legal Counsel and, if necessary, review by an internal 'Committee on Private Sector Collaboration'. This committee examines the proposed collaboration and advises the Director-General for final approval or rejection. The determination whether specific forms of interaction with the private sector are acceptable and in the interest of WHO is thus not left to the appreciation of the individual units concerned, but is rather centralized and subject to a final determination by the Executive Head of the Organization.

176. The guidelines identify the following main forms of collaboration for the purpose of their application: *donations*, which may be accepted from companies whose activities are not incompatible with WHO's work and which do not have a direct commercial interest in the outcome of the activity supported; *contributions in kind*, which in general terms may be accepted if they can be utilized and if any conditions which may be attached to them are consistent with the objective and policies of the Organization;[1] *secondment of personnel* from companies to WHO, subject to the absence of a conflict of interests on the part of the seconding company or the seconded person; *product development*, which has been discussed *supra* and which should in principle only be carried out on the basis of a collaborative research and development agreement spelling out all relevant conditions; *cost recovery* from companies whose products are being evaluated by WHO; *co-sponsorship of meetings*, which is normally not considered acceptable.

1. The donation of drugs is also subject to the criteria referred to *supra*, para. 172.

177. To protect WHO's image, independence and objectivity, caution is normally also exercised as to the use that private companies make of their collaboration with WHO, to avoid that such interaction may be exploited for commercial or promotional purposes or construed as endorsement by WHO of particular products or processes over others. In this connection, while donations are acknowledged by WHO and may be referred to by the companies concerned in their corporate reports or similar documents, they cannot be used for commercial or promotional purposes. Similarly, the use of WHO's name and emblem by supporting companies is normally not allowed. The protection of the name and emblem is particularly important, in view not only of their function as primary identifier of the Organization, but also of their association to its reputation and standing.

178. Mention should also be made of the recent emphasis, not only in WHO but throughout the UN system, on building longer-term 'public-private partnerships' (PPPs). The proliferation of such partnerships is a relatively recent phenomenon and its analysis and conceptualization in scholarly literature is still limited. However, a recent definition states that: '[h]ealth GPPPs are collaborative relationships that transcend national boundaries and bring together at least three parties – among them a corporation and/or industry association and an intergovernmental organization – so as to achieve a shared health-creating goal on the basis of a mutually agreed and explicitly defined division of labor'.[1] It is important to note that PPPs do not only involve a public and a private for-profit partner, but also frequently a private not-for-profit entity such as philanthropic foundations which support financially such enterprises. The activism of foundations, especially those based in the US such as the Bill and Melinda Gates Foundation and the Rockfeller Foundation, has actually served as a catalyst to promote and financially sustain PPPs.

1. K. Buse, G. Walt, 'The WHO and Global Public-Private Partnerships', in: M.R. Reich (ed.), *Public-Private Partnerships for Public Health* (Cambridge, Massachusetts, Harvard University Press, 2002), p. 171.

179.   The establishment of longer-term collaborative arrangements whereby public and private actors cooperate in the pursuit of specific health goals – mostly but not exclusively the development of new drugs or vaccines – reflects two distinct but interrelated phenomena. The first, more general, relates to the impact of globalization and its effects – e.g., a relative retrenchment of the authority of states, the overall reduction in government spending for international assistance, the increasing prominence of multinational companies and of corporate interests in global governance. This has led, *inter alia*, to a reconsideration by the United Nations and its agencies of their traditionally suspicious relationship with private companies and to a growing interest in exploring interactions which would support broad public goals while at the same time meeting corporate goals. Large multinational companies have shown interest in this offer of dialogue largely because of the pressure exerted upon them by civil society organizations to behave like good 'corporate citizens' and follow basic ethical principles. The best example of this trend is the so-called 'Global Compact', launched by the UN Secretary-General in 2000 to promote the observance by participating companies of nine core principles on human and labour rights and environmental protection.[1]

1. *See* <http://www.unglobalcompact.org>.

180.   The second phenomenon pertains more specifically to the area of public health and thus concerns directly WHO. It has been observed that the gap in health indicators between developed and the developing world is steadily growing. Of particular concern is the yawning gap between the mortality and morbidity engendered by infectious diseases in developing countries (affecting almost 90 per cent of humankind) and the research and pharmaceutical resources spent on them – no more than ten per cent. This is what is commonly referred to as the '90/10 divide'.[1] It has recently been observed that major gaps occur along the drug development process. While basic research often takes place in university or government laboratories, development is almost exclusively done by the pharmaceutical industry, and the most significant gap is in the translation of basic research into drug development from the public to the private sector. Another critical point is the launching of clinical trials for promising candidate drugs, a decision taken by the pharmaceutical industry which is based mainly on potential financial return to shareholders. The situation, in the view of many advocates, represents not only a failure of the market but also of public policy, because society has chosen to leave pharmaceutical research and development (R&D) to the private sector and to reinforce its return on investment through patents, grants, tax credits, and state-subsidized health care.[2]

1. The NGO Médecins sans frontières has been particularly active in denouncing this situation and promoting broader global access to drugs.
2. *See* <http://www.neglecteddiseases.org/summary.pdf> (visited on 1 July 2002), containing the summary of a conference on neglected diseases convened by the NGO Médecins sans frontières in March 2002.

181.   As a consequence of this situation, both public agencies, private foundations and commercial companies have recently launched initiatives to bridge the traditional gap caused by the aforementioned division of labour. Indeed, there has been such a proliferation of health-related PPPs that the Geneva-based 'Initiative on Public-Private Partnerships for Health' lists almost 80 such partnerships, with WHO listed as a participant in more than 30.[1]

1. <http://www.ippph.org/PartnershipDB/partner_lst.cfm?TAB=MAJOR_PARTICIPANTS&id=2> (visited on 1 July 2002).

182.   The establishment or participation in PPPs by the WHO Secretariat has been seen as an important tool to mobilize private industry for priority health goals in innovative ways, which would adapt models of corporate governance and rely on the comparative advantages of partners. In fact, TDR has been indicated as the earliest example of PPP involving WHO.[1] Even though the programme is only co-sponsored by 'public' entities, it has since its early days developed an overall positive relationship with more than twenty pharmaceutical companies which have, for example, provided scientists for TDR's meetings as well as Good Manufacturing Practice facilities for biological reagents and, most importantly, have collaborated in clinical evaluation of new drugs.

1. A.O. Lucas, 'Public-Private Partnerships: Illustrative Examples', in M.R. Reich (ed.), *Public-Private Partnerships for Public Health, supra*, pp. 20–26.

183.   Of the more recent PPPs, a brief review of two cases may outline some of the diverse models chosen by their sponsors. The two examples are the Global Alliance for Vaccines and Immunization (GAVI) and the Medicines for Malaria Venture (MMV).

184.   GAVI was launched in January 2000 thanks to an initial grant of US$ 750 million for five years from the Gates Foundation. The main objective of GAVI is to improve access to sustainable immunization services in the poorest developing countries, following a decade of falling immunization coverage levels and a growing 'vaccine gap' between developed and developing countries. GAVI also focuses on the development of new vaccines and the promotion of safe injection equipment. The membership of the Alliance has grown to encompass, besides the Gates Foundation, WHO, UNICEF and the World Bank, the governments of developed and developing countries, NGOs, vaccine manufacturers from both developed and developing countries, and research institutes. The steering organ of the Alliance is a Board composed of fifteen members, some of which are permanent (such as the

Gates Foundation and WHO) while others are rotating; a small Secretariat is housed in UNICEF.[1] The Alliance as such is not a legal entity, hence the decision to rely on UNICEF to provide the necessary contractual capacity and privileges and immunities. The main philosophy of GAVI is to improve donor collaboration, enhance coordination among governments and development partners, and aim at a sustainable balance between affordable prices for vaccines and adequate investment in supply capacity and R&D of high-priority vaccines.

> 1. The rotating members of the GAVI Board are the following:
> **Foundation**: Rockefeller Foundation;
> **Government – developing countries (two)**: Bhutan and Mali;
> **Government – industrialized countries (three)**: Canada, the Netherlands, and Norway;
> **Nongovernmental organization (NGO):** Gates Children's Vaccine Program at PATH;
> **Pharmaceutical industry – industrialized country**: Aventis Pasteur;
> **Pharmaceutical industry – developing country**: Center for Genetic Engineering and Biotechnology (CIGB);
> **Research institute**: US National Institutes of Health (NIH); and
> **Technical health institute:** US Centers for Disease Control (CDC).

185. Applications for support from developing countries must include an assessment of existing immunization services, an immunization plan for which support is needed, and evidence of an Interagency Coordination Committee led by the Ministry of Health, which is the main coordination and monitoring mechanism of GAVI-funded activities. Applications are screened by an Independent Review Committee and then by the Board. The recommendations of the Board are forwarded to a formally separate and independent Vaccine Fund, which has its own Board that takes the final decision on whether to grant awards to applicant countries. The main reason for this division is to preserve tax-exempt status for the Fund in the US. Awards are then given either as direct financial support with no particular requirements for use, or in the form of vaccine procurement by UNICEF, or both. It should be noted that UNICEF holds and manages a separate fund, through which monies from the Vaccine Funds are channelled and into which governments have been making additional donations for GAVI-related activities. As the Director-General has noted: 'This support, based on the principle of a performance-based reward, constitutes a departure from traditional funding systems: instead of prescribing how resources should be used, it relies on governments and interagency coordination committees to set targets and monitor progress'.[1] The Director-General has been the first Chair of the GAVI Board; moreover, the WHO chairs one of the four Task Forces established by GAVI, on country coordination.

> 1. WHO Doc. A55/10, p. 2.

186. GAVI has given particular emphasis to a quick and flexible review and implementation process, and has attracted international attention because of its success in channelling support in immunization coverage for poor countries. Its resources have expanded to USD1.2 billion and more than USD820 million have been awarded to 54 countries as of May 2002.

187. MMV has a narrower focus than GAVI, and its founders have chosen an entirely different partnership model. MMV has been conceived because of the failure of the market to provide the required incentives for wide scale R&D in new medicines to treat malaria. The idea of a 'public venture capital fund' to encourage R&D and commercialization of new antimalarial drugs initially originated from discussions between WHO and the International Federation of Pharmaceutical Manufacturers Association (IFPMA). MMV was launched in November 1999: its aim is to lead to the discovery and eventual regulatory approval of one new afford-able antimalarial drug every five years.

188.   MMV was established as a Geneva-based not-for-profit foundation under Swiss law. It is thus a separate legal entity, which enjoys a favourable tax status under Swiss law. It is run in its day-to-day operation by a management team, headed by a Chief Executive Officer, which is independent from MMV's donors and stakeholders. It operates more like a small virtual R&D company than a public sector scientific funding agency, hence the need for an independent legal structure, unrelated to a hosting public organization. MMV receives funding and support from a variety of sources, mainly public or philanthropic: the Bill and Melinda Gates Foundation, ExxonMobil Corporation, Global Forum for Health Research, IFPMA, WHO, the Rockefeller Foundation, the World Bank, Roll Back Malaria Global partnership, TDR, the United Kingdom Department for International Devel-opment (DFID), Swiss Agency for Development and Cooperation and the Nether-lands Minister for Development Cooperation. MMV also receives contributions in-kind, such as management expertise, access to chemical libraries, high through-put screening and data handling, from several pharmaceutical companies, univer-sities and research institutes.

189.   MMV's governance structure consists of a twelve member Board, which has ultimate authority in the selection of projects to finance and their monitoring; an Expert Scientific Advisory Committee (ESAC) composed of scientists from both corporations and academia, which advises the Board on the selection and review of projects; and the aforementioned management team. Two staff members of WHO, from TDR and the Roll Back Malaria Programme (RBM), respectively, represent the Organization on the Board.[1]

   1. WHO Doc. EB105/8 Add.1.

190.   In view of its focus on the discovery and commercialization of new drugs in the face of an inertial pharmaceutical market, MMV operates by funding projects on a competitive basis. Applicants are required to sign an initial letter of intent, are made aware that continued funding depends on progress and on maintaining com-petitiveness with other MMV-funded projects, and are subject to regular review and scrutiny to assess progress. It has built a 'drug portfolio' that currently consists of six discovery projects and five development projects.

191.   One distinctive element of MMV and other similar partnerships is the use of intellectual property rights as a strategic element of its operations, so as to ensure some control over the eventual development of new drugs. The balance between ensuring an adequate return for participating companies and the affordability of the new drugs for developing countries revolves around the public source of funding, the not-for-profit nature of MMV, and the selection of appropriate intellectual property rights. In view of MMV's work mainly with large companies, which are not required to make substantial investments in R&D projects, the venture secures downstream rights to develop compounds, either through patent ownership or through a free licence on drug-development candidates that result from the research project. The main condition, in any case, is that MMV retains the right to take over development should a particular commercial partner withdraw.

192.   While it is not possible to review all recent PPPs and WHO involvement therein, it can be stated on a general basis that the Organization has on several occasions acted as the initiator and host of the partnership, provided its secretariat and implemented or coordinated technical activities. On some occasions, for example in connection with partnerships focusing on R&D of new drugs, it has also provided funding or assumed operating costs to facilitate the pursuit of their goal.

193.   Recent studies on PPPs have underlined a number of issues that WHO has been or should be considering with a view to a more strategic participation in partnerships. The most urgent is finding a balance between outreach to industry and maintaining credible safeguards for the integrity of the core functions of the Organization, especially its standard-setting ones.[1] Another issue of primary importance for WHO is a general policy vision of what should and could be achieved by sharing costs and benefits of public health activities with corporate partners, in view of the irreducible differences in goals and expectations. It is fair to say that, after a wave of enthusiasm in embracing 'partnerships' at the end of the 1990s, WHO has recently been considering them with more caution.

1. K. Buse, G. Walt, 'Public-Private health partnerships: a strategy for WHO', 79 *Bulletin of the World Health Organization*, No. 8, 2001, p. 751.

194.   Besides the more general issue of WHO's relations with the private sector, there are industries with which WHO will not, as a policy, entertain relations and whose activities are considered incompatible with those of the Organizations. The guidelines, restating a consistent if unwritten policy, clarify that relations should be avoided with the tobacco or arms industries.

195.   Particular mention should be made of the particular situation of tobacco companies. WHO has for a long time been critical of the conduct and role of tobacco companies for selling an inherently unhealthy and dangerous product with disregard for its impact, and carrying a heavy responsibility for the massive health damage inflicted by the consumption of tobacco products. The position of WHO has traditionally been that the tobacco industry lacks legitimacy as a counterpart and that it could not be trusted to support WHO in the search for ways and means to decrease the impact of the tobacco epidemic. Upon her assumption of office in 1998, Director-General Brundtland decided that tobacco control would be one of the top priorities of the Organization. According to the latest WHO estimates, tobacco use kills 4.2 million people annually with projections of up to ten million deaths a year by 2030 if smoking trends continue unabated. Through the establishment of the Tobacco Free Initiative, WHO established itself with renewed vigour at the forefront of international tobacco control efforts. This has led to a strong advocacy role on its part and a more aggressive and critical attitude against the tobacco industry.

196.   Reference may be made to a statement by the Director-General in 2001, which reads in relevant part: 'When challenged, tobacco companies choose to divert attention from the dramatic public health consequences of tobacco use. They talk of the "right to smoke" and of benefits to economies. They have denied the dangers of their products. They have systematically discredited individuals, institutions and processes that genuinely seek to improve people's well being through the control of tobacco. We know that they have tried to undermine the World Health Organization and the office of the Director General. In the public hearings that took place here in Geneva last week, some tobacco companies proposed joint work with the public health community. However, at the same time, they oppose the interventions that we know to have a measurable and sustained impact on tobacco. So, I urge cautious responses to overtures from tobacco companies. Ask them: are they offering to work on measures that really will have an impact on people's well-being? If so, they would seek less tobacco use and thereby fewer tobacco deaths. This would mean fewer smokers, and lower profits. Thus far, companies are offering to work on measures that have only a limited impact on youth and adult consumption. Let us remember – tobacco remains the only legal consumer product that kills half of its regular users.'[1]

> 1. The speech can be browsed at <http://www.who.int/director-general/speeches/2000/english/20001016_tobacco_control.html> (visited on 15 July 2002).

197.   The disclosure of a large amount of previously classified internal documents by some large tobacco companies, as part of a settlement reached in 1998 between them and several states of the US allowed tobacco control advocates, policy-makers, public health specialists and researchers a previously unimaginable insight into the marketing and public relations strategies orchestrated by the companies concerned and their early knowledge of the addictive effects of nicotine.[1] The documents revealed that several tobacco companies regarded the World Health Organization as one of their leading enemies, and that they had planned a strategy to 'contain, neutralise, reorient' WHO's tobacco control initiatives and had systematically worked to undermine and discredit WHO. Faced with this disclosure, and the doubts it could cast as to the actual influence by the tobacco companies over WHO's policy, the Director-General appointed in 1999 a committee of independent experts to search the available tobacco industry documents and report its findings. The committee concluded its work in July 2000 by releasing a massive report containing a scathing indictment of the tactics used by the companies concerned to undermine and neutralize WHO. The Committee stated *inter alia* that:

> 'The documents show that tobacco companies fought WHO's tobacco control agenda by, among other things, staging events to divert attention from the public health issues raised by tobacco use, attempting to reduce budgets for

the scientific and policy activities carried out by WHO, pitting other UN agencies against WHO, seeking to convince developing countries that WHO's tobacco control program was a "First World" agenda carried out at the expense of the developing world, distorting the results of important scientific studies on tobacco, and discrediting WHO as an institution.'[2]

1. The documents are stored at two repositories in the United States and the United Kingdom, respectively. Most of them have been scanned and posted on the internet by academic or advocacy institutions. *See* for example the internet site maintained by the University of California at San Francisco Library and Center for Knowledge Management, at <http://legacy.library.ucsf.edu/>, and that maintained by the US Centers for Disease Control at <http://www.cdc.gov/tobacco/industrydocs/index.htm> (visited on 15 July 2002).
2. *Tobacco Company Strategies to Undermine Tobacco Control Activities at the World Health Organization, Report of the Committee of Experts on Tobacco Industry Documents*, July 2000, available on-line at <http://www5.who.int/tobacco/repository/stp58/who_inquiry.pdf>, p. 13 (visited on 15 July 2002). The committee made a number of recommendations to address the question and consequences of corporate misbehaviour by tobacco companies, at *ibidem*, pp. 228–244.

198.   The findings of the committee have reinforced the perception by WHO of a lack of legitimacy of the tobacco industry as an interlocutor. In this context, WHO has recently produced a report exploring in general terms the potential of litigation against tobacco companies and public inquiries into their behaviour to foster broad tobacco control goals.[1]

1. *Towards health with justice – Litigation and public inquiries as tools for tobacco control* (Geneva, WHO, 2002).

Part V. Competence

Chapter 1. The Concept of Health

199. The central provisions for the definition and delimitation of WHO's mandate are Articles 1 and 2 of the Constitution in the light of their context including the preamble, which serves as an important interpretative element to fully appreciate the mandate of the Organization. Whereas Article 2 spells out in considerable details the functions through which the Organization pursues its goal, Article 1 broadly sets its objective as 'the attainment by all peoples of the highest possible level of health'. The preamble, as a matter of fact, contains some of the most advanced and visionary expressions underlying the establishment of WHO and defining its mission. Particular reference is made to the three initial paragraphs, which read as follows:

> 'Health is a state of complete physical, mental and social well-being and not merely the absence of disease or infirmity.
>
> The enjoyment of the highest attainable standard of health is one of the fundamental rights of every human being without distinction of race, religion, political belief, economic or social condition.
>
> The health of all peoples is fundamental to the attainment of peace and security and is dependent upon the fullest co-operation of individuals and States.'

200. The grant of authority given by Member States to WHO and enshrined in its Constitution, is then developed through the practice of the Organization. As international jurisprudence and scholarly literature have amply demonstrated, international organizations are living and dynamic organisms, which adapt and evolve their constitutional mandate in the light of historical and political developments as well as – in the case of technical agencies such as WHO – of technical and scientific developments. Such a process is carried out by the governing bodies of the Organization through the setting of policies and the orientation of its programme of work. It is also carried out by the Secretariat in its implementation of the mandates entrusted to it by the Constitution and the governing bodies, as well as in its pursuit and proposal of new or renewed areas of work. Besides relying on the generally accepted theory of implied powers, this evolutionary process is strengthened by Article 2(v) of the Constitution, which lays out as a residual function of WHO '... to take all necessary action to attain the objective of the Organization'.

201. The foregoing statements may lead to the conclusion that the competence of WHO coincides in practice with its functions and the activities carried out by it, which are reviewed in the next Part. However, this Part would like to offer some considerations on the 'outer limits' of WHO's mandate and on some of its essential components.

202. A glance at the functions listed in Article 2 and the issues concretely tackled by WHO since its establishment shows that health is an intrinsically complex and multi-faceted topic, which straddles many areas of human activity and which has undergone a deep technical and philosophical evolution during the last few decades. At the same time, it shows how interlinked and overlapping WHO's mandate is with that of most other agencies and bodies of the United Nations system. Besides FAO, UNDP and UNICEF, whose interactions with WHO have been mentioned in Part IV, interactions and overlaps are evident with, for example, the UN Environment Programme (UNEP) in the area of environmental risks to health; ILO as regards occupational health; the International Atomic Energy Agency (IAEA) concerning the health aspects of radiation safety and the medical applications of radioisotopes; and the United Nations as regards, for example, the increasingly evident relations between health and human rights.[1]

> 1. On coordination and cooperation with other organizations, *see supra* Part IV and, in the literature, Y. Beigbeder, *supra*, pp. 171–186.

203. The extent of the mandate of WHO is thus defined, *inter alia*, by the notion of 'health' contained in its Constitution, as the central object of its mission, and by its position as a specialized agency of the United Nations. Under the first point, the most relevant elements are the vision of health as a positive state encompassing both the individual and the community, as well as its definition, albeit with some important qualifications, as a human right.

204. The notion of a 'right to health', or at least a right to the protection and advancement of health through the provision of adequate services, is a nineteenth century development having as its origins the public health movement in Europe.

205. The Technical Preparatory Committee for the International Health Conference had proposed that 'health' as such should be stated to be the subject of a human right, in a declaration to the effect that 'The right to health is one of the fundamental rights to which every human being is entitled.' This proposal was eventually not adopted by the International Health Conference; nevertheless, since that time, the WHO definition has often been encapsulated in the phrase 'the right to health', both in the United Nations and in WHO itself. Thus, on two separate occasions (in 1970 and 1977), the World Health Assembly proclaimed that 'health [*without qualification*] is a human right'.[1] The same assertion was made by the International Conference on Primary Health Care, held in Alma-Ata in what was then the USSR in September 1978. In Article I of the Alma-Ata Declaration, the Conference reaffirmed that health in the positive sense codified in WHO's Constitution, 'is a fundamental human right and that the attainment of the highest possible level of health is a most important social goal . . .'.[2] In the 1998 World Health

Declaration, moreover, the Member States of WHO reaffirmed their commitment 'to the principle enunciated in its Constitution that the enjoyment of the highest attainable standard of health is one of the fundamental rights of every human being; in doing so, we affirm the dignity and worth of every person, and the equal rights, equal duties and shared responsibilities of all for health.'[3]

1. *See* Resolutions WHA23.41 of May 1970, in OR 184, p. 21, and WHA30.43 of May 1977, in OR 240, p. 25. In the preamble of the latter resolution, the Assembly considered that 'health is a basic human right and a world-wide social goal . . .'.
2. *Report of the International Conference on Primary Health Care* (Geneva, WHO, 1978), p. 2.
3. Health Assembly Resolution WHA51.7 of 16 May 1998, Annex, in WHA51/1998/REC/1, p. 4.

206. In the absence of any reported discussion in the *travaux préparatoires* or elsewhere on the precise scope of the WHO definition, or indeed on subsequent occasions when the right to health has been referred to in the terms indicated, it has been suggested that what is effectively intended is a right to the provision of health services, since health cannot be objectively defined and cannot therefore be the subject of a duty to provide it. One of the participants at a Workshop on The Right to Health as a Human Right, held in the Hague in 1978, Professor W.P. Von Wartburg, commented on this point as follows: 'Since health, unlike a commodity, is not available on demand, it follows that any attempt to interpret the basic rights of the citizen in a modern society as giving him an active claim to the enjoyment of good health must be regarded as mistaken from the very outset. The State cannot be held liable to the citizen in respect of any claims for the maintenance or restoration of health or for the alleviation of ill-health.'[1]

1. *See* Von Wartburg's contribution in R.-J. Dupuy, (ed.), *The Right to Health as a Human Right.* Proceedings of a Workshop convened by the Hague Academy of International Law and the United Nations University, The Hague, 27–29 July 1978 (Alphen aan den Rijn, the Netherlands, Sijthoff & Noordhoff, 1979), pp. 117–119; *see also* C.H. Vignes, 'Droit à la santé et coordination', *ibidem*, p. 304.

207. Most commentators have viewed the 'right to health' as implying a 'right to health services'. For example, Marmor suggests that '[a]lmost all of the twentieth century debate over the "right to health" in fact has addressed issues concerning not health *per se* but the distribution of access to medical care.'[1] Others suggest that a requirement to provide healthy living conditions is extremely vague and impossible to satisfy fully and that the rights relating to health set out in the international instruments are in too general terms for them to be invoked as international rules before a domestic judge.[2]

1. T. Marmor, 'The right to health care'. In: T.J. Bole, III & W.B. Bondeson (eds.), *Rights to Health Care* (Dordrecht, the Netherlands, Boston and London, Kluwer, 1991), p. 23.
2. J. Hersch, 'Human rights in Western thought: conflicting dimensions'. In: *Philosophical Foundations of Human Rights* (Paris, UNESCO, 1986), p. 144.

208. The WHO definition has not gone without other criticism. For example, it has been suggested that the inclusion of the reference to social well-being amounts to the 'over-medicalization' of the domain of social philosophy.[1] However, in the same vein, while the WHO definition has discerned the intimate communication between the good of the body and the self (and not only the individual self but the social community of selves), 'health' does not necessarily imply a state of complete physical, social and mental well-being since this demands that life deliver perfection.

1. N. Daniels, 'Health care needs and distributive justice'. In: R. Bayer, A.L. Caplan & N. Daniels, *In Search of Equity: Health Needs and the Health Care System* (Hastings-on-Hudson, NY, The Hastings Center, 1983), p. 13.

209. However, the suggestion that the 'right to health' implies only the provision of health services does not really satisfy the intent and substance of the relevant provision of the WHO Constitution. Such a construction does not correspond with the wishes of the founders of WHO and, as in the case of all human rights, the scope of the right is probably wider than the scope of the corresponding duties on the state. Furthermore, it is to be recalled that in the social context it has been expected that individuals would at least attempt to protect and promote their own health and that health cannot be promoted and protected solely by preventive and curative services; health does depend on lifestyles, personal attitudes and disciplines, and awareness of this can be aroused through programmes of health information and education. A striking example of this is UNAIDS, where with the present unavailability of effective prophylaxis or treatment, efforts were concentrated on preventive measures, together with a drive, under international human rights instruments, to avoid discrimination against and marginalization of individuals and groups engaging in high-risk behaviour.

210. A possible interpretation would be to consider the WHO definition and subsequent declarations as having the twofold purpose of setting a social goal and at the same time establishing a right under positive law to those services and encouragements as will help to attain that goal.

211. The definition of health and what is commonly referred to as the 'right to health' cannot be seen in a vacuum. The right to health has also been included in numerous human rights instruments adopted by the United Nations, which complement and interrelate with the WHO Constitution to provide a framework shaping both the international obligations of states as well as WHO's mandate. Besides Articles 25.1 of the Universal Declaration of Human Rights and 12 of the ICESCR, reference can be made to Article 5 of the International Convention on the Elimination of All Forms of Racial Discrimination;[1] Articles 11 and 12 of the Convention on the Elimination of All Forms of Discrimination against Women;[2] and Article 24 of the Convention on the Rights of the Child.[3]

1. Adopted on 7 March 1966, in UNTS, Vol. 660, p. 195.
2. Adopted on 18 December 1979, in UNTS, Vol. 1249, p. 13.
3. Adopted on 20 November 1989, in UNTS, Vol. 1577, p. 3.

212. The above-mentioned provisions and the practice concerning their interpretation appear to clarify that the right to health, in UN practice, is not tantamount to a right to health care, but has a broader and more complex content encompassing other human rights as well as a host of economic, social and political determinants.

At the same time, recent UN and WHO practice, as well as scholarly literature, have elucidated the numerous and deep linkages between health and the respect, protection and fulfilment of human rights.[1] The foregoing considerations on the contents of the right to health and the linkages between health and human rights may have substantial consequences for the definition of WHO's mandate as well as its role and position within the UN system. In particular, they strengthen WHO's role in dealing with the health-related aspects of social and economic situations which affect the enjoyment of human rights, including the right to health.

1. In the literature, *see in particular* J.M. Mann, S. Gruskin, M.A. Grodin, G.J. Annas (eds.), *Health and Human Rights* (New York/London, Routledge, 1999).

213. An important statement in this connection is General Comment No. 14 on 'the right to the highest attainable standard of health', adopted in May 2000 by the Committee on Economic, Social and Cultural Rights.[1] The committee monitors the implementation of the ICESCR and, *inter alia*, adopts general comments on the rights and obligations contained in the Covenant. General comments serve to clarify the nature and content of individual rights and obligations and are generally considered as authoritative interpretations issued by the expert body concerned.

1. UN Doc. E/C.12/2000/4, CESCR, of 4 July 2000, available on-line at <http://www.unhchr.ch/tbs/doc.nsf/view40?SearchView> (visited on 4 September 2002).

214. General Comment No. 14 opens by stating that 'health is a fundamental human right indispensable for the exercise of other human rights'. It recognizes that the right to health is closely related to and dependent upon the realization of other human rights, including the right to food, housing, work, education, participation, life, non-discrimination, privacy, access to information, and the freedoms of association, assembly and movement.[1] Further, the Committee interpreted the right to health as an inclusive right extending not only to timely and appropriate health care but also to the underlying determinants of health, such as access to safe and potable water and adequate sanitation, an adequate supply of safe food, nutrition and housing, health occupational and environmental conditions, and access to health-related education and information, including on sexual and reproductive health. The right to health contains both freedoms, including sexual and reproductive freedom, as well as entitlements such as the right to a system of health protection which provides equality of opportunity. The committee goes on to state that the right to health must be understood 'as a right to the enjoyment of a variety of facilities, goods and services and conditions necessary for the realization of the highest attainable standard of health'.[2]

1. *Ibidem*, para. 3, p. 2.
2. *Ibidem*, para. 9, p. 3.

215. The General Comment recognizes the central responsibility of WHO in realizing the right to health and refers to the Alma-Ata Declaration as providing 'compelling guidance' on the core obligations arising from Article 12 of the ICESCR.[1] By so doing, the General Comment frames WHO's technical assistance and cooperation as a form of implementation of a human right and implicitly acknowledges its role in the UN human rights system. The synergies between the UN and WHO in this respect could further be strengthened through the appointment by the Commission on Human Rights, at its 58th Session in 2002, of a special rapporteur on the right to health. The resolution requests the special rapporteur, *inter alia*, to develop a regular dialogue and discuss possible areas of cooperation with a number of actors, including notably WHO.

1. Even though the General Comment does not contain a specific reference to the Declaration, mention should be made in particular of Recommendation 5 on 'the content of primary health care', which reads as follows: '. . . primary health care should include at least: education concerning prevailing health problems and the methods of identifying, preventing, and controlling them; promotion of food supply and proper nutrition, an adequate supply of safe water, and basic sanitation; maternal and child health care, including family planning; immunization against the major infectious diseases; prevention and control of locally endemic diseases; appropriate treatment of common diseases and injuries; promotion of mental health; and provision of essential drugs.' *Report of the International Conference on Primary Health Care, supra,* p. 24.

216. WHO has, since the late 1990s, begun to explore more systematically than in the past the linkages between health and human rights in the context of the implementation of its constitutional mandate and of the implications of its policies and programmes. While the Health Assembly has not yet considered the desirability of adopting a general WHO human rights policy, it has on occasion considered the human rights implications of policies or programmes adopted in specific areas.[1] The Secretariat, particularly after the appointment of Director-General Brundtland, has been working towards the mainstreaming of human rights considerations into its programmes and strategies. The 'Corporate Strategy for the WHO Secretariat', submitted to the 105th Session of the Executive Board in January 1999, mentions as one of the new emphases for the Organization the adoption of 'a broader approach to health within the context of human development, humanitarian action and human rights . . .'.[2] Similarly, in an important report submitted at the same session concerning WHO's renewed focus on poverty and health, the Director-General emphasized the integration of gender and human rights perspectives in strategies for country support.[3]

1. Two recent examples are Resolutions WHA55.10 of 18 May 2002 on mental health, and WHA55.12 of the same date on HIV/AIDS. The latter resolution states that 'the full realization of human rights and fundamental freedoms for all is an essential element in a global response to the HIV/AIDS pandemic'. Unpublished but available on-line at <http://www.who.int/gb> (visited on 5 September 2002).
2. WHO Doc. EB105/3, p. 3.
3. WHO Doc. EB105/5, p. 5.

217. More generally, the WHO Secretariat has identified the following six broad areas of work for the 2002–2003 biennium with a view to strengthening its focus on human rights:

– Development of a WHO health and human rights strategy;
– Enhancement of the knowledge base of rights-based approaches to development and their application to health;
– Development of tools to integrate human rights in health development policies and programmes;

- Strengthening WHO's capacity to identify and address the human rights implications of its work;
- Providing technical support to Member States to integrate human rights in health development policies and programmes;
- Supporting the United Nations human rights system and other partners in advancing health as a human right and other health-related rights.[1]

> 1. Written submission by the World Health Organization to the 58th Session of the Commission on Human Rights, on file with the authors.

218. Assertions of WHO's competence to deal with certain issues have not gone unchallenged. In fact, as early as the 1946 International Health Conference, a proposal was made to extend WHO's regulatory powers under Article 21 of the Constitution to the prevention of the importation by states of biological, pharmaceutical, and similar products which did not conform to standards adopted by the Health Assembly. The proposal was rejected as it was felt by several states that it dealt with matters of commercial policy outside the jurisdiction of WHO. Another challenge to WHO's competence concerned the proposal for an International Code of Marketing of Breastmilk Substitutes: during the debates at the 34th Health Assembly, a few delegations objected that WHO was moving into the area of 'commercial codes', which did not pertain to it.[1]

> 1. WHA34/1981/REC/3, p. 200 (United States). On the International Code, *see infra*, Part VI.

Chapter 2. The Advisory Opinion of 8 July 1996

219. In this connection, an important if problematic episode for the delimitation of WHO's constitutional mandate was the response on 8 July 1996 by the International Court of Justice (ICJ) to a request by the Health Assembly, contained in Resolution WHA46.40 of May 1993, to deliver an advisory opinion on the following question: 'in view of the health and environmental effects, would the use of nuclear weapons by a State in war or other armed conflict be a breach of its obligations under international law including the WHO Constitution?'[1]

1. WHA46/1993/REC/1, p. 43. For the 'non-advisory opinion' of the Court, *see* ICJ Reports, 1996, pp. 66–85.

220. The request must be placed within a trend in the Health Assembly to consider certain political and subsequently legal aspects of war and of certain categories of weapons in the context of their health effects. In 1970, for example, the Assembly had adopted Resolution WHA23.53 concerning chemical and biological weapons, on the basis of a landmark study by the Secretariat on their health effects.[1] The Assembly, *inter alia*, emphasized 'the need for the rapid prohibition of the development, production and stockpiling of chemical and . . . biological weapons . . . as a necessary measure in the fight for human health'. A similar trend also took place concerning nuclear weapons and nuclear war. This was summarized by the Legal Counsel, Claude-Henri Vignes, during the oral pleadings before the ICJ, when he stated that 'Dans une première phase, l'OMS étudie "les effets des radiations ionisantes". Dans une seconde, elle examine "les effets de la guerre nucléaire". Dans une troisième, elle se préoccupe de "licéité de l'utilisation des armes nucléaires"'.[2]

1. OR 184, p. 29. The study in question is *Health aspects of chemical and biological weapons* (Geneva, WHO, 1970).
2. Available on-line at <http://www.icj-cij.org/icjwww/icases/ianw/ianw_cr/iANW_iCR9522_19951030.PDF>, p. 22 (visited on 5 September 2002).

221. The Assembly had adopted, in May 1987, Resolution WHA40.24 on health effects of nuclear war on health and health services, on the basis of a report by a Management Group appointed by the Director-General. The proposal to seek an advisory opinion on the legal consequences of the use of nuclear weapons arose in 1993 in the context of the follow-up to that resolution. The proposal, submitted in 1992 and 1993 by a number of developing countries with the decisive external support of several NGOs, sparked an intense debate as to the competence of WHO to deal with a legal/political question that seemed to pertain to the UN. The then

Legal Counsel, Anthony Piel, expressed doubts about the competence of WHO to deal with the 'legality' of the use of nuclear weapons and consequently to refer that question to the ICJ, noting that the issue appeared to fall within the jurisdiction of the UN General Assembly. At the same time, he qualified his views concerning the question whether the use of nuclear weapons would violate the WHO Constitution, by suggesting that the Health Assembly would have the competence to address it directly rather than referring it to the Court.[1] Before adopting the resolution, Committee B rejected a motion by the United States that the draft resolution was not within the competence of WHO.

   1. WHA45/1992/REC/3 pp. 4–5; WHA46/1993/REC/3 pp. 257–258 and 265–266.

   222.   The Court, by a comfortable majority of eleven to three,[1] argued that it lacked jurisdiction, under Article 96 of the UN Charter, to respond to WHO's question because the legality of the use of nuclear weapons did not fall within the competence of the Organization. This conclusion was based on the following main arguments:

(a) The interpretation of Article 2 of the Constitution, in the light of Article 31 of the Vienna Convention (which gives weight to the practice of the Organization to construe the meaning of the Constitution) as well as of the Court's jurisprudence concerning the particular nature of constitutive instruments of international organizations, leads to the conclusion that none of the functions of WHO is dependent upon the legality of the situation upon which it must act. Article 2 authorizes WHO to deal solely with the effects on health of human activities, including the use of nuclear weapons, since the Organization would be called to provide assistance in the case of such use whether it was legal or illegal: 'whether nuclear weapons are used legally or illegally, their effects on health would be the same.'[2] These conclusions are borne out by an analysis of the practice of WHO, which does not amount to an agreement among its members to interpret the Constitution as empowering the Organization to deal with the legality of the use of nuclear weapons.[3]

(b) Also the reference in Resolution WHA46.40 to primary prevention (i.e., the prohibition of nuclear weapons in the intentions of its sponsors) as the only means to deal with their health and environmental effects does not enlarge WHO's competence, because preventive actions can only refer to the functions provided for in Article 2 of the Constitution.

(c) The reference to the WHO Constitution in the WHA's question does not modify the main conclusions, as WHO is not empowered to seek an opinion on the interpretation of its Constitution in relation to matters outside the scope of its functions.

(d) The Court also dismisses the determination by the WHA of its own competence as somehow determinative of the competence of the Organization, in that it cannot prevent the Court from indepedently satisfying itself that the conditions for the exercise of its advisory jurisdiction are met.

(e) Although the Court recalls its established jurisprudence concerning the implied powers enjoyed by international organizations, it concludes that WHO, as a specialized agency belonging to a coherent institutional system laid out under the UN Charter, is rather subject to a 'principle of speciality'. The application of such principle, expressly enunciated by the Court for the first time, means that the specialized agencies are endowed with complementary and sectorial powers, which may neither encroach with each other nor with the general powers of the United Nations. Questions concerning the use of force and disarmament lie within the competence of the United Nations; any other conclusion would render meaningless the notion of a specialized agency.[4]

1. Judges Koroma, Shahabuddeen and Weeramantry voted against and appended lengthy dissenting opinions, in ICJ Report, *supra*, pp. 97–224.
2. *Ibidem*, p. 77.
3. *Ibidem*, p. 81.
4. *Ibidem*, pp. 78–80.

223. It is the first time that the ICJ refuses to accede to a request for an advisory opinion.[1] The dissenting judges and most scholars who have commented on the Court's decision have criticized it on several accounts. In particular, there has been an impression that the Court has 'sacrificed' WHO by adopting an extremely strict approach, in the light of the political sensitivities surrounding the parallel similar requests from both WHO and the UN General Assembly.[2]

1. The Permanent Court of International Justice had declined to give an advisory opinion in the 1923 case concerning the Statute of Eastern Carelia, in PCIJ, B Series, No. 5.
2. *See for example* V. Leary, 'The WHO Case: Implications for Specialized Agencies', in L. Boisson de Chazournes, P. Sands (eds.), *International Law, the International Court of Justice and Nuclear Weapons* (Cambridge, Cambridge University Press, 1999), p. 116.

224. Both Judges Shahabuddeen and Koroma, as well as Prof. Leary, have argued that the Court placed too much emphasis on the issue of 'legality versus illegality' of nuclear weapons *per se* to justify its conclusions, while the question by the Assembly focused on the legal consequences of the use of those weapons under international law and, most importantly, under the WHO Constitution. The dissenting judges, in particular, disagreed with the ICJ's cursory dismissal of the argument that WHO would in any case be competent to seek an opinion about the interpretation of its own Constitution.[1] In connection with the scope of its constitutional mandate, the argument that WHO may only be concerned with the effects of certain human activities has been defined as formalistic. The rules of international law applicable to those activities may be relevant for WHO's mandate in that they could, for example, affect its assistance to states in prevention, planning and preparedness, determine who would be financially responsible for certain measures, and clarify the scope and context of medical advice (e.g., on the effects of nuclear weapons).[2] Finally, it has been argued that the Court could have reformulated the question and framed it in a way which would have enabled it to fully exercise its advisory jurisdiction. In fact, the Court did just that with the question posed by the WHA in 1979 concerning the WHO-Egypt agreement.

1. *Ibidem*, p. 114. *See* ICJ Reports, *supra*, p. 35 (Judge Shahabuddeen) and p. 140 (Judge Koroma).
2. M. Bothe, 'The WHO Request', in L. Boisson de Chazournes, P. Sands (eds.), *supra*, pp. 104–105.

225.   Also the construction of the 'principle of speciality', as opposed to the theory of implied powers consistently advocated by the Court with regard to the United Nations, has been criticized as being based on an unrealistic vision of the UN system as composed of bodies and agencies with an exclusive and clearly delimited technical (i.e., non-political) mandate. Reality, they argue, has instead revealed how overlapping and interconnected the competence and functions of specialized agencies can be, and how the emphasis should rest on coordination and coherence.[1] Some commentators have wondered about the implications of the advisory opinion for specialized agencies in general, in particular whether it implies a message by the Court that it is not their principal judicial body and that it may assume the role of guardian of the division of powers within the UN system.[2]

1. *Ibidem*, pp. 108–111.
2. G. Griffith, C. Staker, 'The Jurisdiction and Merits Phases Distinguished', in L. Boisson de Chazournes, P. Sands (eds.), *supra*, p. 75.

226.   It does not seem that the advisory opinion has led to a dramatic reconsideration by WHO of its overall mandate, and the observation may be correct that the opinion has to be seen in its political context to appreciate its value as a precedent. It is fair to say in any case that the legal status of certain situations and activities, beyond the strict dilemma of 'legality versus illegality', may be a legitimate concern of WHO within the ambit of its constitutional functions. Rules of international law prohibiting or restricting certain activities play a protective and preventive role which may indeed be relevant for WHO's technical functions. Equally, they may provide for forms of assistance with a definite impact on health.

227.   The Secretariat published in 2001 a thoroughly revised edition of its 1970 study on chemical and biological weapons.[1] The new edition contains a chapter on the legal aspects of those weapons, focusing on the 1972 Biological Weapons Convention and the 1993 Chemical Weapons Convention. While mostly devoted to recommendations on preparedness and the mobilization of resources for assistance, a public health approach to the possible use of those weapons could not ignore the crucial importance of prevention and protection, based on the applicable legal instruments. The publication thus contains a chapter that reviews the main legal and institutional features of the principal international treaties prohibiting the use or possession of chemical and biological weapons. Moreover, one of the recommendations emerging from the study reads as follows:

'With the entry into force of the 1972 and 1993 Conventions and the increasing number of states that have joined them, great strides have been made towards "outlawing the development and use in all circumstances of chemical and biological agents as weapons of war", as called for in the 1970 edition of the present report. . . . All Member States should therefore implement the two Conventions fully and transparently; propagate in education and professional training the ethical principles that underlie the Conventions; and support measures that would build on their implementation.'[2]

1. *Public Health Response to Biological and Chemical Weapons* (2nd edition, Geneva, WHO, 2001). Available on-line at <http://www.who.int/emc/book_2nd_edition.htm> (visited on 6 September 2002).
2. *Ibidem*, p. iv.

228.   Similar considerations could be made in connection with the on-going negotiation of a Framework Convention on Tobacco Control (*infra*, Part VI). In view of the particular status of tobacco and tobacco products as commodities or manufactured products of mass consumption manufactured and marketed by a group of powerful multinational companies, which at the same time are inherently harmful for health, a purely medical or advocacy approach has proved to be inadequate. Consequently, WHO Member States have chosen to pursue an international regulatory approach aiming at the market mechanisms which may influence tobacco demand. In this connection, WHO's consideration of the rules governing such mechanisms has been seen as closely related to the ultimate public health objective pursued by the Organization.

Part VI. Functions

Chapter 1. General Considerations

§1. WHO's Functions and their Categorization

229. The functions entrusted to WHO are listed in Article 2 of the Constitution. Article 2 should, in turn, be read in the light of other constitutional provisions bestowing certain powers or functions to specific organs. Particularly relevant in this connection are Article 18 concerning the Health Assembly, Article 28 concerning the Executive Board, and Article 50 concerning the regional committees.

230. These provisions make it clear that the founders of WHO saw the new institution as a central catalyst for the reconstruction and development of health systems devastated by the Second World War, and assigned to it a wide range of functions culminating with the authority to adopt binding regulations.

231. Article 2 contains 22 paragraphs which list in some detail a random range of functions and activities, not ordered according to any particular priority. Some of the items are actually examples of activities rather than functions in their own right – for example, paragraphs (g), (h) and (i). In this respect, the formulation of Article 2 is probably not entirely felicitous and may have been the result of compromises during the negotiation of the Constitution. However, the paramount and most important function is arguably that laid out in paragraph (a), 'to act as the directing and co-ordinating authority on international health work', which appears to embody the essential task of the Organization. It is interesting in this respect that the Technical Preparatory Committee, in its proposal for the WHO's Constitution, listed as an overarching function that 'the World Health Organization should be the general and co-ordinating authority in international health work . . .', while other functions were listed as a means to pursue this central aim.[1]

1. OR 1, p. 70.

232. The drafting technique of Article 2 does not facilitate a categorization and grouping of WHO's constitutional functions and the activities carried out in their implementation. Although categorizing is always somehow arbitrary, since many activities may fall within different functions or are not easy to label, grouping WHO's diverse activities around some main groups of functions is a useful intellectual reference for the purpose of reviewing or assessing those activities. It should be noted that the drafters of the Constitution themselves had felt the need to rationalize and categorize the disparate functions appearing in Article 2. To that purpose, the summary report of the International Health Conference refers to six interrelated categories: (1) general and co-ordinative; (2) co-operation with other organizations; (3) research and technical services; (4) promotional and educational activities; (5) field operations; and (6) regulatory measures.[1]

  1. OR 2, p. 17.

233. However, the development of WHO's activities and policies since its inception has consolidated the view, expressed on some occasions by the Director-General, that the main dichotomy in WHO's functions is between technical co-operation and normative or directing/coordinating work. Implicit in this division has been the idea that normative or directing functions are carried out primarily at headquarters, and that technical cooperation describes the work of regional and country offices.

234. For the purpose of the present contribution, WHO's functions will be grouped into four main categories, under which most of the functions listed in Article 2 fall. These were identified by the Director-General in a report to the 97th Session of the Board, as follows:

'a role of direction and coordination on international health work (paragraphs (a), (b) and (j));
a role of assistance (paragraphs (c), (d), (e), (q)), including maintaining epidemiological and statistical services (paragraph (f));
a role of research (paragraphs (j) and (n)); and
a normative role (primarily paragraphs (k), (o), (s), (t) and (u)).'[1]

  1. WHO Doc. EB97/9, p. 2.

235. It should be recalled that the relevance of the functions codified in Article 2 were subject to a critical revision by a Special Group for the review of the Constitution, which conducted at the request of the Board a general review of the Constitution and of regional arrangements with a view to their possible adaptation to global changes. The group recommended a revision of Article 2 which would reflect the evolution in health policy since 1948 as well as future prospects, and embody broad and flexible functions defined as general principles rather than specific activities. It also proposed an alternative but very lengthy text of Article 2.[1] The Board eventually decided not to submit the amendment to the Health Assembly, noting that Article 2, while certainly not a perfect provision, had served well the goals of the Organization.[2]

  1. EB101/1998/REC/1, Annex 3, p. 52.
  2. EB103/1999/REC/2, p. 139.

§2. PROGRAMMING AND PRIORITIES

236.   WHO has, since its inception, organized its work around a number of
programmes and priorities which appeared the most relevant or urgent at any particular time. The only constitutional provision concerning the programming of its
activities is contained in Article 28(g) of the Constitution, whereby the Executive
Board submits to the Assembly 'for consideration and approval a general programme of work covering a specific period'.

237.   General Programmes of Work (GPWs) have been used throughout the life
of the Organization as a general device to provide a policy framework for WHO's
activities for a definite period of time, which historically has oscillated between
four and six years. The first GPW was adopted in 1951; that currently in force is
the tenth and covers the period 2002–2005.[1] The Director-General has stated that
the GPW does not only establish the programme framework for WHO's work
but, in view of its approval by the global intergovernmental body in the field of
health and the involvement of a wide variety of actors in its implementation, also
establishes 'the global health policy framework for action by the world health
community.'[2]

   1. Adopted by Resolution WHA54.1 of 18 May 2001, in WHA/54/2001/REC/1, p. 1.
   2. *Ninth General Programme of Work*, WHO Doc. GPW/2002–2005, p. 1.

238.   The essential programming tool for WHO's activities, however, is the
programme budget, which is approved by the Health Assembly for biennial cycles
starting in even years (on financial matters *see infra*, Part VII). The preparation of
the programme budget, which virtually starts shortly after the adoption of the
previous one, is the principal process through which the Secretariat, with the input
of the Board and of the regional committees, proposes the main operational directions of the Organization as well as the main priorities for the period concerned.
The decentralized nature of WHO and the power and autonomy of the regions
poses a challenge to the integration and coherence of the planning process. In the
past, as a matter of fact, the regional offices prepared a draft programme budget for
their respective regions, which were commented on by the regional committees and
then consolidated into a single document at headquarters. This process did not
always ensure the formulation of a coherent and strategically balanced programme
but resulted in the amalgamation of different regional and global priorities.

239.   To better appreciate the working of WHO's programming process as well
as the definition of its current areas of work and priorities, reference can be made
to the process of rationalization and reform launched by Director-General Brundtland.
The Director-General, aware of the need to consolidate and promote the comparative
advantages of WHO within a changing global environment, submitted to the 105th
Session of the EB in January 2000 her vision of a 'corporate strategy' for WHO.[1]
The corporate strategy was presented as a process of organizational development and
reform, both in internal decision-making and in the process of priority-setting. It
was also seen as the first step in a process of harmonization of WHO's work, which

would have led to the elaboration of a GPW, a programme budget and biennial work-plans complementing each other.

1. WHO Doc. EB105/3.

240. The corporate strategy was not submitted for approval by the Board, but its content was included almost *verbatim* into the current GPW, and thus approved by the Assembly. The strategy proposes new ways of working to enable WHO to respond effectively to a changing international environment. In particular, a strong emphasis was placed by the Director-General on adopting a broader approach to health within the context of human development and human rights, on the links between health and poverty reduction, on increasing equity in health, and on playing a greater role in establishing an international consensus on health policy, strategies and standards. These are the areas in which WHO arguably enjoys a comparative advantage. The corporate strategy identifies the following four strategic directions, which will guide WHO at least until 2005:

> '**Strategic direction 1:** reducing excess mortality, morbidity and disability, especially in poor and marginalized populations.
> **Strategic direction 2:** promoting healthy lifestyles and reducing risk factors to human health that arise from environmental, economic, social and behavioural causes.
> **Strategic direction 3:** developing health systems that equitably improve health outcomes, respond to people's legitimate demands, and are financially fair.
> **Strategic direction 4:** framing an enabling policy and creating an institutional environment for the health sector, and promoting an effective health dimension to social, economic, environmental and development policy.'[1]

1. *Ibidem.*

241. As noted, the first product of the corporate strategy has been the GPW 2002–2005. Its duration has been limited to four years to make it coincide with the programme budget cycle. On the basis of the changes introduced with the corporate strategy, the Director-General launched an organization-wide process linking regions and headquarters, for the preparation of the draft programme budget 2002–2003. In particular, for the first time, the regional committees could review and comment on the draft budget in its entirety rather than on the specific regional budget. The programme budget flowed from the corporate strategy, and complemented the GPW in dividing WHO's activities into 35 areas which strive to represent the activities of WHO's Secretariat at all levels and provide a degree of continuity with the previous programme budget.[1] The GPW and the programme budget identify the following eleven priority areas which would have received increased allocations:

Malaria;
Tuberculosis;
HIV/AIDS;
Cancer, cardiovascular diseases and diabetes;

Tobacco;
Maternal health;
Food safety;
Mental health;
Safe blood;
Health systems;
Investing in change in WHO.[2]

> 1. The areas of work cover a broad range of activities, from surveillance, prevention and management of communicable diseases and sustainable development, to research policy and promotion and immunization and vaccine development.
> 2. *Proposed Programme Budget 2002–2003*, WHO Doc. PB/2002–2003, pp. 7–9.

242. The Director-General based the identification of priorities on a number of criteria, such as the potential for significant changes in the burden of disease with cost-effective interventions; the urgent need for new technologies; the opportunities to reduce health inequalities within and between countries; WHO's comparative advantages and major demands for its support from Member States. The Director-General, in the preparation (on-going at the time of writing) for the programme budget 2004–2005, proposed the replacement of the last priority, which was more managerial than programmatic, with 'environment and health'.[1]

> 1. WHO Doc. EB109/9. Requests for the inclusion of that priority were coming from the African, European and Eastern Mediterranean regions.

243. Yet another break with previous practice concerned the operational planning stage after the adoption of the programme budget, i.e., the elaboration of detailed work plans breaking down objectives and expected results into clear activities. This concerned in particular country programmes, which were not included on purpose in the draft budget document in view of its different approach, in particular to stress the unity of the Organization as 'one WHO'. One of the problems encountered in the implementation of the programme budget in the past was that, in view of its lengthy preparation and its approval by the Assembly in May for the following year, the time of preparation and that of implementation were quite removed. This made it difficult to adapt programmes to intervening circumstances and sometimes rendered the relevant parts of the programme budget already obsolete at the start of the implementation phase. In the last programme budget exercise, instead, the negotiation of country programmes by regional and country offices started after the Board's review of the budget estimates in January 2001, i.e., much closer to the implementation phase, with initial reporting to the regional committees during the same year. Moreover, to avoid the fragmentation which prevailed in the past among regions, the Director-General's policy was that the country programmes should take their inspiration and point of departure from the policies agreed upon by the Board and the Assembly, in particular the 35 areas of work applicable to the whole of WHO.

Chapter 2. Normative Functions

244. There is no doubt that WHO was conceived as an organization with a primarily directing and normative role. As the single universal public health agency, which was supposed to replace the previous international bureaux administering the sanitary conventions, WHO was granted extensive powers to set health-related standards and ensure their uniformity at the global level. This design transpires from both paragraphs (k), (o), (s), (t) and (u) of Article 2 as well as Articles 19 to 23 concerning the functions of the Health Assembly. Chapter V clearly centres the normative functions of the Organization in the Health Assembly and provides for three types of legal instruments: conventions and agreements; regulations; and recommendations.

§1. International Conventions and Agreements

I. General Considerations

245. The authority of WHO to adopt international agreements is enshrined in Article 19 of the Constitution. The formulation of that provision was the result of a compromise among different proposals and concerns at the 1946 Conference. The delegation of Belgium, in particular, had proposed an article which largely repeated the formulation of Article 19 of the ILO Constitution.[1] The preference of most participants, however, was for a shorter and more general provision which would leave substantial discretion to the Assembly. Where the Conference appears to have been more clearly influenced by the ILO Constitution is in Article 20, which requires members to 'take action relative to the acceptance' of conventions adopted by the Assembly within eighteen months from their adoption and to notify the Director-General accordingly.

1. Doc. E/H/F/W.6 of 27 June 1946.

246. Whereas the Constitution prescribes the necessary majority for the valid adoption of conventions, it appears to leave the Assembly full discretion in determining the conditions for their signature, deposit, entry into force and so on. The final part of the article, in particular, clarifies that Member States can only become bound by conventions and agreements through their acceptance thereof, but does not refer to the entry into force of agreements as such. That will depend from the final clauses of each convention, which are not prejudiced by Article 19. Why the Constitution should restate a basic principle of the law of treaties is made clear by the preparatory works of the Constitution, especially those of Committee II of the 1946 Conference. On the one hand, participants wanted to underline the difference between conventions and regulations as to their entry into force for individual Member States. On the other hand, the language in question represents a reaction to a proposal which had been discussed in the Technical Preparatory Committee, to the effect that the Constitution would have authorized delegates to the Assembly to sign conventions without reservation of further ratification. This proposal was considered as going too far in the light of the consensual principle of the law of treaties, hence the reference to the constitutional processes of each Member State.

247. The drafters of the Constitution clearly intended to circumscribe the treaty-making authority of WHO to the global level represented by the Health Assembly. It was not envisaged that regional committees could exercise such a normative authority; the regions would rather devote themselves to technical and policy considerations which did not imply the adoption of binding norms at the international level. The fear of a dangerous fragmentation among WHO regions is evident in that decision. The question of the rationale and the legal basis for the adoption of international conventions at the regional level, which had been dormant for 50 years, was raised in 1999 by developments which occurred in the European Region. Reference is made, in particular, to the support given by the Regional Office for Europe, jointly with the Secretariat of the United Nations Economic Commission for Europe (UN-ECE), to the drafting of a Protocol on Water and Health to the 1992 Convention on the Protection and Use of Transboundary Watercourses and International Lakes.[1] The Protocol was adopted on 17 June 1999 by a ministerial conference jointly convened by the WHO Regional Director for Europe and the UN-ECE Executive Secretary. The process followed prevents the Protocol from being considered a 'WHO treaty' under Article 19 of the Constitution. However, that event and the provision in the declaration adopted by the conference about the possible negotiation of a pan-European framework convention on transport, environment and health, prompted the Secretariat to submit to the Executive Board at its 105th Session in January 2000 the general question of whether to grant legal authority to the regional committees to conclude conventions on matters of strictly regional interests. The Executive Board, however, decisively rejected the idea of granting any general treaty-making authority to the regional committees, limiting itself to envisaging the possibility of *ad hoc* authorizations. The arguments raised during the short debate focused on the danger of hindering or compromising the integrity of global policies by the Organizations. No particular added value was seen in allowing the regions to regulate matters of local concern. Interestingly, also European States such as Norway and the Russian Federation declared themselves against the idea.[2] It should be added that the decision taken by the Board does not affect the authority of PAHO, which is a separate international organization endowed by its statute with the competence to conclude treaties. This competence has been expressly recognized by WHO in Article 3 of the cooperation agreement concluded in 1949.[3]

1. The text appears in ECOSOC Doc. MP.WAT/AC.1/1999/1 of 24 March 1999. The Protocol had 36 signatories and seven contracting parties as of August 2002.
2. Doc. EB/105/2000/REC/2, pp. 136–139.
3. Reproduced in *Basic Documents*, *supra*, p. 38.

II. The Framework Convention on Tobacco Control

248. The Member States of WHO never seriously considered the idea of adopting conventions under Article 19 until the 1990s. The replacement of the regime of sanitary conventions was supposed to be achieved through the regulations envisaged by Article 21. Moreover, the emphasis of the Organization for many years was placed on the eradication of diseases or the setting of global health policy through non-binding resolutions and declarations, thus the pursuit of health goals at the global level through the adoption of treaties was not seriously considered.

249. This situation changed during the 1990s, when the Organization faced the compelling need to respond to the challenge of the growing tobacco pandemic. The progressive worsening of the global tobacco pandemic has turned tobacco control into an area of growing importance and urgency for WHO. The health impact of tobacco use and the development of strategies for tobacco control have figured on the agenda of the World Health Assembly since 1970.[1] Still, notwithstanding WHO's accomplishments in this area, the Director-General had to admit in 1994 that comprehensive and sustained national tobacco strategies meeting WHO's recommendations existed only in a few countries.[2]

1. Resolution WHA23.32, in OR 184, p. 15.
2. WHO Document EB95/27, cited in Allyn L. TAYLOR, 'An International Regulatory Strategy for Global Tobacco Control', *Yale Journal of International Law*, 1996, pp. 257–304.

250. The lack of uniformity of national tobacco control legislation and programmes have compounded the difficulty for WHO to elaborate an effective international strategy, also in view of the policies of multinational tobacco companies which have always striven to weaken and fragment tobacco control regulations. Major tobacco companies, faced with increasing public hostility and shrinking markets in developed countries, have been aggressively pursuing the markets of developing countries and countries with economies in transition, which were often ill-prepared in the area of tobacco control. Export subsidies and political pressures by the major exporting nations have led to overall lower prices and increased availability and demand.[1] Finally, as a result of a number of lawsuits in the United States which led to the release to the public of a large number of internal documents of tobacco companies, it became increasingly clear that the latter had not only concealed for decades the addictive and dangerous effects of tobacco, but had also tried to circumvent and destabilize tobacco control policies by individual states as well as by WHO.[2]

1. A.L. Taylor, R. Roemer, *International Strategy for Tobacco Control*, WHO Doc. WHO/PSA/ 96.6, p. 2.
2. S.A. Glantz, 'Looking through a Keyhole at the Tobacco Industry: the Brown and Williamson Documents', *Journal of the American Medical Association*, 1995, pp. 219–224. *See also Tobacco Industry Strategies to Undermine Tobacco Control Activities at the World Health Organization, supra*, Part III.

251. All such elements militated for a change of strategy in favour of an international regulatory approach to tobacco control. The 48th World Health Assembly requested the Director-General, by Resolution WHA48.11, to report on the feasibility of an international instrument of a non-binding or binding nature. The 49th Health Assembly, acting upon a report by the Director-General[1] and a technical paper by the Secretariat,[2] requested by Resolution WHA49.17 of 25 May 1996 the Director-General to initiate the development of a framework convention. Finally, on 24 May 1999, the 52nd World Health Assembly launched, by Resolution WHA52.18, the drafting and negotiation of a framework convention on tobacco control (FCTC).

1. WHO Document A/49/4, pp. 2–6.
2. A.L. Taylor, R. Roemer, *supra*.

252. The WHO Secretariat, in its report to the 49th World Health Assembly, supported the idea of a framework convention of a broad nature, to be supplemented by a number of thematic protocols. The recommendation to aim at a framework convention rather than a single comprehensive agreement was seen as a compromise solution between a purely recommendatory instrument and a single convention, so as to engage states in an incremental and flexible normative exercise in a novel area. The creation of an institutionalized forum for cooperation would progressively build support for reaching agreement on substantive commitments. The legal argument was based on an analogy with recent environmental conventions and their protocols, which were seen as the most suitable model. As in the case of environmental conventions, a framework convention on tobacco control would facilitate 'a cognitive and normative consensus' on facts and measures, thus building momentum among states and helping to overcome the resistance of the tobacco industry.[1]

1. D. Bodansky, *The Framework Convention/Protocol Approach*, WHO Doc. WHO/NCD/TFI/99.1, p. 18.

253. The Health Assembly established an open-ended Working Group 'which will prepare proposed draft elements of the WHO framework convention . . .'. Only after this preparatory step, an Intergovernmental Negotiating Body (INB) open to all Member States would 'draft and negotiate' the FCTC and possible related protocols. The Working Group held two sessions, from 25 to 29 October 1999 and from 27 to 29 March 2000. The Secretariat submitted to the first session a report[1] containing an analysis and examples of the elements considered typical of a framework convention, drawing mainly from environmental conventions as a basis for its suggestions of structure and text. At the second session, the Secretariat focused the work of the group by submitting a set of 'provisional texts of proposed draft elements' for the FCTC, largely based on the discussion at the first session.[2] The Working Group held a general discussion on such elements and offered a number of comments. The 'pre-negotiation' process thus produced a catalogue of draft elements which, however, were not the object of negotiations or an agreement. Consequently, they did not limit the authority of the INB to agree on completely different language, to exclude some of the elements or to include new provisions.

1. WHO Doc. A/FCTC/WG1/6.
2. WHO Doc. A/FCTC/WG2/3.

254. The 53rd World Health Assembly, held in May 2000, adopted Resolution WHA53.16, which requested the INB, among other things, to initially focus on the

draft convention, without prejudice to future discussions on possible protocols. The INB held its first session from 16 to 20 October 2000 and elected a bureau composed of a chairperson and six vice-chairpersons. The INB acted in principle under the Rules of Procedure of the Health Assembly, which were applicable to it as a subsidiary body of the Assembly. At the same time, and in conformity with the flexibility offered by the Assembly's rules, the INB adapted some of the rules and working processes to fit its exigencies.

255.   The process in the INB was influenced since the beginning by the perception that many delegations wanted to approach negotiations in a step-by-step and progressive fashion to enhance the INB's ownership of the negotiating text. Consequently, the INB at its first session (INB1) held a general debate based on the draft elements produced by the Working Group, and agreed that individual comments and textual proposals would be factually recorded in separate conference papers.[1] At the end of the first session, moreover, the INB agreed that the Chairperson would draft a text reflecting his perception of the debate, drawing on the draft elements considered by the Working Group and the proposals made by delegations during INB1.

   1. A/FCTC/INB1/Conf.Papers Nos. 1 to 15.

256.   The Chairman tried, in his draft text of January 2001,[1] to simplify and rearrange the material emerging from the draft elements and from the discussions at INB1. At the same time, based on the discussion at INB1, the Chairman proposed that initial consideration should be given to three protocols on, respectively, tobacco advertising, promotion and sponsorship; elimination of illicit trade in tobacco products; and regulation of the contents and disclosure of tobacco products, including labelling and packaging.

   1. A/FCTC/INB2/2.

257.   The Chair's text was submitted to the second session of the INB (INB2), held from 30 April to 5 May 2001. In order to progress more expeditiously, the INB established three Working Groups, each led by two co-chairpersons elected according to criteria of geographic distribution among WHO's six regions.[1] The Chair's text was divided among the three groups so as to maintain a balance in their respective workloads and to group together items presenting common elements.[2]

   1. The Co-chairpersons of Working Group 1 were from France and Thailand; those of Working Group 2 from Canada and Zimbabwe; and those of Working Group 3 from Egypt and New Zealand.
   2. The initial distribution of items is contained in Doc. A/FCTC/INB2/DIV/6.

258.   At its third and fourth sessions, held from 22 to 28 November 2001 and from 18 to 23 March 2002, respectively, the process followed by the Working Groups mainly consisted of rounds of textual proposals by Member States, which the Co-Chairs then attempted to consolidate into progressively more accepted texts. The Co-Chairs' texts were then submitted again to their respective working groups for comments and further textual proposals. The Working Groups held both formal

and informal meetings, with the informal ones dedicated to discussions on substantive issues. At the end of the fourth session, to facilitate the progress of work and consolidate the various parts of the draft text into a single coherent negotiating text, the Chair undertook to prepare a new Chair's text to be submitted to the fifth session (INB5) in October 2002.[1]

1. The new Chair's text was issued in July 2002 as Doc. A/FCTC/INB5/2 and can be browsed at: <http://www.who.int/gb/fctc/PDF/inb5/einb52.pdf> (visited on 1 September 2002).

259. It should be noted that the regional groups have been actively involved in the negotiating process. All regional groups, as well as some sub-regional groupings such as the Latin American and Caribbean countries as well as the ASEAN countries, met between sessions and reviewed in various ways the Chair's text or the texts emerging from the various phases of the negotiations. They also formulated regional proposals, which allowed them to participate in INB3 and INB4 with unified or coordinated positions.[1] A particularly intense consultation process was undertaken by the countries of the European Union and the institutions of the European Community, in particular the Commission. According to the distribution of competence on specific items, either the Commission or the country holding the rotating presidency of the Union would make proposals and comments on behalf of the Community and/or its Member States.

1. For example, the countries of the African region met on 2–4 October 2001 and produced an agreed text referred to as the 'Algiers text'. Texts emerging from such regional consultations can be browsed at <http://www5.who.int/tobacco/page.cfm?sid=66> (visited on 6 June 2002).

260. Coming now to a brief review of the contents of the text under negotiation as of the time of writing, this is largely based on the proposals of the Chair in his texts of January 2001 and July 2002. The draft texts were, by and large, organized along the following substantive elements:

(1) Objective. The provision retained in the Chairman's text focused on continually and substantially reducing the prevalence of tobacco use;
(2) Guiding principles, such as the importance of technical and financial assistance, the responsibility of the tobacco industry for the harm its products cause to public health, and the participation of civil society in achieving the objective of the Convention;
(3) General obligations, mainly concerning the establishment of national measures, institutions and policies;
(4) Price and tax measures to reduce the demand for tobacco. The draft texts provided for imposition of taxes to achieve reduction in tobacco consumption, progressive harmonization of price measures and the prohibition of duty-free sales;
(5) Non-price measures to reduce the demand for tobacco. A number of measures were placed under this rubric, such as protection from passive smoking; regulation of tobacco products contents and their disclosure; packaging and labelling; education and training; advertising, promotion and sponsorship. Among these, the prohibition or restriction of advertising, promotion and sponsorship has a crucial importance for its international implications and its proved effectiveness in decreasing smoking rates;

(6) Demand reduction measures concerning tobacco dependence and cessation, mainly focusing on the integration of tobacco dependence treatment into national health programmes;

(7) Measures related to the supply of tobacco. Areas such as illicit trade, sales to and by young persons, and government subsidies for tobacco growing and manufacturing were grouped in this section. A particularly sensitive topic in this respect is illicit trade in tobacco products. Evidence shows the magnitude of the problem, whereby billions of cigarettes disappear from the normal chain of legal transactions and are smuggled through a variety of mechanisms by organized criminal groups;

(8) Surveillance, research and exchange of information, encompassing general obligations to cooperate in surveying key epidemiological indicators of tobacco consumption, and in exchanging a broad range of information.

261. Scientific, technical and legal cooperation. This section focused on measures to support tobacco workers and growers in the development of alternative livelihoods, which have been defined as essential to secure participation by many tobacco-growing developing countries.

262. Following the model of several environmental conventions, the Chairman's text[1] foresaw a number of institutional arrangements to support and monitor the implementation of the FCTC and its protocols. In particular, it provides for a conference of the parties (COP) with a rather extensive authority including the power to establish monitoring and advisory bodies. It is foreseen that a secretariat would be established by the convention to service the meetings of the parties and provide technical cooperation at their request. The draft texts also envisaged that WHO and other international organizations would provide technical and financial cooperation. Reporting by the parties to the COP is provided as the main tool for monitoring implementation. Draft Article 27 introduces a settlement of disputes clause which concentrates on non-binding mechanisms, such as conciliation, but foresees arbitration for those parties which make an optional declaration of acceptance to this purpose.

1. WHO Doc. A/FCTC/INB2/2, *supra*, pp. 9–12.

263. A credible financial mechanism and clear commitments on the part of developed countries will be of crucial importance for the viability of the convention, especially considering the economic dependence of many developing countries on tobacco. The establishment of a financial mechanism, and the special financial responsibility of developed countries in supporting transition from tobacco growing and alternative livelihoods for tobacco workers in developing countries, are unsurprisingly issues of central importance in the FCTC process. The draft texts contained various alternatives such as the establishment of a multilateral global fund or the reliance on existing bilateral or multilateral channels.[1]

1. *See* for example Doc. A/FCTC/INB4/2(b), pp. 7–9.

264. The responsibility of the tobacco industry for the health damage it causes through its products appears in the 2001 Chairman's text as one of the FCTC's guiding principles.[1] This topic has proved complex and potentially controversial during its consideration in the INB. To facilitate discussions and offer a technical overview about the status of international law in this area, the WHO Secretariat convened in April 2001 a consultation of legal experts who discussed the implications of existing models of liability under domestic law or international responsibility in the context of tobacco control. A summary of the outcome of the consultation was presented to INB3.[2]

1. WHO Doc. A/FCTC/INB2/2, p. 2.
2. Doc. A/FCTC/INB2/5 Rev. 1.

265. Finally, a point still not thoroughly discussed until INB4 concerns protocols to the FCTC, which should become an integral part of its architecture in view of its nature as a framework convention. This is a multi-faceted issue, as it concerns the relationship between convention and protocols, the latter's contents and procedure for negotiation, as well as possible general criteria to be followed in deciding subject matters to negotiate into protocols rather than the main convention. The references made in the Chair's text to possible initial protocols have been mentioned, as well as the fact that Resolution WHA53.16 instructed the INB to initially focus on the convention. Some delegations, notably Australia, have taken the initiative in urging the INB to work towards agreed principles for the definition of criteria and conditions that would warrant the negotiation of protocols. The United States, moreover, has convened a technical conference on the illicit manufacturing and trafficking of tobacco products, with a view to a possible future protocol on this important topic. The conference was held in New York at the end of July 2002, and its outcome will be reported to INB5.

§2. REGULATIONS

I. General Considerations

266. Authority to adopt international regulations in five specified areas is contained in Article 21 of the WHO Constitution. It should be noted that there is an apparent inconsistency in the WHO Constitution between Article 21 and Article 2(*u*); the latter includes food together with biological, pharmaceutical, and similar products as items in respect of which international standards may be developed, established, and promoted. The *travaux préparatoires* provide no clear indication as to the background of the discussions that led to the non-inclusion of food in Article 21(*d*) and (*e*). This may in fact have been due to problems arising from the coordination of the work of two different committees of the Conference, or possibly a reluctance to see WHO having express binding authority in the area of food. Another proposal made in the course of the conference was that the subject-matter of regulations should extend to the prevention of the importation by states of biological, pharmaceutical, and similar products which did not conform to standards adopted by the Health Assembly. This suggestion was objected to by a number of delegations, in particular those from Latin America, on the grounds that it dealt with questions of commercial policy which did not fall properly within the jurisdiction of WHO.

267. The granting to WHO of exceptional regulatory powers whereby decisions adopted by a simple majority of members would automatically become binding on the whole membership was, unsurprisingly, one of the most debated items at the International Health Conference. One of the precedents that delegates looked at was the Chicago Convention on International Civil Aviation, which established the International Civil Aviation Organization. Certain delegations, in particular Ukraine and Belgium, considered that the 'contracting-out' provisions incorporated in the Constitution (Article 22) amounted to an infringement of national sovereignty or could lead to a state being bound 'by oversight'. It certainly places on every Member State the burden of taking action within a certain deadline to avoid being bound by the regulations. Various other proposals were made but eventually not agreed upon, including:

– the compulsory inclusion in all international health regulations of a denunciation clause whereby any member bound by such regulations could denounce them within three years after their entry into force upon six months' notice;
– a provision whereby members would acknowledge receipt of regulations notified by the Director-General, the period for rejection or reservation then running from the date of such acknowledgement;
– an arrangement whereby only temporary regulations applying new knowledge and techniques to the control of the international spread of disease would enter into force automatically for all members, such temporary regulations being binding upon members for one year only. Other regulations would require formal acceptance by governments.[1]

1. OR 2, pp. 20–21.

II. The Nomenclature Regulations

268. The Assembly has adopted two international regulations under Article 21(*a*) and (*b*) respectively. The first of these were WHO Regulations No. 1 regarding nomenclature (including the compilation and publication of statistics) with respect to diseases and causes of death, which was adopted under Article 21(b).[1] The regulations were given the short title of 'the Nomenclature Regulations', thus compounding the unfortunate confusion in terminology in Article 21(*b*), since the subject-matter of the instrument is not in fact the nomenclature of diseases but rather the unification of the statistical classification of morbidity and mortality for purposes of comparability. The confusion probably arose from the fact that early work in this area was carried out in French and its outcome was usually referred to as 'Nomenclature internationale des maladies et des causes de décès'. It should also be noted that Article 2(s) foresees as one of the functions of the Organization the establishment and revision of 'international nomenclatures of diseases, of causes of death . . .'.

1. OR 13, Annex 1, pp. 349–352.

269. The Nomenclature Regulations represent the continuation of work commenced in the nineteenth century. The first International Statistical Congress (ISC) was held in Brussels in 1853. The second International Statistical Congress was held in Paris in 1855, at which a compromise list adopted by the Congress served as the basis for an international list of causes of death, the preparation of which was entrusted in 1891 to the International Statistical Institute (ISI) as the successor of the ISC. The idea of decennial revisions came from the American Public Health Association in 1898 and such revisions were subsequently made in Paris in 1900, 1910, and 1920. When the League of Nations came into being, its Health Organization cooperated with the ISI in the further development of the international lists. This led to the Fourth and Fifth Revisions in 1929 and 1938, respectively. This work was taken up by WHO after its creation.

270.   The 1948 Regulations incorporated the work of the Sixth Revision of the International List of Diseases and Causes of Death, which was prepared by an international conference held in Paris in April 1948. No particular provisions were included in these regulations to deal with the question of reservations, permitted by Article 22 of the Constitution. As a consequence of this, those reservations that were made were, on the advice of the United Nations, considered as having been accepted in advance. Despite the relatively flexible procedures of the regulation-making process, the Nomenclature Regulations were found in practice to be excessively regulatory and unduly constraining in that, with a decennial revision process, the specific international classification incorporated in the regulations would necessarily be the subject of constant revisions, thus reopening the question of rejection or reservations as such and the consequent risk of a multiplicity of incompatible regimes.

271.   The Nomenclature Regulations were firstly amended in 1956 by the Ninth World Health Assembly with Resolution WHA9.29. When the regulations were reviewed more thoroughly in 1966 and 1967, the Health Assembly decided to reconsider their detailed approach and to separate matters that required mandatory regulation – such as the requirement that member countries use the International Classification of Diseases for official mortality and morbidity statistics – from other matters that could be the subject of recommendations.[1] Accordingly, the Twentieth Health Assembly in 1967 adopted a completely revised Nomenclature Regulation[2] together with a separate set of recommendations concerning topics such as the responsibility for medical certification of causes of death, and the definition of the underlying causes of death together with short lists for tabulation of causes of mortality and morbidity.[3]

1. Resolution WHA19.45, OR 151, p. 22.
2. By Resolution WHA20.18 of 22 May 1967, in OR 160, p. 9.
3. Resolution WHA20.19, in OR 160, p. 11. The text of the recommendations is reproduced in OR 160, Annex 18, pp. 106–107.

272.   The 1967 Nomenclature Regulations, which are still in force, require Member States to compile mortality and morbidity statistics using the revision in force at any given time of the International Classification of Diseases (ICD). Subsequent revisions of the classification could thus be adopted by the Health Assembly without having at the same time to revise the regulations. The language of Article 2 of the regulations gives binding force to the ICD as periodically revised. For this reason, Articles 7 and 8 of the regulations provide for the determination

by the Health Assembly of a date of entry into force of any revision of the ICD and, respectively, for an extension to them of the right under Article 22 of the Constitution to file objections or reservations. Consequently, the regulations require the Director-General to notify all Member States of their adoption as well as of the adoption of any revision of the ICD.

273.   Whereas revisions of the ICD had historically been undertaken at ten-year intervals, it became clear after the Ninth Revision (1975) that such intervals were too short, and that work on the subsequent revision had to start before the current version of the ICD had been in use long enough to be thoroughly evaluated. Consequently, on the recommendation of the Director-General, an International Conference for the Tenth Revision of the International Classification of Diseases was held in Geneva from 26 September to 2 October 1989 (instead of 1985) and its recommendations were adopted by the World Health Assembly in May 1990.[1] Volume 1, a tabular list of the International Statistical Classification of Diseases and Related Health Problems (ICD-10), was published in 1992 (the Nomenclature Regulations are reproduced in an Annex). Volume 2, an instruction manual, was published in 1993, and Volume 3, an alphabetical index, was published in 1994.[2] Notwithstanding the ten-year cycle of formal revisions, the Assembly endorsed, in Resolution WHA43.24, the establishment of an updating process within the cycle.

1. Resolution WHA43.24, in WHA43/1990/REC/1, p. 24.
2. *International Statistical Classification of Diseases and Related Health Problems, Tenth Revision*, 3 vols. (Geneva, World Health Organization, 1992–1993–1994).

274.   A spin-off from the ICD which may be mentioned here has been the elaboration by WHO of a supplementary classification of impairments, disabilities and handicaps. The International Conference for the Ninth Revision of the ICD drew the attention of the Health Assembly to the fact that the ICD concerned the identification of life expectancy and causes of death, but the data collected thereby gave no further indications on the health status of the living population. The Assembly aimed at filling this gap by approving, with Resolution WHA29.35 of 17 May 1976, the publication of supplementary classifications of impairments and handicaps and of procedure in medicine as supplements to, but not as integral parts of, the ICD. As a result, WHO published in 1980 the International Classification of Impairments, Disabilities and Handicaps (ICIDH), which underwent a long testing and revision process. The second edition of this classification tool was endorsed by the 54th Health Assembly with Resolution WHA54.21 under the title 'International Classification of Functioning, Disability and Health' (ICF). Notwithstanding the endorsement of the Health Assembly, however, the ICF does not share the same legal nature of the ICD under the Nomenclature Regulations. Resolution WHA29.35 made it clear that the new classification would not be an integral part of the ICD; moreover, it deals with a different though complementary topic from the ICD.

III. The International Health Regulations

275.   WHO inherited from its predecessors the responsibility for the management of the international regime for the control of the international spread of disease. This regime was based on a series of international conventions and agreements dating from 1892, each of which had a specific objective in view.[1] The inconsistency of the earlier regime under the succession of conventions and agreements was apparent, considering that none of these entirely replaced each other, they did not take account of new methods available for the control of the diseases they covered, and they were not framed to deal adequately with a greatly increasing volume and speed of international traffic.

1. For a historical survey of these instruments, *see* N. Howard Jones, *The Scientific Background of the International Sanitary Conferences*, 1851–1938. (Geneva, WHO, 1975).

276. The revision and consolidation of these international conventions was undertaken by WHO from 1948 onwards, and regulations were first adopted by the Fourth World Health Assembly in 1951 as WHO Regulations No. 2, the International Sanitary Regulations.[1] These regulations covered the so-called 'quarantinable diseases', namely plague, cholera, yellow fever, smallpox, louse-borne typhus, and louse-borne relapsing fever. The regulations declare that, as between their parties, they replace earlier conventions and agreements, including those parts of the Pan American Sanitary Code dealing with international disease control, the remainder of the code remaining in force as the fundamental instrument governing PAHO.

1. Resolution WHA4.75 of 25 May 1951, in OR 35, p. 50.

277. At the same session, the Health Assembly established by a separate resolution a consultative procedure for the settlement of disputes or questions under the new regulations and set up a monitoring body, known as Committee on International Quarantine and later as Committee on International Surveillance of Communicable Diseases, to regularly review the regulations and make recommendations on practices, methods and procedures related to their implementation.[1]

1. Resolution WHA4.77, in *ibidem*.

278. The regulations have been subjected to several revisions, generally resulting from global improvements in the knowledge and control of epidemic diseases. Thus, special provisions covering the Mecca Pilgrimage, adopted provisionally in 1951, were repealed in 1956,[1] the concept of large tropical areas being considered as perennially 'yellow fever endemic zones' was dropped in 1955, and louse-borne typhus and relapsing fever were removed from the scope of the regulations in 1969, when a major revision of the text was undertaken and the regulations renamed the 'International Health Regulations' (IHR).[2] Smallpox was removed entirely from the scope of international quarantine control in 1981, consequent upon the global elimination of this disease following WHO's eradication programme.[3]

1. By Resolution WHA9.49, of 23 May 1956, in OR 71, p. 34.
2. By Resolution WHA22.46 of 25 July 1969, in OR 176, p. 22.
3. By Resolution WHA34.13 of 20 May 1981, in WHA34/1981/REC/1, p. 10. The 1969 Regulations have also been amended in 1973 with regard to cholera: Resolution WHA26.55 of 23 May 1973, in OR 209, p. 29. The current text of the International Health Regulations, with annotations, the applicable standard forms, and a number of annexes, appears in *International Health Regulations* (3rd annotated edition, Geneva, WHO, 1982).

279. As a result of the foregoing revisions, the IHR as currently in force apply to only three diseases: plague, cholera and yellow fever. They contain general provisions applicable to all covered diseases (Part IV) and special provisions relating to each specific disease. At the same time, they allow additional measures in relation to migrants, seasonal workers or 'persons taking part in periodic mass congregations', for example with regard to malaria (Article 84). They also authorize the conclusion of special treaties or arrangements in order to facilitate their application in a number of areas, provided that they are not in conflict with the IHR (Article 85). The main regulatory feature of the IHR is that, in order to reconcile the prevention of the spread of diseases with minimizing interference with traffic in goods and persons, they provide maximum measures applicable to international traffic. Measures going beyond those foreseen in the regulations, or imposed against the spread of other diseases, are not authorized under the regulations. The application of the IHR is predicated upon the core obligations for Member States to immediately report to WHO cases of the three covered diseases. They include a range of measures such as:

– The disinsecting, disinfection, and deratting of ships, aircraft and, at least in some cases, containers;
– The reporting of cases of illness and related information by officers of arriving ships and aircraft;
– The provision of sanitary conditions, facilities and certain services at some sea- and airports;
– Circumstances under which some examinations or other measures may be performed on travellers, conveyances and trade;
– Some circumstances under which aircraft or ships may be denied on public health grounds the right to land or dock and/or commence operations;
– Health documents which may be required of travellers to enter a Member State.

280. The provisions of the regulations are complemented and integrated by the interpretations and recommendations made by the aforementioned committee and adopted by subsequent Health Assemblies. They are reproduced in the published text of the IHR in the form of annotations to specific articles. The legal status of such interpretations and recommendations may be open to questions – it seems dubious, in particular, that they share the same binding force of the regulations in view of the lack in the latter of an explicit grant to the Assembly of a power of authentic interpretation or of the authority to take binding decisions. However, their adoption by the Assembly and their connection with the regulations gives them a somehow enhanced status and raises an expectation of compliance on the part of Member States. As an example, reference could be made to the interpretation of Article 24 of the regulations, which provides that 'Health measures shall be initiated forthwith, completed without delay, and applied without discrimination'.[1] The Committee on International Quarantine interpreted it in 1965 as not exempting travellers with diplomatic status from the full application of the regulations. Some articles of the IHR, moreover, contain cross-references to recommendations by WHO, thus indirectly upgrading their legal status for the purpose of compliance with the regulations. An example is offered by Article 67 paragraph 4, under which aircraft in certain circumstances 'shall be disinsected . . . using methods recommended by the Organization'.

1. *Ibidem*, p. 18.

281. Viewed as an international instrument, the IHR contain two sets of provisions that are of special interest. The somewhat laxist position that was taken over reservations in the Nomenclature Regulations clearly would not do for the Health Regulations, in view of the problems of reciprocity arising if, despite measures having been taken in accordance with them on or before departure, travellers and means of transport were to be subject to additional measures not provided for in the text through uncontrolled reservations. The regulations therefore contain provisions under which reservations are to be reviewed by the World Health Assembly before they come into effect (Articles 88 and 91). If the reservation is not accepted by the Assembly, the regulations will not enter into force for the reserving state (which then remains bound by earlier instruments in its relations with other states). This procedure has led in practice to a form of consultation between the reserving state and the Organization under which a number of reservations have been withdrawn or attenuated, or accepted subject to a time limit, followed by further review. The authority enjoyed by the Assembly in this regard is quite exceptional and distinguishes the special regime of the regulations from that applicable to reservations to multilateral treaties under general international law and Articles 19 to 23 of the Vienna Convention on the Law of Treaties.

282. Initially, 25 Member States submitted some 73 reservations to the regulations. These were examined by the Health Assembly and 38 were rejected as incompatible with the purpose of the regulations. By 1958, the Director-General of WHO was able to report that most of the rejected reservations had been withdrawn so that the Member States concerned had become bound by the regulations. In 1970, in connection with the adoption of the 1969 Regulations, an *ad hoc* Working Group reported to the Assembly on the reservations filed by a number of states. Based on its recommendations, the Twenty-third Health Assembly did not accept the sweeping reservations entered by Australia, which remains to date the only WHO Member State not bound by the regulations.[1] The only Member States still listed as participating under reservations are Egypt, India and Pakistan.[2]

1. WHA23.57 of 22 May 1970, in OR 184, p. 31. The report of the Working Group is reproduced *ibidem*, Annex 12, pp. 83–94.
2. *See International Health Regulations, supra*, pp. 51–54.

283. The most intractable problem with regard to reservations has been the yellow fever situation, where certain countries free of the disease are believed to have the conditions that would be favourable to its uncontrollable spread if introduced. These are countries where mosquito vectors are present but not the disease, or where the mosquito vectors have been eliminated. Because of the remaining risk of either the disease itself or its vectors, or both, being accidentally introduced or reintroduced, a risk which it is difficult to assess objectively, these countries have, understandably, been reluctant to accept modifications of the international regime without offering reservations for their own protection.

284. As in the case of the international sanitary conventions and agreements, WHO has had to face the problem of excessive measures, either prohibited by the regulations or not justified by the epidemiological situation. This problem came to the fore in the 1960s and early 1970s following the westward spread of the El Tor strain of *Vibrio cholerae*. This led to the imposition in some cases of unjustified measures on travel and commerce and to the consequent reluctance of some health authorities to report the presence of the disease, or its acknowledgement as 'summer diarrhoea' or some equivalent euphemism. The problem of excessive measures once again emerged in 1994 in response to an outbreak of the plague in India. Despite the fact that the epidemiological situation in the country did not warrant such responses, major impediments to the flow of commerce resulted (e.g., closing of airports, barriers to importation of foodstuffs). The financial impact of the excessive measures was enormous, costing the country an estimated US$1.7 billion export loss during a two month period. The regulations therefore contain detailed provisions for dispute-settling, with a first reference to the Director-General followed by a reference, if the dispute is not so settled, to an 'appropriate committee' or 'other organ' of the Organization for settlement. However, the dispute-settlement mechanism has remained largely underutilized.

285. A further difficulty is that of the control of diseases not expressly covered by the provisions of the regulations. While some measures are permissible in respect of certain 'non-quarantinable' diseases, such as destruction of malaria vectors, or measures predicated upon 'a grave danger to public health', the situation is not entirely clear in other circumstances, such as for example global epidemics of influenza or the arrival at frontiers of persons infected with the HIV virus. WHO's position has been that restrictive measures at frontiers are generally ineffective and costly, lead to a false sense of security, and will inevitably result in concealment and corruption.

286. In this regard, WHO has expressed its views on the imposition of health measures on international travellers in respect of HIV/AIDS transmission, pointing out that, under Article 81 of the regulations, no health documents, other than those provided in the regulations, may be required in international traffic. There is consequently no provision for any certificate guaranteeing that a person entering any country or coming from any country is free from a given disease. A certificate stating that a person is not carrying HIV would in no way prevent the introduction and spread of AIDS and would afford no protection.

287. In the administration of the regulations, WHO produces a number of publications for the use of its Member States and others. Information on the incidence of disease, including communicable diseases under surveillance, is published in the *Weekly Epidemiological Record*.[1] Health-related information is also available in *International Travel and Health*, revised annually.[2]

1. Available on-line at <http://www.who.int/wer/> (visited in August 2002).
2. Available on-line at <http://www.who.int/ith/> (visited in August 2002).

288. The developments referred to above led to an acknowledgement by WHO's members in the 1990s that the regulations, while preserving their usefulness as an accepted template for routine measures, had become marginal as an instrument to respond to major outbreaks of communicable diseases in a globalizing world. Outbreaks of new or re-emerging diseases, such as ebola and other haemorrhagic fevers, underscored this consideration. In response to the 1995 request of the World Health Assembly (embodied in Resolution WHA48.7), the International Health Regulations (IHR) are currently being revised. The purpose of the revision is to reflect the significant changes in disease patterns for emergence and re-emergence, medical science, communications technology and shipping methods for goods and cargoes, since the adoption of the IHR in 1969.[1]

1. For a complete critical discussion and analysis of the regulations *see* A.L. Taylor, 'Controlling the global spread of infectious diseases: Toward a reinforced role for the International Health Regulations'. In: *Houston Law Review*, Vol. 33, No. 5, pp. 1327–1362, (1997); B.J. Plotkin, 'Mission Possible: The Future of the International Health Regulations'. In: *Temple International and Comparative Law Journal*, Vol. 10, pp. 503–515 (1996); and B.P. Fidler, 'Return of the Fourth Horseman: Emerging Infectious Diseases and International Law'. In: *Minnesota Law Review*, Vol. 81, No. 4, pp. 771–868 (1997).

289. The revision process, undertaken since late 1995, has proved long and complex. The Secretariat convened a number of technical meetings followed, in November 1998, by a meeting of the Committee on International Surveillance of Communicable Diseases. The initial focus was on the replacement of the three named diseases with the concept of 'syndrome notification'. Five syndromes were initially identified to cover the diseases of potential public health importance. A pilot study in 22 countries field-tested this approach, but it was decided not to pursue it because of difficulties in reporting syndromes and because they could not be linked to pre-set rules for the control of spread of diseases.[1] Consequently, a different and more promising global approach is being developed since 1999 with the hope of launching a round of intergovernmental discussions on revised draft Regulations by 2003 and having them approved by the Assembly in 2004.

1. *See* WHO Doc. A/54/9, p. 3.

290. In order to select a normative, conceptual and operational approach which would respond to developing health threats and global trade trends, WHO has been consulting and exploring synergies with a variety of partners, including notably WTO and its Committee on Sanitary and Phytosanitary Measures.[1] As a result, a concept has been developed based on the following fundamental areas:[2]

(1) States shall report all public health emergencies of international concern. The revised IHR will contain an algorithm, or decision tree, to help states determine when such an event has occurred. The algorithm focuses on four criteria to be applied to the emergency: seriousness; unexpectedness; capacity for international spread; and possible international restrictions to travel or trade deriving therefrom;
(2) Appointment in each state of a focal point for the IHR, relying on electronic communications for timely provision of information about outbreaks and risks for other countries;
(3) A definition of the capacities that a national disease surveillance system will require in order to detect, evaluate and respond in a timely manner to an

emergency. Such a definition, on the one hand, will provide a clear statement of the minimum standards required of each national health system; and on the other hand, it will allow developing countries to define their core needs when approaching external donors;

(4) Option for states to make a confidential provisional notification to WHO, an option not available under the current IHR. WHO would then work with the state concerned to assess the extent of the risk. This option would ideally insulate a country from international overreactions to events not of international concern. WHO would in any case retain the authority to make a public statement in case of increased risk or spread;

(5) Information other than notification from states could be used by WHO to identify and control health emergencies of international concern. States would be under an obligation to respond to requests for verification from WHO. WHO has already gathered much experience in early detection and assessment of outbreaks through the well-tested Global Outbreak Alert and Response Network of which WHO is an integral part. The Network would in all probability become an integral component of the surveillance system centered on the revised IHR;

(6) WHO would issue in each case of emergency of international concern a recommended template of measures for the protection of other states, based on the actual public health threat and the available evidence. This is a crucial point for the viability of the IHR: states lack an incentive to report promptly emergencies if they fear punishing and maybe disproportionate economic measures from other countries. WHO would try to reconcile opposing concerns by recommending the most appropriate but least traffic-limiting measures;

(7) WHO would be under an obligation to assist Member States in assessing and controlling outbreaks. Working with WHO in this process would also increase the international credibility of the surveillance and response capacity of the states concerned;

(8) The process used within WHO to issue recommendations in case of imminent risk of international spread of disease or disruption of international travel and trade would have to be efficient but above all transparent and legitimate in the eyes of national decision-makers and the public;

(9) The IHR as a legally binding instrument would mainly contain, besides the notification and verification obligations mentioned above, measures destined to prevent the international spread of disease at embarkation, during travel, and at point of entry. This is the kind of measures contained in the current IHR which, while they may need to be updated, maintain their importance. At the same time, the failure of the current IHR and the rigid set of measures contained therein warrants a more flexible approach, whereby WHO could tailor recommendations to the specific features of the event in question. The revised IHR will thus contain a non-exhaustive list of all key measures as well as a protocol for ending them.

1. There is no doubt that the interaction between WHO and WTO will be of extreme importance to ensure the compatibility and complementarity between the future IHR and the SPS Agreement. For an overview of the role of the two organizations as well as of the Codex Alimentarius Commission, *see* 'Revision of the International Health Regulations – Public Health and Trade', in 25 *Weekly Epidemiological Record*, 1999, pp. 193–201.

2. The current working concepts are reviewed in *Global Crises – Global Solutions, Managing public health emergencies of international concern through the renewed International Health Regulations*, WHO Doc. WHO/CDS/CSR/GAR/2002.4. *See also* 'Revision of the International Health Regulations – Progress report, May 2002', in 77 *Weekly Epidemiological Record*, 2003, pp. 157–160.

291. This hands-on approach on the part of WHO will necessitate a permanent and active IHR review body, which will update and clarify the measures and their scope of application.

292. The IHR and their revision cannot be seen in isolation but represent the normative framework and one of the facets of WHO's activities in the area of epidemic alert and response – what the Health Assembly has recently dubbed 'global health security'.[1] WHO's strategy for global health security, in brief, has three main components: (i) specific programmes for the prevention and control of known epidemic threats such as influenza, meningitis or cholera; (ii) detection and response to health emergencies resulting from unexpected circumstances or unknown causes; and (iii) improving preparedness through the strengthening of national infrastructures for disease surveillance and response.[2] Their cohesiveness within the overall strategy is therefore essential to their success. As a consequence of the events on 11 September 2001 in the United States and the perception of increased risks of bio-terrorism, the 55th Health Assembly has requested the Director-General to strengthen WHO's global surveillance of infectious diseases to increase global preparedness towards such occurrences. The revised IHR will arguably play an important role also in this context.

1. Resolution WHA54.14 of 21 May 2001, in WHA54/2001/REC/1, p. 21.
2. 'Revision of the International Health Regulations – Progress report, May 2002', *supra*, p. 158.

§3. RECOMMENDATIONS AND OTHER NON-BINDING STANDARDS

I. Introduction

293. The setting of a wide variety of recommendations and other non-binding standards is without doubt the most prolific and successful normative activity of the Organization. The flexibility deriving from the non-binding nature of the standards in question, and sometimes their non-formal nature, is coupled with the credibility of WHO as a scientifically and technically reliable organization. Purely recommendatory or illustrative documents, have proved to be adaptable to very different national circumstances and to command compliance and adherence through their technical or political soundness. The need for adaptability to local circumstances and historical developments may be one of the reasons WHO gravitated towards non-binding instruments even for issues which could have been the subject of regulations under the Constitution.

294. The standard-setting activities of WHO, or coordinated by WHO, partly overlap in our classifications of the functions of the Organization with the role of direction and coordination assigned to it by Article 2 of the Constitution. Emphasis will thus be placed here on recommendations and standards that purport to regulate a discrete area or issue of public health importance rather than express a general policy of the Organization.

295.   This aspect of the normative functions of WHO (in a broad sense) takes place at different levels both legally, politically and practically. This fact makes it difficult sometimes to determine whether certain recommendations are attributable to WHO or not. To briefly resume, and as will be reviewed more in detail *infra*, the 'standards' in question fall into three broad categories:

– regulatory recommendations adopted by the Health Assembly or, within the limits of its constitutional functions, by the Executive Board. Such recommendations are normally elaborated by the Secretariat, on its own initiative or at the request of a governing body;
– standards and recommendations developed by the Secretariat on the basis of a grant of authority by a governing body but not endorsed or approved as such by the latter;
– standards developed by expert bodies convened by the Secretariat and published by WHO as such, without formal endorsement.

296.   It should be noted at the outset that the Assembly has very rarely explicitly placed some of its recommendations under Article 23 of the Constitution. A search through the records of the Health Assembly reveals only four or five such instances. From a legal point of view, in any case, the invocation of Article 23 or lack thereof does not change the recommendatory nature of the decisions.[1]

1. It has been suggested that the only legal difference is that, with regard to recommendations adopted explicitly under Article 23, Member States would be under an obligation to report annually under Article 62 of the Constitution. However, such a strict reporting requirement has never been enforced in practice, rendering the difference even more insubstantial. *See* S.S. Fluss, F. Gutteridge, J.K. Little, H. Harris, 'World Health Organization' in R. Blanpain, *International Encyclopaedia of Laws* (Deventer, Boston, Kluwer, 1998), p. 29. On the role of WHO in setting non-binding standards and norms, *see* C.H. Vignes, 'Towards the harmonization of health legislation: the role of the World Health Organization', in 46 *International Digest of Health Legislation*, No. 3, 1995, p. 422.

II. The International Code of Marketing of Breast-milk Substitutes

297.   The number and scope of recommendations made by the Assembly since 1948 on the most various topics make an attempted summary purposeless. Attention should be drawn, however, to probably the best-known recommendation by the Health Assembly, namely, the 'International Code of Marketing of Breast-milk Substitutes'.[1]

1. The code was adopted by Resolution WHA34.22 of 21 May 1981, in WHA34/1981/REC/1, p. 21. The text of the code appears in Annex 3 thereof and is reproduced as *International Code of Marketing of Breast-Milk Substitutes* (Geneva, WHO, 1981). The main scholarly work in the recent literature is S. Shubber, *The International Code of Marketing of Breast-Milk Substitutes: an International Measure to Protect and Promote Breastfeeding* (The Hague, Kluwer Law International, 1998).

298. The origin and the history of the Code are complex and rather 'tumultuous' and it is not possible to thoroughly review them here.[1] It may be recalled that the main impetus at the preparation of a code of marketing was the realization at the beginning of the 1970s that breastfeeding rates were declining globally, especially throughout the developing world. While a variety of socio-cultural and other factors may have been at stake, international agencies and NGOs were concerned about the impact of the marketing and advertising of breast-milk substitutes in discouraging breastfeeding. Concern was also expressed at the risks for both mothers and infants from the premature abandonment of breastfeeding. Even though the debate focused on developing countries, where hygienic and economic conditions increase risks, the issue has a global dimension in that the unnecessary interruption of breastfeeding may always have negative health consequences. The processed food industry was thus directly called into question for marketing practices which allegedly encouraged the abandonment of breastfeeding, were considered by many unsuitable for developing countries and could have been responsible for an increase in infant morbidity and mortality.

1. A brief history of the controversies that characterized the international debate on breastfeeding in the 1970s and that led to the adoption of the code is in Y. Beigbeder, *The World Health Organization, supra*, pp. 75–83.

299. Several UN programmes and agencies tried to foster a consensual approach which would balance the essential principle of the superiority of breast milk and breastfeeding with responsible marketing practices for breast-milk substitutes 'when', in the words of the code, 'these are necessary'. This, however, was soon displaced by an increasing polarized confrontation between the processed food industry and a number of activist NGOs.[1] As Beigbeder notes, 'the debate had progressively lost any technical character which would have permitted a sensible dialogue between specialists . . .'.[2] Emotional and political considerations have characterized this aspect of international nutrition policies and continue unabated to the present time.

1. One of the most active NGOs, dedicated mostly to the promotion of breastfeeding and the denunciation of abusive practices by food companies in this respect, is the 'International Baby Food Action Network' (IBFAN). On-line information is available at <http://www.ibfan.org>.
2. Y. Beigbeder, *The World Health Organization, supra*, p. 79.

300. WHO and UNICEF stepped into this increasingly acrimonious environment by organizing a joint meeting on infant and young child feeding in 1979. The meeting was attended by representatives of parties concerned, and was unusual in that Member States, international agencies, NGOs and processed food companies participated on an equal footing. One of the points of agreement at the meeting was to entrust WHO and UNICEF with the preparation of a code of marketing in consultation with all parties concerned. The Health Assembly endorsed that recommendation by Resolution WHA33.32 of 23 May 1980. After lengthy and inclusive consultations during which WHO and UNICEF offered their services to foster dialogue on the form and content of the instrument, a draft Code was submitted to the 67th Session of the EB in January 1981.

301.   One of the main items of discussion at the 67th Session of the EB was whether the code should be adopted as a regulation or a recommendation. The Legal Counsel noted the difference in the Constitution between Article 2(u), which empowers WHO to develop international standards 'with respect to food, biological, pharmaceutical and similar products'; and Article 21(d) and (e) concerning regulations. However, echoing the position of WHO that breast-milk substitutes had to be considered as a 'nutritional medicine', he argued that they fell within the purview of Article 21.[1] The consideration that eventually prevailed in favour of a recommendation was to avoid rejection of a binding code by a number of developed countries trying to safeguard their commercial interests.

1. EB67/1981/REC/2, p. 319.

302.   The Health Assembly adopted the code by Resolution WHA34.22 of 21 May 1981, with the sole dissenting vote of the United States.[1] The preamble of the resolution envisages the code as a 'minimum requirement', while the preamble of the code expresses the guiding principle behind the very concept of a code, namely, that 'the marketing of breast-milk substitutes requires special treatment, which makes usual marketing practices unsuitable for these products'. The Director-General was requested to support Member States in the implementation of the code and to use his 'good offices' for continued cooperation with all parties concerned in its implementation and monitoring.

1. WHA34/1981/REC/1, pp. 21–23.

303.   In view of the confrontational atmosphere dominating the debate and the growing importance of this issue in public health terms, WHO took over the function of mediator between the opposing camps. By promoting its impartiality and objectivity, WHO would offer NGOs and processed food companies an opportunity to meet and discuss with a view to agreeing on public health aspects of child nutrition which could be supported by appropriate epidemiological information. By and large, WHO has continued this role after the adoption of the code and up to the present time.

304.   The aim of the code, as expressed in its Article 1, is the provision of safe and adequate nutrition for infants by the protection and promotion of breastfeeding and by ensuring the proper use of breast-milk substitutes when they are necessary. The code pursues this aim by subtracting a range of products from normal market practices, especially their advertising, promotion and labelling. By treating breast-milk substitutes as a nutritional medicine to introduce only as needed, the code strives for a balance between the protection of breastfeeding, the promotion of informed nutritional choices by mothers, and the regulation of marketing practices so that crucial nutritional choices are not unduly influenced by commercial interests. The code, *inter alia*, states that manufacturers should not seek contacts with pregnant women and mothers (Article 5.1) and restricts them to only providing scientific and factual information, as well as samples only for the purpose of professional evaluation or research, to health workers (Article 7.2). The code also states that health care facilities should not be used for the promotion of products within the scope of the code and that donations or low-price sales of products should be strictly limited (Articles 6.2 and 6.6). The code assigns the main responsibility for monitoring its application to governments 'acting individually, and collectively' through WHO, thus aiming at a form of inducement to compliance through the scrutiny of the Health Assembly.[1] NGOs and other 'civil society organizations' are explicitly given a role in the overall monitoring process (Article 11.4), and this has been seen by the NGO's concerned as a legitimization of their watchdog role towards the processed food industry.

    1. The Director-General, pursuant to Article 11.7 of the code, reports in even years to the Assembly on its implementation.

305.   The code was the product of a difficult compromise between opposite and fiercely maintained positions. As such, its provisions have allowed different interpretations on certain important topics, notably on the scope of the code and on the exact meaning of activities such as advertising and promotion. At the same time, the Health Assembly has adopted numerous resolutions since 1981 which have clarified and expanded certain provisions of the code, albeit without formally amending it. This indirect revision process has also been interpreted differently by the parties concerned, with food companies in particular maintaining that subsequent decisions did not have the same status as the code for the purpose of their compliance. WHO, however, has advocated that they have equal legal status, thus the code has to be applied together with subsequent Assembly decisions.[1] The 54th WHA has indirectly confirmed this interpretation by Resolution WHA54.2 which urges Member States, *inter alia*, '. . . *to ensure compliance with the International Code . . . and subsequent relevant Health Assembly resolutions*, with regard to labelling as well as all forms of advertising . . .' (emphasis added).

    1. *See* most recently WHO Doc. A55/15.

306.   An interesting interpretative point in this regard is whether the code provides an age limit concerning its applicability. This problem has arisen in particular with regard to so-called follow-up formula, defined as a food intended as a liquid part of weaning diet from the sixth month and for young children. The code does not provide in its operative part an age limit of the infant beyond which it would not be applicable. The preamble of the code contains a statement to the effect that appropriate complementary foods could be introduced 'usually when the infant reaches four to six months of age'. The representative of the EB made a similar statement when introducing the draft code at the 34th WHA.[1] Consequently, some food companies maintain that foods destined for children older than six months fall outside the scope[2] of the code and can be freely advertised and promoted as long as they are not represented as breast-milk substitutes. The problem is that these practices may affect sustained breastfeeding beyond the first six months and may have a broader indirect impact that can undermine exclusive breastfeeding of younger infants. Consequently, the Health Assembly has urged Member States to foster 'appropriate complementary feeding practices from the age of about 6 months emphazing continued breastfeeding'.[3] The WHO Secretariat has taken the position that, although strictly speaking follow-up formula does not fall within the scope of the code, national authorities may wish to consider it a '*de facto* breast-milk sub-stitute' taking into account the intent and spirit of the code. On a general basis, both WHO and UNICEF, as well as the recent literature, maintain that nothing in the code places an age limit to its application, as long as any particular food product is marketed or represented as a breast-milk substitute. This approach, besides fall-ing within the letter and the spirit of the code, appears practical because the period of breastfeeding varies widely between countries and cultures, depending on a broad range of circumstances. It would thus be arbitrary for an instrument such as the code to purport to codify this period.[4]

1. WHA34/1981/REC/3, p. 188.
2. An argument strengthened by the relevant Codex Alimentarius standard, which states that follow-up formulas 'are not breast-milk substitutes and shall not be represented as such'. Codex Doc. CODEX STAN 156, 1987, available on-line at <http://www.codexalimentarius.net/standard_list. asp> (visited on 19 August 2002).
3. Resolution WHA47.5 of 9 May 1994, in WHA47/1994/REC/1, pp. 3–5.
4. *See* S. Shubber, *supra*, pp. 67–68 and references in footnote 2, para. 250.

III. The Standard Setting Process

307.   The International Code remains a special instance of a complex recom-mendation issued on a topic of intense political, commercial and emotional interest. Most other recommendations, guidelines and standards do not take the form of a full-fledged regulatory text approved by the Assembly, but rather that of technical documents elaborated by groups of experts or external collaborators. The staff of WHO cannot by itself maintain full knowledge and mastering of diverse, complex and sometimes rapidly developing technical fields. The disciplines involved are also manifold: from biology to statistics, from the most various areas of medical special-ization to economics and ethics. This consideration, and the need to effectively implement its normative functions, have characterized the policy of WHO ever since its inception. This has led to the development of various mechanisms through which the requisite expert advice and support is made available to the Organization.

308.   The most formalized of such mechanisms are expert advisory panels and expert committees, governed by regulations adopted by the Health Assembly.[1] Expert advisory panels are lists of experts appointed by the Director-General, from whom WHO may obtain technical guidance within a particular subject. Members of expert advisory panels are selected by the Director-General for renewable four-year terms; they may be consulted individually or may be invited by the Director-General to participate in expert committees. Both the Director-General as well as the EB and the WHA have the authority to establish and disestablish expert advi-sory panels, thus establishing a form of shared control over the main direction of the scientific policy of the Organization. The establishment and convening of expert committees instead falls under the authority of the Director-General. Expert com-mittees represent the most stable mechanism for the elaboration and validation of technical standards. They do not have a standing membership; their members are selected by WHO for every meeting, thus allowing the Secretariat to balance the search for the required mix of competence with the desirable level of continuity in membership. The outcome of meetings of expert committees are reports that contain conclusions and recommendations addressed to the Director-General. Expert committees are advisory bodies and cannot commit the Organization unless the Director-General specifically approves their findings. Reports of expert committees are normally published as part of the 'Technical Report Series' (even though a final decision rests with the Director-General) and their contents may exercise considerable influence on the scientific development of the issue concerned.

1. 'Regulations for Expert Advisory Panels and Expert Committees', in *Basic Documents, supra,* pp. 101–109.

309.   The Director-General is required to report regularly to the EB about meetings and recommendations of expert committees and to add his observations on their implications as well as his recommendations on any follow-up. Board Members routinely discuss the contents and recommendations of the Director-General's reports, and their views are taken into account by the Secretariat in the follow-up.

310.   A distinctive expert committee is that on drug dependence, in that its recommendations affect the discharge by WHO of certain functions assigned to it by drug control treaties. WHO has been designated as the organization responsible for the evaluation of the medical, scientific and public health aspects of psychoactive substances under the Single Convention on Narcotic Drugs of 1961 (as amended by the 1972 Protocol)[1] and the Convention on Psychotropic Substances of 1971.[2] These conventions entrust WHO with the responsibility of reviewing and assessing any substance which may need to be included in one of their schedules. Such a review can be initiated through a notification to the UN Secretary-General by a party to the conventions or even by WHO. The assessment by WHO is forwarded to the Commission on Narcotic Drugs of the UN (CND), which has the responsibility of taking the decision concerning the international control, and level thereof, of a psychoactive substance. WHO has developed an evaluation and assessment procedure, which was approved by the EB.[3] The central step in this procedure is the review made by the Expert Committee on Drug Dependence, which advises the Director-General on substances being considered for international control and exempted preparations. The Director-General takes the final decision as to whether to forward the Committee's assessment to the CND. Since the functions of WHO, and consequently of the Expert Committee, are based on the provision of the aforementioned conventions, also the advice of the Committee on scientific, medical and public health considerations must comply with the criteria set down therein. For this reason, the EB has adopted specific guidelines for the work of the committee, which complement the general regulations on expert committees.

1. UNTS, Vol. 520, p. 151. On the single Convention and its amendments, *see* C.H. Vignes, 'La Convention sur les substances psychotropes' in XVII AFDI, pp. 641–656, and C.H. Vignes, 'Les modifications apportées a l'organe international de controle par les amendements à la Convention unique sur les stupéfiants', in XVIII AFDI, pp. 629–648.
2. *Ibidem,* vol. 1019, p. 175.
3. The Guidelines for the WHO review of dependence-producing psychoactive substances for international control are reproduced in Doc. EB105/2000/REC/1, Annex 9, p. 49.

311.   As reported to the 109th Session of the Executive Board in January 2002, 49 expert advisory panels with a total of 1,337 experts were in existence as of January 2002. Their areas of competence went from biological standardization and immunology to leprosy and zoonoses (animal diseases which can be transmitted to humans). Moreover, six expert committees met during 2001, covering topics such as food additives (convened jointly with FAO), specifications for pharmaceutical preparations and biological standardization.[1]

  1. WHO Doc. EB109/33 Add. 1.

312.   In addition to expert advisory panels and expert committees, the Executive Board has adopted regulations for other mechanisms of collaboration which play an important role in the development of recommendations and standards. The main types of mechanisms are defined as study groups, scientific groups and collaborating centres, but the Director-General is also granted the general authority to develop collaboration with individual experts, expert groups and institutions in response to particular requirements.[1] Study groups are normally convened instead of expert committees when the knowledge on a given topic is too uncertain to reach authoritative conclusions or when the topic to be studied is very limited in scope. Scientific groups are more focused on research; their functions is usually to review given fields of medical, health and health systems research. As the regulations state, they 'play for research a role comparable to that of expert committees . . . for the Organization's programme in general.'[2] The regulations and Rules for Expert Committees are in principle applicable to these groups.

  1. The regulations were adopted by Resolution EB69.R21 and amended by Resolution EB105.R7. The text is reproduced in *Basic Documents, supra*, pp. 110–117.
  2. *Ibidem*, p. 112.

313.   Collaborating centres are external institutions (e.g., a laboratory, a university department or a research institute) designated by the Director-General through a rather elaborate procedure to form part of an international collaborative network carrying out activities in support of WHO. Collaborating centres serve as an alternative to the establishment of research institutions directly by the Organization and play an essential role in providing services to WHO in support of programmes of global interest. A few collaborating centres, for example, coordinate the global surveillance of, and response to, influenza epidemics.[1] Their relationship with WHO is regulated through the conclusion of an agreement, which allows them to represent themselves as collaborating centres of WHO and to use the WHO emblem within well-defined limits. Although their role in standard setting might not be as relevant as that of expert committees, many examples of collaborative work under the aegis of the Organization for the purpose of standardization may be cited, such as the international classification of diseases, the setting of standards for the pathology of arteriosclerosis, and the establishment of international standards and reference preparations for biological substances used in human and veterinary sciences.

  1. More information on collaborating centres, their functions, criteria for designation and evaluation are provided on-line at <http://whqlily.who.int/> (visited on 20 August 2002).

314. In practice, once they are published, the conclusions and recommendations of the various committees and groups convened by the Secretariat to advise the Organization have become identified as being the positions of the Organization on the scientific issues covered by the meeting concerned. Officially, however, they are merely conclusions and recommendations of the individual experts convened for that purpose. It is fair to say that over the life of the Organization, the Secretariat has encouraged this duality of status, i.e., it has used these groups as a way for the Organization to carry out much of its standard setting work, while still enabling it – when necessary because of some controversy arising – to point out that formally the conclusions of these groups are not necessarily those of the Organization but only the opinion of individual experts. In specific cases where it has been decided that the Organization should not be identified with the conclusions of the particular group, the Director General has not authorized their publication.

315. Occasionally, when for one reason or another it was felt desirable or necessary to obtain a formal political endorsement of the particular 'position' emanating from the experts group system (often involving guidelines or recommended practices), the matter has been submitted to the Health Assembly for endorsement, thereby becoming a formal position or policy of the Organization. An example in this connection is the 'Certification scheme on the quality of pharmaceutical products moving in international commerce', firstly adopted by the Assembly with Resolution WHA28.65 of 29 May 1975,[1] and the guidelines for its implementation as endorsed by Resolution WHA50.3.[2] In other cases, recommendatory standards have been developed by the Secretariat on the basis of a request and a grant of authority by the Health Assembly, which has however also subsequently endorsed the results of the standard-setting function carried out by the Secretariat. This seems to be the case, for example, of the International Nonproprietary Names (INNs), whose elaboration rests on the legal basis of an initial decision by the Assembly in Resolution WHA3.11 of 1950. An INN identifies a pharmaceutical substance or active pharmaceutical ingredient by a unique name that is globally recognized and is a public property. An INN is also known as a generic name. WHO collaborates with INN experts and national nomenclature committees to select a single name of worldwide acceptability for each active substance that is marketed as a pharmaceutical. To avoid confusion, which could jeopardize the safety of patients, trademarks should neither be derived from INNs nor contain common stems used in INNs. The INN system began operating in 1953, when the first list of INNs was published by WHO. The cumulative list of INNs now stands at some 700 names designated since that time, and this number is growing every year by some 120–150 new INNs. The Health Assembly, although it does not endorse the list as such, adopted decisions concerning the procedure for the selection of INNs and for the use of the latter by Member States.[3]

1. OR, 226, p. 35.
2. WHA50/1997/REC/1, p. 2.
3. *See Guidelines on the Use of International Nonproprietary Names (INNs) for Pharmaceutical Substances* (Geneva, WHO, 1997).

316. This system of standard setting – involving on the one hand the recommendations emanating solely from the technical level and on the other hand those having received formal Health Assembly endorsement – has worked reasonably well over the life of the Organization. It does, however, provide an opportunity for a degree of uncertainty on what are the positions of the Organization in specific cases. This situation has been increased by the proliferation of the ways in which reports of various groups of experts and consultations are published, ranging from the most formal, e.g., the Technical Reports Series and the WHO Bulletin, to the least formal, e.g., documents with 'Limited' or 'General' distribution, the Weekly Epidemiological Record, or even the WHO web site.[1]

1. Reference could be made for example, in the area of child nutrition, to the preparation and posting on the WHO web site, of a 'Protocol for adapting feeding recommendations' and the guide entitled 'Complementary feeding: family food for breastfed children'. Both are available at <http://www.who.int/child-adolescent-health/NUTRITION/complementary.htm> (visited on 20 August 2002).

317. WHO's approach to scientific knowledge in support of its normative activities reflects the central importance that the Organization has always attributed to the technical excellence and objectivity of the evidence it uses as a basis for its standards. Public health policies set by the Assembly, and the normative standards developed by the Secretariat, whether or not they are endorsed by the Assembly, must be based on solid, reliable and credible scientific evidence. The mechanisms used by the Secretariat to develop and validate such evidence have tried to ensure that the conclusions and recommendations of experts, and the process to arrive at them, are as objective and impartial as possible and insulated from political or commercial influences.

318. For these reasons, the aforementioned regulations for expert committees and other mechanisms have granted the Secretariat general authority to select experts, to limit participation in technical meetings, and to draw the relevant conclusions from the findings of expert bodies without the need for specific approval by WHO's governing bodies. The governing bodies only exercise general oversight authority on the basis of reports by the Director-General, or consider his recommendations for the purpose of adopting standards and policies. In the case of meetings of expert committees, for example, the regulations and rules only foresee participation by other organizations of the UN system and NGOs in official relations (unless otherwise agreed by the committee and the Director-General), to the exclusion of other stakeholders which could influence the outcome of the meeting. It has also been the policy of the Secretariat in principle not to disclose either the names of experts on expert advisory panels or those of the individuals invited as members of expert committees. It was felt that disclosure could have exposed those experts to pressure by entities having an interest in their particular fields, or in the outcome of a specific meeting. The names of members of expert committees, however, are made public in the report of the committee. Moreover, the practice has been followed to transmit the composition of expert advisory panels to Member States and members of the Board, under certain conditions and upon request.

319. The strict application of this policy has faced, in recent times, challenges based on the importance of ensuring transparency in standard-setting and of considering the views and inputs of stakeholders with legitimate interests in the regulation of certain matters. While the need to ensure the integrity of scientific processes remains a paramount consideration, it has been noted that WHO sets standards which have substantial implications beyond the strict public health domain. Excluding any form of outside scrutiny and input in the standard setting process would decrease the credibility and legitimacy of their outcome and negatively affect their practical impact. This criticism has particularly characterized areas such as access to medicines and food standards, in which the commercial interests of several Member States are particularly acute. In the area of food standards, for example, WHO and FAO have been criticized for the exclusion of outside observers in the meetings of JECFA and JMPR.[1]

    1. On JECFA and JMPR, *see supra* Part IV, section on the Codex Alimentarius Commission.

320. WHO has responded to this challenge in various ways. In the case of the Expert Committee on Drug Dependence, for example, an information meeting may be held before the actual committee meeting, at which relevant NGOs may present additional information to the members of the committee about the substances to be reviewed. Although the scheduling decisions are formally taken by an intergovernmental organ of the UN, the recommendations of the committee may bear substantial implications for the pharmaceutical and chemical industries.

321. An issue of recent debate in this connection has been the revision of the procedure for updating WHO's Model List of Essential Medicines. The model list is probably one of the most important recommendatory standards set by the Secretariat, in this case without case-by-case approval by a governing body. The development by WHO of a model list of essential drugs was requested in 1975 by the Health Assembly with Resolution WHA28.66.[1] The list is revised every two years by the Director-General upon the recommendation of the Expert Committee on the Use of Essential Drugs (now the Expert Committee on the Selection and Use of Essential Medicines).[2] Applications for inclusion or deletion of specific medicines are usually made by WHO departments, NGOs and pharmaceutical companies. Essential medicines (the term 'medicine' is now used instead of 'drugs') have been defined by the Secretariat as 'those that satisfy the priority health care needs of the population'.[3] The model list is a recommended guide for the development of national and institutional essential medicine lists, i.e. of medicines which are intended to be available at all times in adequate amounts and at a price the individual and the community can afford. As such, the model list and its underlying philosophy has been of crucial importance both for the global acceptance of the concept of essential medicines and to guide national health policies. The Secretariat has reported that, by the end of 1999, 156 Member States had official essential medicine lists, which *inter alia* guide the procurement and supply of medicines in the public sector as well as insurance reimbursement schemes. Also international agencies such as

UNICEF and UNHCR have adopted the essential medicines concept and base their procurement system mainly on WHO's model list.[4]

1. The Assembly requested the Director-General to assist Member States by 'advising on the selection and procurement, at reasonable cost, of essential drugs of established quality corresponding to their national needs'. *See* OR 226, p. 35.
2. The model list is available on-line at <http://www.who.int/medicines/organization/par/edl/eml. shtml> (visited on 22 August 2002).
3. WHO Doc. EB109/8, p. 3.
4. *Ibidem*, p. 2.

322.   The Secretariat, on the basis of recommendations from the Expert Commit-tee, has developed a revised procedure for updating and disseminating the model list. Some core components of the new procedure were a shift from consensus-based to evidence-based decisions, a system of global consultation on all proposals before the meeting of the Expert Committee, a better system of reporting and managing any conflict of interest of Expert Committee members, and rapid electronic dissemination of the report in the six official languages of the Organization. Some of the concerns underlying the approach to the revision had to do with the transparency of the process and reflected the intense interest of Member States and the pharmaceutical industry in standards with obvious commercial implications. In particular, the discussion of the 'affordability' element in the criteria for the selection of essential medicines, and the historical preference for generic or multi-source products over more expensive patented ones, have raised the concern of the pharmaceutical industry.

323.   The draft revised procedure was therefore widely circulated for com-ments, and listed as one of its purposes a more transparent process for selecting essential medicines based on a systematic review of all available evidence. Still, at the 109th Session of the Executive Board in January 2002, where the final version of the procedure was discussed, comments were made by some delegations to the effect that the Expert Committee 'should be accountable to all interested parties'[1] and that the membership of the committee 'must be publicized and the procedure for [the] selection should be transparent'.[2] The Board, however, did not endorse those statements. The Expert Committee, which met in April 2002 to test the new procedure, agreed in response to hold an open session to allow all interested stakeholders to present comments on issues on the agenda of the Expert Committee and to participate in discussions related to the model list. The 55th Health Assembly addressed, by Resolution WHA55.14, the general political dimension of this debate by urging Member States 'to establish the necessary mechanisms for essential med-icines lists that are science-based, independent of external pressures, and subject to regular reviews'.[3] The new procedure for updating the model list are now used by the Expert Committee.[4]

1. EB109/2002/REC/2, p. 68 (Japan).
2. *Ibidem* (United States).
3. Unpublished at the time of writing. Available on-line at <http://www.who.int/gb/EB_WHA/ PDF/WHA55/ewha5514.pdf> (visited on 22 August 2002).
4. The new procedure is available on-line at <http://www.who.int/medicines/organization/par/edl/ procedures.html>.

§4. GENERAL CONSIDERATIONS ON THE USE BY WHO OF ITS
    NORMATIVE FUNCTIONS

324. The preceding overview makes it clear that WHO has not yet fully utilized the full range and scope of the normative powers assigned to it by the Constitution. Besides the two existing regulations (one of which has arguably become of marginal importance) and the current negotiations on the FCTC, both the governing bodies and the Secretariat have clearly preferred to pursue a flexible, non-binding recommendatory approach, or to pursue WHO's functions through the dissemination of guides, information or the findings of expert bodies. Even when proposals were advanced to adopt new regulations (as in the case of the International Code of Marketing for Breast-milk Substitutes), the governing bodies have not been prepared to extend the coverage of Article 21, and these matters have been dealt with by the adoption of recommendations or technical standards. The possibility of the preparation and adoption of further regulations has also been discussed in connection with topics such as international maritime venereal disease control; the control of malaria; the International Pharmacopoeia and pharmacopoeial formulas for potent drugs; quality control of drugs; and biological standardization. A proposal was also made by certain Member States for a 'treaty' to cover the international control of the HIV/AIDS epidemic.[1]

1. *See* S.S. Fluss, F. Gutteridge, J.K. Little, H. Harris, 'World Health Organization', *supra*, p. 28.

325. Still, the text of the Constitution and the debates that led to its drafting show that the founders of WHO envisaged the adoption of conventions and regulations as central instruments in the regulation and management of international health issues. The power to issue regulations, in particular, was and remains an exceptional tool for global international organizations. Why, then, did WHO shy away from the use of such powers? Various reasons have been put forward for this apparent failure of the international regulatory technique in the health field. These include the restricted scope of Article 21, as compared with the general statement of WHO's functions under Article 2, the difficulties inherent in formalizing technical requirements in a rapidly evolving domain, the cost of maintaining centralized facilities for the administration of legally binding instruments, the absence of any requirements of reciprocity in many cases, the reluctance of the Organization to indulge in what might be termed the 'making of official science', and the uneven development of states in science and technology.[1] Gutteridge adds the historical consideration that WHO 'began its life with a tendency to direct its major efforts towards direct action in the field, due in part to its inheritance from UNRRA. This tendency became enhanced at a later stage through the admission of . . . developing countries, more inclined to support field work. . . .'[2] The opposition by some major industrialized countries to a regulation on breast-milk substitutes and on essential drugs shows, moreover, the limitations which may be imposed by economic and commercial considerations over the use by WHO of regulatory powers.

1. *Ibidem*, p. 27.
2. F. Gutteridge, 'Notes on Decisions of the World Health Organization' in S.M. Schwebel (ed.), *The Effectiveness of International Decisions* (Leyden, Sijthoff, 1971), p. 282.

326.   The recent literature has proposed other reasons to explain WHO's legal timidity. Thus, Taylor states that it is 'largely attributable to the internal dynamics and politics of the organizations itself. In particular, this unwillingness stems, in large part, from the organizational culture established by the conservative medical professional community that dominates the institution.'[1] Besides the medical-technical ethos of the Organization, Fidler notes the prevalence in WHO for a long time of what he dubs 'eradicationitis', i.e. the impact of the progress in the eradication of infectious diseases in sidelining a legal approach to their control. He also argues that, with the development of powerful medical tools to address infectious diseases, 'developed states gradually lost interest in infectious disease control as an important element of interstate relations'.[2] The latter consideration may be tempered, however, by the impact of the HIV/AIDS pandemic on WHO's thinking in this respect, in particular the use of a human rights approach as an important aspect of an overall control and prevention strategy. That has been seen as an intellectual watershed in WHO concerning the relations between international law and public health goals.[3]

1. A.L. Taylor, 'Making the World Health Organization Work: A Legal Framework for Universal Access to the Conditions for Health', in 18 *American Journal of Law and Medicine*, 1992, p. 303.
2. D.P. Fidler, 'The Future of the World Health Organization: What Role for International Law?' in 31 *Vanderbilt Journal of Transnational Law*, 1998, pp. 1099–1103.
3. *See in particular* J.M. Mann, 'Human Rights and AIDS: The Future of the Pandemic', in J.M. Mann, S. Gruskin, M.A. Grodin, G.J. Annas (eds.), *Health and Human Rights* (New York/London, Routledge, 1999), pp. 216–226.

327.   The authors in question argue in favour of a renewed effort by WHO as a whole to reconsider and, to a certain extent, rediscover its normative powers to make a difference and build on WHO's comparative advantages in a globalizing world. The ever clearer connection between human rights and health is indicated as a case in point for the pursuit of a more deliberate normative strategy by the Organization.[1] In this connection, it should be underlined that, in *Health for All in the 21st Century*, the Director-General states a strong commitment on the part of WHO to '. . . develop international instruments that promote and protect health, . . . monitor their implementation, and . . . encourage its Member States to apply international laws related to health. A strong system of global governance is necessary for implementation of existing international instruments on health and human rights as well as instruments having health implications.'[2]

1. A.L. Taylor, 'Making the World Health Organization Work: A Legal Framework for Universal Access to the Conditions for Health', *supra*, pp. 316–319.
2. *Health for All in the Twenty-first Century*, WHO Doc. A/51/5, para. 52.

328.   Whether WHO will in fact make more use of its normative powers remains a matter for debate and speculation, which is not possible to review in this contribution. Two considerations, however, appear of central importance to any development or discussion in this area. The first is the need for WHO as a whole to be fully aware of the growing overlap and interactions, in a globalizing world, between international health and other areas of international relations and law. A very tentative list would include international trade law, human rights, arms control, with particular regard to weapons of mass destruction, international labour law, maritime and aviation law, environmental law, international humanitarian law, intellectual property law and international law on bioethics. These fields of international law are already regulated through a web of international conventions and other instruments, many of which have been developed and are administered and enforced through international agencies such as the United Nations or WTO. This fact appears to restrict the possibility for WHO to take entirely independent initiatives of a normative nature. At the same time, it could arguably allow the Organization not only to actively support the normative activities of other organizations, but also to fill gaps related to public health left open by the existing instruments. The involvement of WHO in the negotiation of the above-mentioned Protocol on Water and Health can be cited as an example. The latter option obviously makes it imperative for WHO to properly consult and coordinate with agencies competent on 'neighbouring' subject matters, to avoid conflicts and duplications and possible challenges to WHO's competence. In this respect, the consultations taking place between the Secretariat and WTO as well as the World Customs Organization in the context of the FCTC negotiations are a case in point.

329. The second consideration is that, in the end, the decisive factor in this area will be the attitude of WHO's Member States, in particular their confidence in the Organization as an instrument for establishing, monitoring and administering international binding instruments. There is definitely a lack of a 'normative tradition' in WHO's governing bodies, which makes many delegations and ministries of health somehow unfamiliar or even uncomfortable with negotiating and debating international legal instruments. In this regard, the outcome of the FCTC negotiations will probably be instrumental in overcoming or confirming this reluctance. In the meantime, some recent proposals to launch new international conventions on topics of unquestionable public health importance seem to confirm the reluctance of Member States to use WHO as a forum for legally-binding normative initiatives. Reference is made, in particular, to the proposal, made by France and Germany and endorsed in principle by the General Assembly of the United Nations with Resolution 56/93 of 12 December 2001, of an international convention against the reproductive cloning of human beings.[1] The Assembly has convened an *ad hoc* committee to discuss a possible mandate for negotiations which will take place under aegis of the UN. Similarly, by Resolution 56/168 of 19 December 2001, the General Assembly has established another *ad hoc* committee to consider proposals for a comprehensive and integral international convention to promote and protect the rights and dignity of persons with disabilities. The originator of this initiative was Mexico.[2] WHO will participate in the work of the two committees as an observer and will strive to have its positions on both subjects, as well as broader public health considerations, reflected in the forthcoming conventions.

1. The text of the resolution is available on-line at <http://daccess-ods.un.org/doc> (visited on 23 August 2002).
2. *Ibidem.*

Chapter 3. Directing and Coordinating Functions

330. As noted above, direction and coordination of the development and main trends of international cooperation in the field of health was seen by WHO's founders as its essential purpose, in the face of the devastation left by World War Two and the innumerable health problems afflicting humankind. This determination has remained the fundamental mission of the Organization to date. The achievement of the 'highest attainable standard of health' for all human beings is a vision far from being achieved; while the overall health profile of the international community has changed in many respects since 1948 and much progress has been made, many threats to health have remained constant for 50 years, while others have emerged or re-emerged.[1] Moreover, the poverty and underdevelopment that afflicts most of humankind and the widening gap between rich and poor countries present formidable obstacles to the improvement of the health status of billions of human beings.

> 1. It is interesting to note that the 1st WHA had established the following issues as the top priorities for international health in 1948: malaria, maternal and child health, tuberculosis, venereal diseases, nutrition and environmental sanitation. With the exception of venereal diseases, all the other topics remain a challenge and a priority for WHO at the present time. *See* Y. Beigbeder, *supra*, p. 16.

331. Such is the overall importance of the directing and coordinating functions that the Director-General defined it in the Ninth GPW in a way which virtually encompasses all other functions and activities of WHO:

> 'WHO's directing and coordinating functions include the search for international consensus on health problems of global priority and the most effective ways of assisting countries to solve them, and advocacy of measures to mobilize international resources and action for health, including humanitarian assistance. They also comprise what is often referred to as the normative function of WHO, that is, monitoring the health situation and trends throughout the world; proposing conventions, regulations, norms, standards and guidelines related to health; and stimulating research, the advancement and application of knowledge and the sharing of information in the field of health, including the bioethical dimensions.'[1]

> 1. *Ninth General Programme of Work, supra*, p. 24.

332. An analysis of WHO's directing and coordinating functions is thus, in a way, a history of WHO as the global international health agency. For the purpose of the present contribution, only a few selected issues and areas will be reviewed in which the role of WHO appears to be more directly related to policy-making or to the coordination of internal and external actors in the pursuit of a discrete health outcome.

333. Before such a review, however, a reference to the report submitted by the Secretariat to the 110th Session of the Board in May 2002 may give an idea of the scope and breadth of WHO's activities carried out in implementation of the pro-gramme budget 2000–2001, organized along the clusters established by Director-General Brundtland.[1]

    1. WHO Doc. EB110/11.

334. In the area of *communicable diseases*, WHO intensified global and coun-try level efforts for disease control, mainly by encouraging partnerships between a variety of stakeholders. WHO co-sponsored partnerships to roll back malaria and stop tuberculosis, as well as to combat African trypanosomiasis. In 2000, a global alliance to eliminate lymphatic filariasis brought together 30 organizations and channelled free supplies of drugs offered by their manufacturers.

335. In the area of *noncommunicable diseases (NCDs)*, WHO focused attention on four main groups of diseases which share common risk factors, namely, cardio-vascular diseases, diabetes, cancer and chronic lung diseases. The Secretariat elabor-ated a tool to facilitate surveillance and control of NCDs by low and middle-income countries as well as guidelines for policy-makers and health care professionals on improving the delivery of preventive and clinical management.

336. In the area of *family and community health*, the Integrated Management of Childhood Illness had been introduced in over 100 countries by the end of 2001. Work to reduce the practice of female genital mutilation was also intensified, and culminated in the publication of four manuals, one on advocacy and three on training health care workers. The Making Pregnancy Safer initiative began work in ten countries, with the goals of increasing access of mothers and newborns to quality health services. WHO's support for combating HIV/AIDS was scaled up, with a focus on both prevention and care. WHO's contribution to tackling HIV/AIDS in Africa was intensified by providing enhanced support to countries in sub-Saharan Africa particularly affected by the disease.

337. In the area of *sustainable development and healthy environments*, a policy framework on health in poverty reduction was endorsed by the Board at its 105th Session, and health was squarely placed on the agenda of the United Nations General Assembly special session on social development (Geneva, June 2000) and the Third United Nations Conference on Least Developed Countries (Brussels, March 2001). In order to promote policy coherence between the health and trade sectors, WHO cooperated with the WTO in analyzing the relationship between health risks and international trade issues. Normative standards and guidelines were drawn up for nutrition, energy requirements of all age groups, vitamin and mineral requirements, management of nutrition in major emergencies, and safe levels of vitamin A for pregnant women and children, in addition to preparing a global strategy for feeding infants and young children. As part of WHO's action to protect the human environment, more than 250 chemical and other high-risk pollutants were evaluated and the findings published. Amendments to WHO's guidelines for drinking water quality were also finalized and published, and guidelines issued for air quality at global and regional levels. In addition, the first WHO's food safety strategy was finalized through a broad consultative approach, and was endorsed by the Board at its 109th Session in January 2001. WHO coordinated or conducted more than 50 interventions in emergencies around the world, with support from donors.

338. In the area of *social change and mental health*, mental health was the theme for the 2001 World Health Report and for the ministerial round tables during the 54th WHA. As a result, mental health has become a priority on the health agenda of many states. Work on healthy ageing in 2001 involved preparation of WHO's contribution to the UN Second World Assembly on Ageing (Madrid, April 2001). The programme on substance abuse compiled and disseminated a global database on alcohol consumption, prepared a multinational study on drug injecting, and launched a global initiative on the primary prevention of substance abuse. The draft of the world report on violence and health was prepared after thorough regional consultations. The report was published in late 2002. WHO also provided support to the United Nations Special Rapporteur in monitoring implementation of health related aspects of United Nations standard rules on persons with disabilities. Strategies and programmes to prevent blindness and deafness were further developed and strengthened. In the case of trachoma, seventeen endemic countries started implementing the WHO-recommended SAFE strategy (surgery for trichiasis, antibiotics, facial cleanliness and environmental improvement). The Fifth Global Conference on Health Promotion (Mexico, June 2000) reviewed best practices and endorsed work for national capacity building. The 17th World Conference on Health Promotion and Health Education (Paris, June 2001) launched a global forum for health promotion dialogue. WHO continued to foster effective school health programmes in the context of health promoting schools.

339. In the area of *health technology and pharmaceuticals*, WHO's activities focused on the four components of its strategy for improving access to essential and other medicines: rational selection of medicines, affordable prices, sustainable financing, and reliable supply and delivery systems. Medicine selection has been improved by updating the procedures of the Expert Committee on the Selection and Use of Essential Medicines. WHO encouraged lower medicine prices in poor countries by advocating differential pricing and by making price information widely available. It also raised awareness of certain provisions of WTO's Agreement on Trade-Related Aspects of Intellectual Property Rights (TRIPS) which affect the affordability of medicines. Voluntary contributions in support of the eradication of poliomyelitis more than doubled in comparison with the 1998–1999 biennium. Although the target of eradicating poliomyelitis in all regions by the end of 2001 was not met, two out of the six regions were certified polio-free and the disease remained endemic in only ten countries. WHO aimed at increasing the use of new or underutilized vaccines through the GAVI partnership (*see supra*, Part IV). This included accelerating introduction of hepatitis B vaccine, which was accomplished through major donor support. WHO provided auto-disable syringes systematically to all countries receiving support from GAVI and the Vaccine Fund. World Health Day 2000 raised global awareness of blood safety, and several regional offices provided support to countries in formulating national plans to ensure quality and safety of the blood supply. Launching of the project on HIV/AIDS diagnostic support raised awareness and ensured the development of expertise. Prequalification of diagnostic tests is in place and WHO bulk purchasing has resulted in much-reduced prices for HIV tests.

340.   In the area of *evidence and information for policy*, new lifetime tables were estimated for all countries and published in the World Health Report 2001. The International Digest of Health Legislation (*see infra*, Part VIII) became available on the internet in May 2000. More than 70 countries took part in the creation and field-testing of the International Classification of Functioning, Disability and Health, the first such classification. The concept of health system responsiveness was devised, and methods to assess it were developed after an analysis of 60 country surveys, undertaken as part of the WHO multicountry survey 2000–2001. WHO increasingly focused on the organization of health services. Conceptual frameworks were designed for assessing and improving health provider performance, for measuring coverage of key health interventions, and for categorizing health care delivery models. The Commission on Macroeconomics and Health (*see infra* in this Part), established in 1999 to examine the extent to which ill-health contributes to poverty and underdevelopment, published a report in late 2001 that provided important guidance for WHO's follow-up.

341.   One of the innovations in the overall management of WHO's activities in 2000–2001 was the establishment of three *cabinet projects*: Roll Back Malaria, the Tobacco Free Initiative, and the Partnership for Health Sector Development. The establishment of such projects was seen as a way of rapidly creating visibility and impact in selected priority areas and to create a uniformity of purpose throughout WHO.

342.   The main benefit of designating Roll Back Malaria (RBM) as a cabinet project was that it fostered a greater understanding in WHO of the long-standing problem of malaria and led to an agreement on actions needed. The project adopted a four-prong strategy: prompt access to treatment, prevention with insecticide-treated nets, epidemic prediction and response, and malaria in pregnancy. The project has been successful in building and coordinating partnerships and facilitating cross-cutting work. For example, the prompt access to treatment encourages governments and national RBM partnerships to monitor the development of parasite resistance to antimalarial drugs, to replace drugs which are no longer effective, and to increase access to effective treatment. The product development group, organized under the auspices of TDR in collaboration with industrial partners, identifies potential antimalarial drugs and provides support for the necessary clinical trials. Similar collaboration on essential medicines led to work with regulatory authorities on such issues as drug registration in developing countries. During 2001, an extended group worked with the governments of Burundi, Ethiopia, Rwanda, South Africa, United Republic of Tanzania and Zambia on changes in policy for malaria treatment. RBM has succeeded in raising awareness of malaria at high political levels and successfully placed malaria on the global agenda, as reflected by the Abuja Declaration on Roll Back Malaria in Africa (2000), and the proclamation by the UN General Assembly of the period 2001–2010 as the Decade to Roll Back Malaria in Developing Countries, Particularly in Africa.[1] The heightened awareness of malaria and the potential to control it, led to the inclusion of the disease as one to be tackled by the Global Fund to Fight AIDS, Tuberculosis and Malaria.[2]

1. Resolution 55/284 of 7 September 2001.
2. More information on the Global Fund can be obtained on-line at <http://www.globalfundatm.org/>.

343.   The *Tobacco Free Initiative* was launched as a cabinet project to provide global leadership and to mobilize national and international action for preventing and reducing tobacco use. Besides supporting the negotiation of the Framework Convention on Tobacco Control (*supra*), the initiative organized the first public hearings on tobacco consumption in October 2000. Also, the *Ad Hoc* Interagency Task Force on Tobacco Control, chaired by WHO, initiated studies on the economic implications of tobacco reduction; employment issues related to tobacco control; smoke-free policies in the United Nations workplace; smuggling; trade issues related to the framework convention; and economic analysis of tobacco control that focuses on demand-side issues; and privatization and illicit trade. The Global Youth Tobacco Survey was completed in over 50 countries,[1] and a report was issued on the impact of tobacco on children and young people; a report on the Convention on the Rights of the Child and its relation to tobacco was issued in 2001.[2]

1. *International consultation on tobacco and youth: what in the world works?*, WHO Doc. WHO/NMH/TFI/00.1.
2. *Tobacco and the rights of the child*, WHO Doc. WHO/TFI/01.3 Rev.1.

344.   The purpose of the cabinet project on *partnerships for health sector development* was to develop a corporate approach to country work in general, and to country cooperation strategies in particular. It examined the way in which different parts of the Organization work with each other, with countries and with development partners. Three interrelated components were defined: to develop a more strategic approach to country work, to promote a health sector perspective, and to strengthen WHO's dialogue and engagement with development agencies. By the end of 2000, four experimental country cooperation strategies had been formulated and the institutionalization phase began. By July 2001, country cooperation strategies had been initiated in 25 countries in the six regions, and country support units had been established or strengthened at headquarters and the regional offices.

§1. HEALTH FOR ALL

345.   The most important and long-lasting contribution of WHO to international health policy is arguably the process defined as 'health for all' (HFA), as well as the concepts and reorientation of WHO's activities and priorities underscoring that

process. Even though the initial ambitious goal of health for all 'by the year 2000' has proved unachievable, the policy has been revised and reaffirmed in 1998 as one of the main inspiring principles for WHO's activities.

346.   The historical origins of the HFA lie in the dissatisfaction prevailing in the mid-1970s about the static, fragmented ways of dealing with health, and WHO's role therein. In the developing world, expensive city hospitals were absorbing an inordinate share of the national health budget while smaller health posts and clinics, both urban and rural, were scarce and starved of resources. Even countries that had made serious gains through separate programmes to combat malaria, leprosy and yaws, for example, were increasingly aware of the duplication and even competition inherent in such a fragmented set-up. At the same time, important health needs were not being catered for at all. Millions of people had no access to even rudimentary health services and scarce attention was given to the root causes of their ill health such as malnutrition caused by the growing of cash crops instead of staple foods.

347.   In the industrialized world, many health systems had become top-heavy. Sophisticated hospital care had expanded faster than health promoting and clinical services where people actually worked and lived. People were becoming passively dependent on the 'medical miracle' to cure the effects of a lifetime of unhealthy living, while at the same time they were not happy with the impersonality of high-technology medicine.

348.   In the same period, WHO began to study and document the innovative, successful approaches to health that were being pioneered in some developing countries. The findings showed that while these alternative approaches were highly specific, they had certain key elements in common. One was an explicit commitment to universal coverage: bringing essential health care to not just some but all of the population, with special attention to those in greatest need. Another was the active involvement of individuals, families and communities; health workers increasingly engaged in dialogue with the community to determine what health needs it perceived as most urgent. When the surprising health gains made by several developing countries were studied, it turned out that these were societies that encouraged schooling for both girls and boys, and where female autonomy was sufficient for mothers to act with some independence in caring for themselves and their children. What these successful innovations pointed to was a new way of perceiving, promoting and protecting health. The time was ripe for an approach to health not only based on sound technology but centered on people and inspired by the values of universality and equity.

349.   WHO became progressively aware of the flaws of some of its previous policies and the need for a profound rethinking of its role. In his annual report for 1975, Director-General Mahler stated that

'separate programmes, each designed for the control of a specific disease, are not likely to solve the overall problem . . . We must also remind ourselves that the urgent health problems of developing countries relate to poverty, to infection, to malnutrition and undernutrition, to lack of accessible potable water, and to multiple environmental hazards. Such basic threats to health are unlikely to be countered by conventional health service techniques . . . The main lesson learned is that, in the fight against disease, too much emphasis must not be placed on health technologies alone. What we can achieve in this field depends directly on the level of economic development of the countries concerned.'[1]

1. OR 229, pp. VII, VIII, XI.

350. In May 1977, the 30th WHA declared that the main social target of governments and WHO should be the attainment by the year 2000 of a level of health that will permit all citizens of the world 'to lead a socially and economically productive life', and decided to reorient the work of WHO 'for the development of technical cooperation and transfer of resources for health' in its role as directing and coordinating authority.[1]

1. Resolution WHA30.43, in OR 240, p. 25.

351. In pursuance of this change of strategy, WHO and UNICEF convened in September 1978 in Alma-Ata an International Conference on Primary Health Care. The conference produced a declaration and a number of implementing recommendations which set a new vision for international health.[1] HFA is based on five principles defined in the declaration:

(1) Resources for health should be evenly distributed and essential health care should be accessible to everyone;
(2) People have the right and duty to participate individually and collectively in the planning and implementation of health care;
(3) Promotive, preventive, curative and rehabilitative services for the main health problems in the community should be provided;
(4) Technology should be appropriate for each country concerned and maintainable with resources the country can afford;
(5) The realization of the highest level of health requires the action of many other social and economic sectors in addition to the health sector.

1. *Primary Health Care – Report of the International Conference on Primary Health Care* (Geneva, WHO, 1978).

352. The HFA strategy is based on the primary health care approach – which has been dubbed by critics as 'poor man's medicine'. Primary health care is defined in the declaration as follows:

'Primary health care is essential health care based on practical, scientifically sound and socially acceptable methods and technology made universally accessible to individuals and families in the community through their full participation and at a cost that the community and country can afford to maintain at every stage of their development in the spirit of self-reliance and self-determination.

It forms an integral part both of the country's health system, of which it is the central function and main focus, and of the overall social and economic development of the community. It is the first level of contact of individuals, the family and community with the national health system bringing health care as close as possible to where people live and work, and constitutes the first element of a continuing health care process.'[1]

1. *Ibidem*, p. 3.

353.   Primary health care was, in turn, based on at least eight main components: (1) education concerning prevailing health problems and the methods of preventing and controlling them; (2) promotion of food supply and proper nutrition; (3) an adequate supply of safe water and basic sanitation; (4) maternal and child health care, including family planning; (5) immunization against the major infectious diseases; (6) prevention and control of locally endemic diseases; (7) appropriate treatment of common diseases and injuries; and (8) provision of essential drugs.

354.   The ambitions of the process launched at Alma-Ata are evident. It required not only a radical evolution, but also a 'social revolution', in public health. Its objective was to change the mentality of the population concerning its own health care, to change health services structures and the distribution of resources thereto, and to reorient the role of professional health personnel. The use of health technology and knowledge had to be reintegrated into an infrastructure of basic health services, for whose orientation the communities concerned had a right and a duty of participation. The emphasis of public health care shifted from the medical approach to the determinants of health, which touched deeply the social, political and cultural structure of the societies concerned. The integration of health services into an equitable and sustainable health system was also a central requirement of this approach. At the same time, while not neglecting curative and medical aspects, renewed emphasis was placed on health promotion and the prevention of diseases through basic approaches to the determinants of health (sanitation, education, nutrition, etc.). Most importantly, the implementation of the declaration would have required a significant increase in the resources destined to public health and their redistribution so as to satisfy the basic needs of the population and aim at an equitable access to health and other services.

355.   HFA and its concomitant emphasis on primary health care were endorsed by the Health Assembly in 1979. The assembly decided that WHO's programmes and the allocation of resources should be functional to its commitment to achieve HFA by the year 2000. Much emphasis was placed on the right and responsibility of Member States to formulate their own strategies and plans of action and the related responsibility of the Secretariat in supporting them in this endeavour and in the implementation of strategies and plans.[1] The Assembly adopted, in 1981, the Global Strategy for health for all by the year 2000 for the implementation of the HFA approach, submitted by the Board.[2] The Assembly requested the Board to monitor and evaluate periodically the strategy and to formulate future General Programmes of Work in its support. Under the Global Strategy, Member States were to provide representative, accurate and timely information on a set of global indicators to enable WHO to monitor and evaluate progress. However, it soon became apparent that, in many countries, the statistical infrastructure required to generate and compile the data was not yet operative, reflecting the logistic and financial difficulties associated with the establishment of an adequate health information system.[3]

1. Resolution WHA32.30, in WHA32/1979/REC/1, p. 27.
2. Resolution WHA34.36 in WHA34/1981/REC/1, p. 35.
3. Y. Beigbeder, *supra*, p. 26.

356. The ambitious – some would say utopian – blueprint adopted in Alma-Ata soon revealed the difficulties underlying its implementation. By way of example, primary health care requires that medical doctors be redistributed more equitably between urban and rural areas, which is only possible in the public sector. Medical associations of western countries had many reservations at the assignment of medical functions to 'second-category' health personnel foreseen in the strategy to spread the access to basic health services, while large pharmaceutical companies were similarly hostile to the 'essential drugs' component of the strategy. Even determined political will by governments found substantial obstacles at changing the fundamental political, economic and social dynamics of countries. The Director-General summarized as follows the main obstacles to progress towards HFA:

(1) insufficient political commitment to the implementation of HFA;
(2) failure to achieve equity in access to all Primary Health Care elements;
(3) the continuing low status of women;
(4) slow socioeconomic development;
(5) difficulty in achieving intersectoral action for health;
(6) unbalanced distribution of, and weak support for, human resources;
(7) widespread inadequacy of health promotion activities;
(8) weak health information systems and no baseline data;
(9) pollution, poor food safety, and lack of safe water supply and sanitation;
(10) rapid demographic and epidemiological changes;
(11) inappropriate use of, and allocation of resources for, high-cost technology;
(12) natural and man-made disasters.[1]

1. *Health for All in the Twenty-first Century, supra,* p. 6.

357. However, the overwhelming obstacle to the progressive pursuit of the HFA Strategy was economic. The Health Assembly acknowledged in various resolutions that the economic situation of many developing countries was a serious constraint to the achievement of HFA goals and was actually leading to cuts in national health budgets.

358. Against this backdrop, the Board submitted to the Assembly in 1995 a proposal to revise and renew the HFA strategy, which would build on the conceptual and political changes brought about by the Alma-Ata Declaration, and by its achievements, while drawing lessons from its shortcomings and taking account of a changing international environment.[1] The Health Assembly, by Resolution

WHA48.16, stressed the continued validity of HFA as a 'timeless aspirational goal' and agreed that a new global health policy should be elaborated. Such policy would give priority attention to the most seriously deprived in health care, should be based on the concepts of equity and solidarity, emphasize the responsibility of individuals, families and communities, and place health squarely within the overall development framework.

1. EB95/1995/REC/1, Annex 5.

359. After a thorough consultation process, the Director-General submitted his report to the 51st WHA, which adopted on 16 May 1998 a synthetic 'World Health Declaration' (reproduced in Annex 3).[1] The report and the declaration develop the main principles and approaches which are guiding WHO's action at the present time, and which constitute the foundations, for example, of the corporate strategy and the 9th GPW. Along the lines of the previous HFA strategy, the declaration stresses the place of health in social and economic development and a collective commitment to the ethical concepts of equity, solidarity and social justice. It also introduces a gender perspective which was missing from the Alma-Ata Declaration, while it emphasizes WHO's commitment to address poverty and the basic determinants of health. The main emphasis of the declaration lies on the need to strengthen, adapt and reform through appropriate investments and private and public actions health systems 'in order to ensure universal acess to health services that are based on scientific evidence, of good quality and within affordable limits, and that are sustainable for the future.' Sustainable health systems have to guarantee equitable access to essential health functions, including making quality care available across the life span; preventing and controlling disease, and protecting health; developing health information systems and ensuring active surveillance; and securing adequate and sustainable financing. While the availability of 'the essentials of primary health care' is explicitly affirmed as a foundation to build on, there is less emphasis on it as the key to the attainment of HFA.

1. The report is contained in WHO Doc. A/51/5, *supra*. The Declaration is annexed to Resolution WHA51.7, in WHA51/1998/REC/1, p. 5.

§2. POVERTY AND HEALTH

360. It has been estimated that 1.3 billion people (about twenty per cent of the world population) live in absolute poverty, with an income of less that USD1 per day, while almost half of the world population survives on USD2 per day. The results in terms of health outcomes are dire. For example, those living in absolute poverty are five times more likely to die before reaching the age of five, and two-and-a-half times more likely to die between the ages of fifteen and 59, than those in higher income groups. Differences in maternal mortality are even more dramatic: the risk of dying in pregnancy in parts of sub-Saharan Africa, where almost 50 per cent of the population live in absolute poverty, is one in twelve, compared to one in 4,000 in Europe. Ill-health is both a cause and a consequence of poverty. Illness can reduce household savings, lower learning ability, reduce productivity and lead

to a diminished quality of life – thus creating or perpetuating poverty. The poor in turn are exposed to greater personal and environmental risks, are less well nourished, have less exposure to information, and are less able to access health care. They are therefore more at risk of illness and disability.

361. In view of this inextricable linkage, it is not surprising that WHO has focused its attention since its inception on the diseases or other conditions which affect disproportionately the poor, or on the inequities that the functioning of health systems can generate. On the one hand, the campaign to eradicate river blindness (*see infra*), the strategy of directly observed treatment to combat tuberculosis, the implementation of essential medicines policies, and the promotion of research on medicines for tropical diseases, are just a few examples. On the other hand, promoting equity is a cornerstone of the HFA and as such has been a part of WHO's programmes for over twenty years. Moreover, addressing inequities in health is central to the work of several WHO regions and features in the HFA targets set by many Member States. These efforts have been underpinned by a series of Health Assembly resolutions, for example the aforementioned 'World Health Declaration' of 1998. Nevertheless, WHO has been paying increasing attention to poverty and health issues, attempting to approach health as a means of combating absolute poverty.

362. The reduction or even eradication of absolute poverty has become one of the main goals of the international development agenda, and as such has featured prominently in the international conferences convened by the UN in the 1990s and the beginning of the present decade, such as the United Nations Conference on Environment and Development (1992), the International Conference on Population and Development (1994), the World Summit for Social Development and its follow-up Conference (1995 and 2000), the International Conference on Financing for Development (Monterey, Mexico, 2002) and the World Conference on Sustainable Development (Johannesburg, South Africa, 2002). The culmination of this process has been the proclamation by the General Assembly in the year 2000 of the UN Millennium Development Goals, which list the eradication of extreme poverty and hunger as their first goal. It is significant that three of the eight development goals concern health: reduction of child mortality, improvement of maternal health, and combating HIV/AIDS, malaria and other diseases.

363. Still, until recently health did not figure in the development agenda as one of the determinants of development. The common wisdom was that increasing levels of development would improve the health situation of the population. The other side of this equation – that better health can prevent or offer a route out of poverty – has been given less attention. However, evidence gathered during the 1990s showed with increasing clarity that better health translates into greater and more equitably distributed wealth by building human and social capital and increasing productivity.

364. One of the main initiatives of Director-General Brundtland at the beginning of her term of office, therefore, was to place squarely health within the global development agenda and to make it more central to economic and human development.

Her approach was spelled out in a seminal report she submitted to the 105th Session of the Board in January 2000.[1] The report foresaw a role for WHO in influencing international action to reduce poverty, namely, to generate and disseminate evidence on the relationship between health and development; to establish partnerships with the main development actors; and to catalyse action on the part of governments to make the health of the poor a priority.

1. WHO Doc. EB105/5.

365. The most appropriate strategies in reducing poverty identified in the report balance the need to gather sound evidence of why the poor suffer greater mortality and morbidity with the consideration that to only focus on health systems would not be sufficient, since many of the determinants of ill-health will depend on developments beyond the health sector. The report charts an ambitious course for WHO, by focusing on the determinants of health and on the need for WHO to influence development policies both at national level and through a widening network of international partnerships. WHO should aim at reducing risks through a broader approach to public health, going beyond the traditional domains and encompassing, for example, safe food and clean water. Particular emphasis is placed on the functioning of national health systems, especially their capacity to ensure equitable access, to treat clients with respect and to protect them from impoverishment. At the same time, the report contains a determination which has inspired recent health and poverty policies, namely, that the health of the poor is disproportionately affected by a limited number of conditions for which cost effective health service interventions generally exist. The development community, and not exclusively WHO, should thus target those conditions in an integrated manner.

366. The pursuit of poverty-reducing strategies raises a number of issues for WHO. For example, while most development organizations have started to concentrate their resources almost exclusively on the reduction of absolute poverty, WHO has a global health mandate which goes beyond poverty reduction. The incorporation of this new priority necessitates therefore finding a balance with the other strategic directions in the corporate strategy.

367. The directions followed by WHO to follow up on this policy statement have been manifold: increasing advocacy to obtain support from other international agencies and donors; gathering sound and precise evidence to underscore the validity of such a policy; mobilizing resources to scale up interventions in favour of poverty reduction; and identifying the best approaches to support countries in developing policies adapted to local contexts.

368. A particularly important initiative taken by the Director-General has been the establishment in January 2000 of a Commission on Macroeconomics and Health (CMH), chaired by Prof. Jeffrey Sachs and comprising eighteen leading economists, public health experts, development professionals and policy-makers. The commission's terms of reference were to assess the place of health in global economic development. The commission carried out an overall thematic analysis by organizing itself in six working groups, which published as many separate reports on their respective topics. The consolidated report of the commission, issued in December 2001, provides compelling evidence that better health for the world's poor is not only an important goal in its own right, but can act as a major catalyst for economic development and poverty reduction.[1]

1. *Macroeconomics and Health: Investing in Health for Economic Development – Report of the Commission on Macroeconomics and Health* (Geneva, WHO, 2001).

369. The commission, by examining in detail the links between health, poverty reduction and economic growth, concluded that economic losses from ill health had been underestimated and that the role of health in economic growth had been grossly undervalued. It thus challenged the traditional argument that health will automatically improve as a result of economic growth, demonstrating clearly that, on the contrary, improved health is a prerequisite for economic development in poor societies.

370. The commission confirmed that a few health conditions accounted for a high proportion of avoidable deaths, in particular communicable diseases, maternal and perinatal conditions, childhood infections, tobacco-related illnesses and nutritional deficiencies. The main operational focus of the report was on the financial dimension. It showed that the level of spending on health in low income countries is insufficient but also that, by using their existing resources more efficiently, they can increase of up to one per cent of GNP by 2007 and two per cent by 2015. However, even such an increase would leave a major financing gap; the commission recommended an increase of USD27 billion per year in donor grants by 2007, rising to USD38 billion in 2015, to finance necessary interventions. The report estimates the aggregate additional cost of scaling up interventions in the order of USD66 billion per year, with around half of this amount coming from donors. The predicted result, however, is to save around eight million lives a year and generate economic benefits of USD360 billion – i.e. a sixfold return on investment.

371. Concerning the 'investment strategy' of the necessary resources, the commission recommends that investments be increased in several sectors – such as crucially education – and that, within the health sector, the highest priority should be for a 'close-to-client' system. The bulk of the additional funding should be spent on country-level programmes. However, the report also encourages increased investment in essential public goods for health, such as research and development for diseases of the poor. Emphasis is also placed on the need to increase poor people's access to affordable life-saving medicines through full utilization of the safeguards contained in the TRIPS agreement.

372. The WHO Secretariat has been using the findings and recommendations of the Commission to scale up its agenda on poverty reduction and the mobilization of the necessary resources. The report had a major positive impact internationally. It received special attention at the Monterey Conference, where the need for increased spending on health was a central theme, and was central to WHO's contribution to the Johannesburg Conference. Senior representatives of governments and other donors met in Geneva in June 2002 to discuss ways on how to take the CMH process forward at country level. Donor support has been offered to support the development of a CMH workplan to be implemented by WHO.

373. At country level, several governments, with WHO support, have established or were in the process of establishing (as of August 2002) National Commissions on Macroecomics and Health (e.g., Ghana, Mexico and Thailand), while others have begun using existing mechanisms to build on the CMH recommendations (e.g. Indonesia and Sri Lanka). Requests for WHO assistance in implementing the CMH process had been received by several other countries, e.g. Ethiopia, Malawi and Mozambique.

374. WHO, among other initiatives, has renewed its efforts to tackle the three communicable diseases which disproportionately affect poor countries and which have proved particularly challenging to control: HIV/AIDS, malaria and tuberculosis. In a recent document, the Secretariat articulated the rationale of a scaled-up campaign against these diseases and the unacceptable burden of death and suffering which they cause.[1] Targeting these diseases can help directly the most vulnerable, for whom poor health is a constant threat to survival. Controlling AIDS, tuberculosis and malaria can remove significant obstacles that keep people in poverty, while preventing families from falling into poverty and decreasing business costs deriving from health related absenteeism and greater expenditures on medical costs for employees. An intensified campaign would prevent the international community from losing further ground against drug resistance, which threatens to undermine the limited supplies of low cost drugs for the effective treatment of TB and malaria. It would also reduce risks of disease spread as a consequence of population mobility and prevent HIV/AIDS from engulfing Asia and eastern Europe. Finally, it can strengthen health services, for example by training and posting more medical personnel in rural areas, so that they can focus not only on the three diseases in question, but also on the many other needs of the low income communities they serve. Several success stories are mentioned, which show the potential benefits of political commitment, effective partnerships and appropriate strategies.[2]

1. *Scaling up the response to infectious diseases* (Geneva, WHO, 2002).
2. For example, the DOTS strategy against TB has substantially reduced the number of deaths in Nepal and halved TB incidence in Peru. *See ibid.*, p. 18.

375. Placing health on the development agenda, and increasing its own credibility and effectiveness as a development actor rather than only as a medical agency, has arguably been one of the major achievements of WHO during the tenure of Dr. Brundtland. Still, political support has to translate in fresh resources to realistically scale up the campaign against diseases of the poor. One important sign of an increased commitment to investing in health has been the decision, initially taken in principle at the 2000 G8 meeting in Okinawa and followed up in 2001 with the support of Secretary-General Annan and Director-General Brundtland, to establish a Global Fund to Fight AIDS, Tuberculosis and Malaria as a new global funding mechanism.

376.   The fund is not meant as a programme but rather as a financial instrument designed to collect, manage and disburse funds which would be additional and complementary to other forms of development assistance. The intention of the 38 countries and organizations – including WHO – which constituted themselves in a transitional working group in August 2001 was to break from 'business as usual' and aim at an innovative and effective funding mechanism. The fund was formally established in January 2002 as a foundation under Swiss law, to underscore its independence from governments or existing international institutions. At the same time, to reduce management costs, it relies on WHO to provide its Secretariat as well as administrative services on a contractual basis. It has also agreed that the World Bank will serve as the fiduciary agent of the fund. The governance mechanism of the fund consists of a Board comprising seven representatives of donor countries, seven of developing countries, two of NGOs, one of a private foundation and one of the private sector.

377.   The main operational principle of the fund is that its grants will be linked to the achievement of results. To this end, the Board has established a Technical Review Panel to screen funding proposals and make recommendations to the Board. WHO supported the establishment of the panel. The fund agreed on rather stringent conditions from applicants, asking them to establish a country coordinating mechanism including civil society representatives. WHO has supported several countries in the preparation of their proposals. As of September 2002, pledges to the fund exceeded USD2 billion. The Board, at its second meeting in April 2002, approved 40 proposals from 31 countries, amounting to a commitment of USD378 million over two years.[1]

   1. *See* WHO Doc. A55/8 and Add. 1. More information on the Fund are available on its web site at <http://www.globalfundatm.org>

§3. THE FIGHT AGAINST DISEASE

378.   Fighting diseases is one of the natural primary functions of a health agency such as WHO. Article 2(g) of the Constitution, lists as one of WHO's functions 'to stimulate and advance work to eradicate epidemic, endemic and other diseases'. Indeed, one of the first achievements of the Organization was the control of yaws, a crippling and disfiguring tropical disease mainly affecting the skin and bones. A single injection of long lasting penicillin was enough to cure it. Between 1950 when the first yaws campaign was launched in Haiti and 1965, a total of 46 million patients in 49 countries were successfully treated and the disease was no longer a significant public health problem in most of the developing world. However, this early success created an ill-founded optimism among health workers and policy-makers that other diseases could be controlled as easily.

379.   WHO has undertaken the responsibility of coordinating or catalysing programmes and campaigns to either eradicate or manage and control a large number of diseases, from influenza to poliomyelitis, from childhood diseases such as measles and whooping cough, to a range of tropical diseases. Each of these diseases presents different characteristics and relates to different socioeconomic contexts. Part of the challenge for WHO, therefore, has always been to devise effective strategies, aim at realistic goals and mobilize the necessary political support as well as financial and human resources.

380. The first decades of WHO's history are marked by successive campaigns against the most important diseases from a global public health perspective, in particular tuberculosis, malaria and smallpox, with mixed success. Later, the mass immunization campaigns against single diseases were replaced by a single integrated Expanded Programme on Immunization, aimed at protecting by the year 2000 all children against six vaccine-preventable diseases – measles, diphtheria, pertussis, tetanus, poliomyelitis and tuberculosis – in their first year of life. Global coverage with the vaccines reached its peak at the end of 1990 when the goals of immunizing 80 per cent of all children by the age of one was achieved. The main factors inhibiting further progress have been insufficient political commitment by countries, civil unrest, donor fatigue and lack of resources.

381. The concentration on vertical programmes dedicated to single diseases was later criticized as contradicting the HFA strategy, which privileges a horizontal, integrated approach to health promotion on the basis of primary health care.[1] The drawback of a sectoral approach is reportedly to create specialized medical teams in the countries concerned, which may neglect the preventive approach to the detriment of basic health services. On the other hand, disease-related programmes have a specific and measurable target, and enjoy the advantage of relating to known technical means to control or eradicate it. In this regard, a successful international campaign against a disease requires unity of direction and decision, which did not always prove compatible with the decentralized nature of WHO, with ensuing conflicts between Headquarters and the regional offices.

1. Y. Beigbeder, *supra*, p. 125.

382. For the purpose of the present contribution, the approach of WHO to a few selected diseases will be reviewed. This is largely to offer an example of the variety of methods and scenarios confronting WHO and used by it in its search for effective prevention, treatment or control. By no means the examples offered below cover the whole spectrum of WHO's activities. In particular, lack of space prevent us from reviewing in detail WHO's activities to control and prevent the spread of HIV/AIDS within the context of UNAIDS. Suffice it to mention that the mission statement for UNAIDS, as provided by the programme in its first Strategic Plan for 1996–2000, is 'As the main advocate for global action on HIV/AIDS, UNAIDS will lead, strengthen and support an expanded response aimed at preventing the transmission of HIV, providing care and support, reducing the vulnerability of individuals and communities to HIV/AIDS, and alleviating the impact of the epidemic.'[1] The global mission of UNAIDS is to lead, strengthen and support an expanded response to the epidemic that will:

– prevent the spread of HIV;
– provide care and support for those infected and affected by the disease;
– reduce the vulnerability of individuals and communities to HIV/AIDS;
– alleviate the socioeconomic and human impact of the epidemic.

1. <http://www.unaids.org/about/files/strat.html> (visited on 20 May 2002).

I. Onchocerciasis

383. One of the most important cosponsored programmes executed by the Organization is against a parasitic disease, onchocerciasis. Onchocerciasis is caused by a worm (filaria), transmitted from one person to another through the bite of a small blackfly, the *simulium damnosum*. Onchocerciasis used to be a major public health problem. Commonly known as river blindness, a name that expresses its endemic location and its most serious manifestation, the disease gives rise to serious visual impairments and skin lesions. Found in several parts of the world, the disease was mainly prevalent in central Africa. The fertile riverside areas where the black flies abound were abandoned through fear of disease, thus constituting a major obstacle to socio-economic development. In the savannah zone in West Africa, the situation was particularly serious.

384. In the presence of such a situation, several concerned governments expressed their interest in a concerted action against the scourge and approached in the 1960s bilateral and intergovernmental agencies for support. UNDP, FAO, the World Bank and WHO co-sponsored a preparatory mission, following which it was decided to launch the Onchocerciasis Control Programme (OCP). This programme started operations in 1974 covering an area of approximately 1,235,000 sqkm.

385. The programme was based on a partnership initially bringing together seven and later eleven West African countries ('Participating Governments'), the Governments and Organizations funding the programme ('Contributing Parties') and the four international Organizations already mentioned ('Sponsoring Agencies'). WHO served as Executing Agency, and the World Bank as fiscal agent of OCP.

386. The structure of the programme reflected its nature as a partnership. The overall authority for policy-making, planning, programming, implementation and financing the operations belonged to the Joint Programme Committee (JPC), meeting once a year, consisting of representatives of the Participating Governments, of the Contributing Parties and the Sponsoring Agencies. The Committee of Sponsoring Agencies (CSA), meeting several times a year, was the organ of preparation and execution that monitors the operations and considers management issues. The Expert Advisory Committee (EAC), composed of not more than twelve independent scientists, carries out independent evaluation and gives technical and scientific advice to the JCP and the Programme Director. The Director, located at the OCP headquarters in Ouagadougou (Burkina Faso), leads a Secretariat which provides the programme with permanent and administrative assistance and is in charge of its implementation.

387.   The objective of the programme planned initially to be achieved by 1997 and later extended to the end of the year 2002, was to eliminate onchocerciasis as a disease of public health and socio-economic importance throughout the programme area and to ensure that there is no recrudescence of the disease thereafter. The basic strategy of OCP was to carry out aerial application of insecticides to breeding sites of blackfly larvae in the rivers. Around 50,000 km of river were under control and helicopters were regularly spraying during the rainy season when blackfly breeding is at its highest.

388.   As a result of this operation, it may be considered that the disease is virtually eliminated from the OCP area as a disease of public health importance in conformity with the objective fixed. More than eleven million children born in the area since the beginning of the operation have been spared the risk of onchocercal blindness and more than 35 million people are protected from infection. From a socio-economic perspective, by eliminating the threat of blindness and other severe skin ailments, the programme has permitted the resettlement of populations in the fertile areas along the rivers and a total exceeding 250,000 sqkms of arable land has been made available. It is estimated that the resettled land will produce food to feed seventeen million people. Beyond that the programme has contributed to overall development in the OCP countries, roads have been built, wells have been drilled, schools have been opened.

389.   After 25 years of existence, the objective having been achieved, OCP is at its end and its closure has been fixed on 31 December 2002. However, the fight against onchocerciasis continues in nineteen other African countries from southern, central, west and east Africa, neighbouring the initial area of OCP, through a new programme. This new programme is called the African Programme for Onchocerciasis Control (APOC). The ultimate goal of APOC is the same as OCP, the elimination of onchocerciasis as a disease of public health and socio-economic importance throughout Africa, thus contributing to improving the welfare of its people. A great number of similarities exist between the two programmes, but it cannot be concluded that the two are identical. The basic strategy followed for the control operations is totally different. As already said, OCP was based on the control of the vector, by spraying insecticide. APOC is instead based on the control of the parasites invading the patient by treating them with a drug, ivermectin. The clinical effects include alleviation of discomforts and a significant reduction in the risk of developing eye lesions. The drug is given orally, usually once a year. The new treatment process constitutes precisely another remarkable difference between the programmes.

390.   APOC is based on an innovative partnership bringing together the Participating Countries, the Contributing Parties, the Sponsoring Agencies, as OCP, but also non-governmental development organizations and affected communities. The new programme directly involves the population and the rural communities suffering from the disease whose responsibilities in the operations become essential. The planning for, and distribution of, ivermectin is now carried out by the villagers themselves with supervision and support by the local health services.

This process is known as community directed treatment with ivermectin (CDTI). By the year 2007, the total involvement of these communities will be fully operational. Apart from these main differences, the basic structure of APOC is copied from OCP. The institutional framework comprises also a main committee – the Joint Action Forum (JAF) – consisting of representatives of the usual partners, beneficiaries, donors and sponsoring agencies, but also representatives of non-governmental development organizations. The functions and operation of JAF are very similar to those of JPC. A Committee of Sponsoring Agencies (CSA) has also been established which is practically identical to that of OCP. A technical organ, the Technical Consultative Committee (TCC) plays the role of the EAC. The WHO serves as the Executing Agency and manages the programme, the World Bank being the fiscal agent.

391. APOC is planned to covers three phases: Phase I covering the initial period 1996–2001, Phase II for 2002–2007 and the Phasing out Period covering the years 2008–2010 for winding up APOC. At the end of APOC, hopefully, the ultimate goal of the two onchocerciasis programmes implemented by the WHO will be reached: to protect 50 million Africans from onchocerciasis and at the same time to contribute to improving the health status of the rural population and the socio-economic development

II. Smallpox

392. The fight of WHO against smallpox, the first disease that has ever been eradicated by man, began in 1958, when the Soviet Union delegate to the Eleventh World Health Assembly proposed to undertake a global programme to eradicate smallpox. The author of the proposal believed that smallpox eradication was far more attainable than malaria eradication, which had been undertaken in 1955, and that the costs of eradication would be much lower than the ones necessary for vaccination, which was the only way to cope with this untreatable disease.

393. Following the Soviet Union proposal, the Eleventh World Health Assembly requested the Director-General to investigate the means of ensuring the world-wide eradication of smallpox.[1] The next year, the Assembly called for the urgent eradication of the disease, declaring that it could be accomplished 'by successfully vaccinating or revaccinating 80 per cent of the population within a period of four to five years'.[2]

1. Resolution WHA11.54, OR 87, p. 41.
2. Resolution WHA12.54, OR 95, p. 47.

A. The Global Smallpox Eradication Programme, 1959–1967

394. The strategy for smallpox eradication was based on the idea that eradication could be accomplished in a comparatively simple manner by rendering immune, through vaccination, a sufficiently large proportion of the population so that transmission would be interrupted.[1] On the one hand, Member States would have to take the primary responsibility for the execution of the programme, by bearing the major burden of the programme administration and the costs. On the other hand, WHO would provide technical assistance, fellowship for the training of professionals, as well as assisting in the provision of vaccines. There was no focus on the leadership and coordinating role of WHO.

1. OR 95, pp. 572–88.

395. From 1960 to 1966, the expenditures of the smallpox eradication programme amounted to 0.6 per cent of WHO's total expenditures. Progress was slow, principally due to lack of funds for vehicles, supplies and equipment. For several years, only one medical officer and a secretary were working full-time on the programme at headquarters, there was no staff solely responsible for smallpox eradication in the regional offices, and only five experts were sent to the field.

396. The idea of a special budget for the programme was growing, but the failure of the malaria eradication programme was compromising WHO's credibility. Therefore, the Director-General feared taking the major responsibility of coordinating a second eradication effort. In 1964, a WHO Expert Committee on Smallpox was convened, but its report did not recommend a significantly more active role for WHO: the primary responsibility of the programme still rested on governments.

B. *The Intensified Smallpox Eradication Programme, 1968–1980*

397. In 1965, the programme was given impetus by the United States' commitment to actively support it and to provide technical and material assistance for smallpox eradication and measles control in twenty western and central African countries. The decision by the World Health Assembly in 1966 to intensify the effort to eradicate smallpox[1] was taken with real doubts. However, the intensified programme began in 1967 and ended ten years later with a major success. During these ten years, WHO took the leadership of the international eradication effort. It encouraged governments to undertake programmes, greatly involved the regional offices in the co-ordination and implementation effort, sent staff to help organizing and carrying out the field operations, solicited contributions of vaccine and money and assisted laboratories in starting vaccine production. WHO's real commitment and support, both though technical assistance and motivation, was the breakthrough for success.

1. Resolution WHA19.16, OR 151, p. 8.

398. The Director-General's report to the Nineteenth World Health Assembly[1] described the strategy for the eradication of smallpox as two-fold:

(1) mass **vaccination campaigns** in which vaccine of assured quality was employed and which were assessed by specially trained teams;
(2) the development of a **surveillance system** for the detection and investigation of cases and the containment of outbreaks.

    1. OR 151, pp. 106–121.

399.   To promote a common vision and understanding of the strategy and procedures of the eradication programme, a manual entitled *Handbook for Smallpox Eradication Programmes in Endemic Areas* (hereafter referred to as WHO Handbook) was issued by WHO in 1967[1] and broadly distributed in endemic countries.

    1. SE/67.5 Rev. 1 (Geneva, WHO, 1967).

1. Vaccination Campaigns

400.   Mass vaccination campaigns were usually conducted by national health staff, paid by the respective government, with technical advice and material assistance from WHO and other agencies. After 1973, WHO employed many temporary workers to intensify the programme in the remaining endemic areas. International assistance bore the costs of all supplies and equipment in most countries.

401.   For most national programmes, special training was organized and coordinated by WHO, to familiarize the staff with their duties and responsibilities. Provision was made for the cold storage of vaccine in the capital city, as well as in state and district centres. The reserve supplies of vaccines and needles at WHO Headquarters, from which deliveries could be made within 48–72 hours, proved to be very helpful to overcome shortages.

402.   WHO decided that field activities should usually begin in the areas with the greatest population density and the highest smallpox prevalence, and last one to three years. Most countries used mobile vaccination teams, which usually consisted of two to eight persons. In India, for example, 28 mobile teams were established in 1973, consisting of one medical officer, one paramedical workers and a driver. WHO provided fourteen epidemiologists while the government agreed to take care of the rest.

403.   Two basic approaches to mass vaccination were employed. In Africa and South America, the assembly point system, in which many people gathered for vaccination at a designated point, was widely employed. In Asian countries, house-to-house visits were usually made by vaccinators, although the assembly point system was also sometimes used.

404.   On balance, the mass vaccination campaigns were remarkably successful in most countries, and cost most countries not more than what they used to spend on control measures.

2. Surveillance-containment

405.   The importance of surveillance and containment was emphasized by the World Health Assembly in 1968, 1969 and again in 1970 when it requested 'all countries to take appropriate steps to improve further case-reporting and adopt as an objective the immediate investigation and containment of all reported cases and outbreaks of smallpox from 1970 onwards'.[1] The decision to emphasize surveillance as an important component of the strategy proved to be effective. Reporting systems were developed to detect such smallpox foci as remained and to eliminate them. By isolating the patients and vaccinating their contacts, outbreaks could be rapidly contained. In this way, even in areas were the vaccination coverage was poor, the transmission could be stopped quickly.

   1. Resolution WHA23.46, OR 184, p. 24.

406.   It soon appeared that mass vaccination campaigns were less important than the discovery and containment of outbreaks. By 1967, half or more of the population of most countries had been vaccinated, and it was found that the interruption of smallpox transmission was less closely related to an increase in vaccinial immunity than to better reporting and containment measures. From 1969 onwards, smallpox eradication staff at WHO Headquarters recommended that surveillance-containment measures should be given priority over mass vaccination and, from 1972 on, even proposed to direct all resources on surveillance-containment activities.

407.   Special surveillance teams were trained, following the WHO Handbook recommendations. They visited each health unit in an area to ensure that reports on the number of cases seen were submitted each week. Thereafter, the teams worked with local health authorities to contain the outbreaks. Enquiries in schools and marketplaces were very helpful, and children in particular proved to be a very good source of information.

3. Collection of Data

408.   The first step in the implementation of the programme consisted in defining which countries had endemic smallpox. The first evaluation of the situation was made in a report by the Director-General to the 41st Session of the Executive Board, which met in January 1968.[1] The 31 countries finally classified as endemic were in four epidemiological zones sufficiently separate to make it unlikely that one could be reinfected by another after having been freed by smallpox.[2] Consequently, WHO decided to give priority to eradication programmes in the smaller epidemiological zones – Brazil and Indonesia – believing that a success there would encourage the other countries and more resources would become available to tackle the larger and more difficult regions.

   1. WHO Doc. EB41/12.
   2. The four areas were: 1) Brazil; 2) Indonesia; 3) Africa south of the Sahara; 4) a group of Asian countries extending from Afghanistan to East Pakistan (now Bangladesh).

4. Information and Education

409.   On the one hand, an informed and educated population is more likely to seek vaccination and to continue to participate in all phases of the campaign. On the other hand, in countries where there was no qualified national health education staff, it was important to give assistance in the collection of information, in the assessment of resources and their means of utilization, in the assessment of likely obstacles and the ways to overcome them.

410.   To reach the first objective, a complete publicity machinery was put in place. Radio broadcasts, street banners, personal letters and placards were used regularly to motivate people to get themselves immunized and to report cases which would come to their knowledge.

411.   As to the information to be given to local authorities and health staff to motivate them and enable them to plan efficiently their work, meetings were organized by WHO not only at national level with local representatives of medical bodies, other government agencies, volunteer groups and influential personalities, but also at regional level, between senior staff from different national programmes. Each country representative was asked to present papers illustrating specific findings, the outcome of particular strategies and interesting new approaches. Several specific changes in national programmes occurred after these meetings.

412.   WHO directly provided much information to the countries. Not only basic strategies and principles for the implementation of the eradication programme were issued in 1967 in the WHO Handbook, but reports giving epidemiological information and documenting progress in the countries were published every two to three weeks and widely distributed to senior eradication staff throughout the world. In addition to providing information to the health staff, the reports also served to inform public officials and the press, with sometimes unexpected results.

413.   Finally, WHO was seeking publicity through the mass media to make what was happening in the eradication programme well known to potential donors. In 1974, a series of article published in the *New York Times* documented the importance of the programme that was being carried out. The consequent international publicity brought an increased support from senior government officials and substantial additional voluntary contributions.

5. International Support

414.   The vast majority of endemic countries did not have the necessary resources to carry out their national programmes and were therefore dependent on international support. In the Director-General's original plan, as presented to the World Health Assembly in 1966,[1] four sources of support were foreseen: 1) the WHO regular budget; 2) contribution to the WHO Voluntary Fund for Health

Promotion, Special Account for Smallpox Eradication; 3) bilateral contributions; and 4) contributions from other international agencies.

1. OR 151, pp. 106–121.

415.   It was expected that two-thirds of the total costs of the smallpox eradication programme would be met by international agencies other than WHO, bilateral support and voluntary contributions to the Special Account for Smallpox Eradication. In fact, from 1967 to 1973, the WHO regular budget covered nearly half of the costs of the programme, the other half being mainly covered by bilateral support. The voluntary contributions to the Special Fund raised significantly only from 1974, and two-thirds of the costs of the eradication programme were eventually covered by bilateral aid, contributions to the fund and international agencies other than WHO.

416.   The supply of vaccine was also essential to success. Vaccine was obtained entirely from voluntary contributions or local production. From 1967 to 1979, 27 countries contributed 407 millions doses of vaccine to the Voluntary Fund, more than 60 per cent of this coming from the former USSR.

6. Research

417.   At the beginning of the Intensified Smallpox Eradication Programme, the majority of scientists believed research in the field of smallpox was not necessary anymore. The vaccine existed and the feasibility of eradication had been demonstrated. However, research proved to be seriously needed, also to reassure the international community on more than one occasion.

418.   The main area where research was needed was to seek firm evidence that there was no animal or other natural reservoir of the virus. In March 1969, a first series of biennial meetings of an informal group of researchers was convened by WHO in Moscow to plan and implement a collaborative research programme to discover whether any reservoir of variola virus existed. A new concern emerged in 1973 about a possible natural reservoir of smallpox, when what was termed 'whitepox' viruses, which was indistinguishable from smallpox, was isolated. The WHO informal research group, meeting for the third time, considered this issue and could dismiss this concern only several years later.

419.   WHO's research role also included testing better vaccination instruments and practices. In 1968, field studies conducted by WHO showed that a newly developed bifurcated needle could be used to administer vaccines by a new technique: the multiple puncture vaccination. The bifurcated needle soon became the standard method for vaccination. Likewise, another important task carried out by WHO was the systematic control of samples of each of the vaccines donated for the programme.

C. The Global Certification of Smallpox Eradication

420. Brazil's last case was detected in 1971 and Indonesia's in 1972. By the summer of 1973, smallpox had been eradicated throughout Africa, except in Ethiopia and in five Asian countries where activity was still noted. An intensive effort was made in these densely populated areas, and the last case of smallpox occurred in Asia two years later. At the end of 1975, only Ethiopia remained endemic. One year later, when the last case occurred in Ethiopia, smallpox was introduced into Somalia. A national emergency was declared and special assistance was provided by WHO. The last case occurred in Somalia on 26 October 1977. Nevertheless, surveillance teams and search workers continued their work for two years, in order to be sure that no other cases occured.

421. To confirm that transmission had been interrupted, WHO convened a series of International Commissions for the Certification of the Eradication of Smallpox. These were independent of WHO and composed of experts in public health, epidemiology or virology, each with some experience in smallpox control. Twenty-one commissions examined the situation in 61 countries, beginning in South America in 1973 and ending with Somalia in 1979. During the visits, the members discussed all evidence with the health authorities, made visits in the field, concentrating on difficult areas, and then met again to discuss the information and produce their report.

422. In October 1977, when eradication appeared to be achieved, the Director-General convened a consultation of world-known epidemiologists and virologists, for the certification of world wide smallpox eradication. The consultation recommended the setting up of an 'International Commission for the Global Certification of Smallpox Eradication'. The Global Commission met in December 1978 and December 1979 and, after considering the situation relating to smallpox in every inhabited area of the world, certified that 'smallpox has been eradicated in every country in the world'. The report, which also outlined a strategy against future risks of reappearance of the disease for the post-eradication era, was submitted to the Thirty-third World Health Assembly which declared on 8 May 1980 that 'smallpox eradication has been achieved'.[1]

1. Resolution WHA33.3, WHA33/1980/REC/1, p. 1.

423. Thereafter, WHO continued to work on the implementation of the nineteen recommendations of the Global Commission. A six-members committee was established by the Director-General to review the progress made in the implementation of the post-smallpox-eradication programme. The Global Commissions recommended, *inter alia*, the discontinuation of smallpox vaccination and special measures for the use of national stocks of variola virus. In 1981, by Resolution WHA34.13, smallpox was no longer included among the diseases subject to the International Health Regulations.

424. The convening of an expert commission to certify eradication on the basis of available evidence and field visits has become a device utilized by WHO as part of the eradication strategy for other diseases, such as dracunculiasis and poliomyelitis.

425. The eradication of smallpox has saved the world from immeasurable suffering and deaths. In monetary terms, the savings throughout the world were estimated to be USD1,000 million per year, while the total cost of the global eradication programme was just over USD300 million. The history of the global effort to eradicate this disease has been fully described in the publication 'Smallpox and its eradication' published by WHO in 1988.[1] The eradication of smallpox remains undeniably an historical feat in the history of humankind. Tribute must be paid to the determination of WHO and its Member States for achieving the first and so far only instance of complete eradication of a disease from the face of the earth.

1. F. Fenner, D.A. Henderson, I. Arita, Z. Jezek, I.D. Ladnyi, *Smallpox and its eradication* (Geneva, WHO, 1988).

D. The Destruction of the Stocks of Variola Virus

426. At its 33rd Session, the World Health Assembly also endorsed[1] the Global Commission's recommendation that remaining stocks of variola virus should be held at only a limited number of sites. The stocks of variola virus were progressively transferred to two WHO Collaborating Centres, respectively in the USA and in the Russian Federation.[2] These are the only known locations of live virus in the world.

1. Resolution WHA33.4, WHA33/1980/REC/1, p. 2.
2. WHO collaborating centre on smallpox and other poxvirus infections designated at the Centers for Disease Control and Prevention, Atlanta, Georgia, USA, and the Russian State Centre for Research on Virology and Biotechnology, Koltsovo, Novosibirsk Region, Russian Federation.

427. Since then, it has been difficult to reach consensus on the destruction of the remaining stocks of variola virus. In 1996, the 49th World Health Assembly[1] decided that destruction should take place on 30 June 1999, after a decision of the Health Assembly. In 1999, the Assembly reconsidered the issue and decided to 'authorize temporary retention up to, but not later than, 2002 and subject to annual review by the Health Assembly of the existing stocks of variola virus at the current locations'.[2] Retention of the variola virus stocks would permit research for public health purposes, including the development of antiviral agents and an improved and safer vaccine. The resolution also called for the appointment of a new group of experts who would establish what research, if any, would have to be carried out in order to reach global consensus on the timing for the destruction of existing stocks.

1. Resolution WHA49.10, WHA49/1996/REC/1, p. 9.
2. Resolution WHA52.10, WHA33/1999/REC/1, p. 10.

428. In the meantime, a new fear of bioterrorism appeared, following the events of 11 September 2001 and the anthrax attacks in the USA. New concern has grown on the possible use of smallpox as a biological weapon. The Advisory Committee for Variola Virus Research, which met in December 2001, recommended that further goal-oriented research, extending beyond the expected deadline, could be justified so that the world population could be adequately prepared for the unlikely, but potentially catastrophic, event of a re-emergence of smallpox.

429. The 55th World Health Assembly endorsed the recommendations of the Advisory Committee and decided to 'authorize the further, temporary, retention of the existing stocks of variola virus at the current locations, for the purpose of enabling further international research', and that 'a proposed new date for the destruction should be set when the research accomplishments and outcomes allow consensus to be reached on the timing of the destruction of the variola virus stocks'.[1]

1. Resolution WHA55.15, unpublished, but available on-line at <http://www.who.int/gb>.

III. Tuberculosis

430. Two billion people worldwide are carriers of the tuberculosis bacillus, the germ that can lead to active tuberculosis (TB). Every year, about 8.8 million people develop active TB and 1.7 million die of the disease; 99 per cent of all TB sufferers live in developing countries.[1] Most of these are poor people aged between fifteen and 54 years, the most economically productive years of their lives. However, since 1944, when the first antituberculosis medicine was discovered, TB can be cured and almost all TB deaths are preventable. Therefore, the most important obstacles WHO and its partners have to face today in their fight to control TB are not technical, but mainly financial and political.

1. *Scaling up the response to infectious diseases. A way out of poverty*, (Geneva, WHO, 2002), WHO/CDS/2002.7, p. 13.

A. WHO and TB Control

431. In the 1970s in Tanzania, Dr. Karel Styblo of the International Union Against Tuberculosis and Lung Disease (IUATLD) was the first to develop a model of TB control based on a managerial approach. He proposed to use an existing basic management unit (usually the district) which has the staff and material resources necessary to diagnose, initiate treatment, record and report patient treatment progress in a population area of 100,000 to 150,000 people.[1] In the following years, cure rates in pilot projects in Tanzania increased from 43 per cent to nearly 80 per cent.

1. D. Maher, M. Mikulencak, *What is DOTS? A Guide to Understanding the WHO-recommended TB Control Strategy Known as DOTS*, (Geneva, WHO, 1999), WHO/CDS/CPC/TB/99.270, p. 13.

432. Following the resurgence of TB in the late 1980s, the World Health Assembly adopted in 1991 new targets for global TB control, which were to cure 85 per cent of the detected new smear-positive TB cases and to detect 70 per cent of existing cases by the year 2000.[1] The WHO TB programme reassessed the TB control strategy and developed a new framework for TB control, based on Dr. Styblo's method. This strategy was thereafter called DOTS (Directly Observed Treatment, Short-course). In 1993, shortly after WHO declared TB a public health emergency, the World Health Assembly welcomed this 'newly developed cost-effective tuber-culosis programme management strategy', and urged Member States to apply it.[2]

1. Resolution WHA44.8, WHA44/1991/REC/1, p. 6.
2. Resolution WHA46.36, WHA46/1993/REC/1, p. 39.

433. Since the introduction of the DOTS strategy, considerable progress has been made in global tuberculosis control. By 2000, 148 countries had adopted the WHO DOTS strategy for TB control and 27 per cent of the global TB cases were treated under DOTS.[1] Some countries have obtained very successful results. In 1993, the government of Bangladesh adopted WHO's DOTS strategy. A revised National TB Programme was set up, and by 1995 as many as 80 per cent of TB patients receiving treatment were being cured in the parts of the country using DOTS strategy. Over 75 per cent of the country is now using the DOTS strategy. In 1997, WHO described Bangladesh's TB control programme as a model for the entire world.[2]

1. *An expanded DOTS Framework for effective Tuberculosis Control*, (Geneva, WHO, 2002), WHO/CDS/TB/2002.297, p. 3.
2. *TB Advocacy: a practical guide*, (Geneva, WHO, 1999), WHO/TB/98.239.

434. The implementation of a ten years project in China also demonstrated that it is feasible to rapidly expand DOTS on a large scale.[1] In about half of the countries where DOTS has been used, it had an astonishing success. TB drugs were provided to patients free of charge and cure rates as high as 90 per cent were among the best in the world. Nevertheless, in the other half, two factors mainly impede cure: patients are not supervised to ensure that they finish their treatment and are too poor to afford the treatment.[2]

1. X. Chen, F. Zhao, H. Duanmu, L. Wan, X. Du, D.P. Chin, 'The DOTS strategy in China: results and lessons after 10 years', in 80 *Bulletin of the World Health Organization*, no. 6, 2002, p. 430.
2. *TB Advocacy: a practical guide, supra.*

435. However, in the overall, progress has been slow and many developing countries have not been able to achieve the global targets set by the World Health Assembly for the year 2000. In March 2000, Ministers of Health, Finance and Development from twenty high-burden countries gathered in Amsterdam for the Ministerial Conference on Tuberculosis and Sustainable Development. They adopted the *Amsterdam Declaration to Stop TB*,[1] which calls for increased political commit-ment and financial resources to reach the targets set by WHO for global TB control by 2005, instead of 2000. In May 2000, the World Health Assembly reiterated this appeal, by encouraging Member States to endorse the Amsterdam Declaration.[2]

1. Available on-line at <http://www.stoptb.org/conference/Decla.access.html> (visited on 26 September 2002).
2. *Ibid.*

436.   To reach the newly set deadline, national tuberculosis programme managers of the 22 high-burden countries, technical partners, financial partners, and the global TB network of WHO met in Cairo in November 2000 and agreed to develop a Global DOTS Expansion Plan (GDEP). The two pillars of the GDEP are the development of national DOTS expansion plans and partnership-building to control tuberculosis.

B. WHO's DOTS Strategy to Control TB

437.   The WHO-recommended treatment strategy for the detection and cure of TB is DOTS (Directly Observed Treatment, Short-course). It combines five key components:

(1) Government commitment to sustained TB control activities.
(2) Case detection by sputum smear microscopy among symptomatic patients self-reporting to health services.
(3) Standardized treatment regimen of six to eight months for at least all confirmed sputum smear positive cases, with directly observed treatment (DOT) for at least the initial two months.
(4) A regular, uninterrupted supply of all essential anti-TB drugs.
(5) A standardized recording and reporting system that allows assessment of treatment results for each patient and of the TB control programme overall.

438.   Political commitment is essential for the success of the programme. Governments must formulate a national policy, with WHO's technical assistance provided in particular through its Regional Offices, and make every effort to obtain the financial and human resources indispensable to implement the medical part of the project. A relatively functioning health sector is also necessary to detect the disease and to implement the DOTS, where patients must take the medicines in the presence of the medical staff. If the treatment is not correctly followed, it causes a resistant form of TB, which is much more difficult and expensive to cure.

439.   An accurate recording and reporting system is needed to evaluate the overall programme performance, as well as the single patient's progress. It also helps in providing the necessary information to plan and maintain adequate drug stocks. WHO is active in facilitating the supply of essential anti-TB drugs, in particular through the '*Global Drug Facility*' (GDF) project, managed by the Stop TB Partnership Secretariat.

440.   During the last decade DOTS has been widely accepted, and has proved to be effective. However, the progress has been slower than hoped. In particular, new challenges have impeded in the last years a better control of TB, such as the increasing impact of HIV on the incidence of TB and the occurrence of multidrug-resistant cases of TB. To face these new challenges, and on the heels of the Amsterdam commitment, WHO has worked out an elaborated strategy, published in the document '*An expanded DOTS Framework for effective Tuberculosis Control*'.[1]

1. *Ibid.*

441. The expanded framework reinforces the five essential elements of the DOTS strategy, and acknowledges the access to TB care as a human right. This expanded framework should assist countries in implementing their national DOTS expansion plans for the medium-term, which they agreed to adopt in the Cairo meeting in 2000. It provides guidelines for the mobilization of the human and financial resources necessary to expand TB control as part of the national health system. In particular, it recommends a series of key operations that need to be established and sustained until TB is no longer a public health threat, including the establishment of a National Tuberculosis Programme (NTP) with a central unit, the preparation of a programme development plan and a programme manual, the planning and initiation of training programmes, the establishment of a recording and reporting system.

442. In many countries, suspected TB cases are first approached and managed by private practitioners. In India alone, the private sector is believed to manage half of the TB cases. In most countries, however, the private sector is still not aware and/or not familiar with the DOTS implementation and, as a result, case detection rates remain low in many countries. Collaboration with private practitioners is therefore essential to achieve a rapid expansion of DOTS and, thus, to control TB. WHO is currently addressing this issue, through a project called Public-Private Mix DOTS (PPM DOTS).

C. The Global Partnership to Stop TB

443. In May 2000, the World Health Assembly called on Member States, organizations and bodies of the United Nations system, donors, non-governmental organizations and foundations to support and to participate in the global partnership to stop tuberculosis.[1] The response has been exceptional: the partnership now has more than 200 members working together with representatives of the high-burden countries.

1. Resolution WHA53.1, *supra.*

444. The objectives of the partnership are to promote a wider and wiser use of existing strategies to interrupt TB transmission, to adapt existing strategies to address the challenges posed by emerging threats, and to accelerate the elimination of TB by promoting research to develop new and improved diagnostic tests, drugs and vaccines.

445. The STOP TB Partnership's flexible structure comprises a Partners' Forum, a Coordinating Board and a Secretariat. The Forum is the assembly of stakeholders, which meets regularly, at least every two years. It is the main coordinating body of the Global Stop TB Partnership. Its functions are to identify problems and new challenges, to exchange information thereon, to consolidate and increase the partners' commitment and reinforce high-level political commitment to stop TB, to review overall progress and, finally, to make recommendations to the Coordinating Board for concrete action.

446.   The Coordinating Board represents and acts on behalf of the Global Partnership, and its composition reflects both the major groupings and the diversity of the partnership. It formulates priorities for action, in line with health policy and technical advice from WHO and the recommendations of the Partners' Forum. A small secretariat hosted by WHO carries out the day-to-day work, implementing the tasks assigned to it by the Board.

447.   Six working groups provide a focus for coordinated action, each one covering a specific technical area: one concentrates on DOTS expansion, two address the new threats of HIV-related TB and multi-drug-resistant TB, and the other three work for research and development (R&D), respectively in the field of drugs, diagnostics and vaccines. Each working group has an independent governance mechanism.

448.   As a major member of the partnership, WHO coordinates the development of a global strategy and policy for TB control. It is the driving force behind the DOTS Expansion Working Group, which assisted the countries in the drafting of their national DOTS expansion plans.[1] The working group on multi-drug-resistant TB formulates solutions for the spread of this severe type of TB. It has succeeded in reducing the price of second-line TB drugs by up to 94 per cent, through a procurement system run by its Green Light Committee (GLC).[2]

1. J.W. Lee, E. Loevinsohn, J.A. Kumaresan, *Response to a major disease of poverty: the Global Partnership to Stop TB*, in 80 *Bulletin of the World Health Organization*, n. 6, 2002, p. 428.
2. *Ibid.*

449.   The working group on TB and HIV tries to promote joint activities between TB and HIV programmes, and is preparing field guidelines for this purpose. In the field of R&D, an innovative and successful outcome is the Global Alliance on TB Drug Development (GATB), a public-private partnership that aims at accelerating the discovery and production of new TB drugs that are affordable in low income countries. In February 2002, the GATB obtained an exclusive, wordwide licence for a new class of compounds from Chiron Corporation. This is the first ever public-private agreement on TB drugs.[1]

1. *Ibid.*

450.   Another significant initiative of the partnership in which WHO is playing an active role is the Global TB Drug Facility (GDF), a mechanism which aims at expanding access to high-quality TB drugs to facilitate global DOTS expansion. The Global TB Drug Facility provides drugs of high quality free of charge to qualifying countries and NGOs, through a web-based ordering system.[1] By now, 23 countries have qualified for GDF support, and eleven have already received the TB drugs.

1. Access to the system on-line at <http://www.stoptb.org/GDF/default.asp>.

D. Political Commitment and Financial Resources

451.   The Global Stop TB Partnership has set the following targets:

By 2005, 70 per cent of people with infectious TB will be diagnosed, and 85 per cent cured;

By 2010, the global burden of TB disease will be reduced by 50 per cent (compared with 2000 levels);

By 2050, the global incidence of TB disease will be less than one per million population.

452.   For WHO and its partners, the global control of TB is not only a public health necessity, but an imperative for development, human rights, and poverty alleviation. As clearly stated in the report presented by the Commission on Macroeconomics and Health to WHO in December 2001,[1] TB impoverishes dramatically too many countries, together with other diseases such as HIV-AIDS and malaria.

1. *Macroeconomics and Health: Investing in Health for Economic Development, supra,* pp. 22–29.

453.   The Stop TB Partners have demonstrated that a global strategy for TB control exists and has excellent results, if implemented properly. But more financial resources are needed for such implementation. Examples such as the establishment of the Global Fund to fight AIDS, TB and Malaria are promising, but unfortunately not sufficient. With a stronger political commitment and sufficient financial resources, WHO and its partners know that they have the necessary knowledge and field expertise to reach their targets and pave the way to the elimination of tuberculosis as a public health problem.

§4. ACCESS TO MEDICINES

454.   Modern medicine depends heavily on the use of drugs and vaccines to treat or prevent illness. Effective drug treatment exists for most of the leading infectious diseases, including acute respiratory infections, HIV/AIDS, malaria, diarrhoeal diseases, tuberculosis and measles. Life-saving drugs have also been developed for the leading non-communicable diseases, including ischaemic heart disease and cerebrovascular diseases.

455.   WHO's activities concerning pharmaceuticals have been varied throughout its history, with an emphasis on elaborating international standards as well as on advising Member States about the rational and effective use of medicines. In this connection, the establishment and updating of the Model List of Essential Drugs and, indeed, the promotion of the very concept of essential drugs have been reviewed earlier in this Part. Part IV also provided a review of the approaches supported by WHO to allow for the development of medicines and vaccines for the diseases of the poor.

456.   Much has been achieved in pharmaceuticals in the 50 years since WHO began establishing international pharmaceutical standards and guidelines, and since the introduction of the essential drugs and national drugs policy concepts. Nearly

160 countries now have national essential drugs lists, while over 100 countries have national drug policies in place or under development. Similarly, rational drug use concepts and teaching are spreading in all regions. Most importantly of all, though, access to essential drugs grew from 2.1 billion people in 1977 to 3.8 billion people in 1997.[1]

1. *WHO Medicines Strategy: 2000–2003*, WHO Doc. WHO/EDM/2000.1 (Geneva, WHO, 2000).

457.   Yet at the beginning of the 21st century inequities in terms of access to essential drugs, quality and rational use remain widespread in many parts of the world. An estimated one-third of the world population lacks regular access to essential drugs, with this figure rising to over 50 per cent in the poorest parts of Africa and Asia. The reasons often include inadequate financing and poor health care delivery. And even if drugs are available, weak drug regulation may mean that they are substandard or counterfeit. Irrational use – for example, high rates of antibiotic prescription, very short dispensing times and incorrect drug use by patients – is of great public health concern, too. The statistics are particularly alarming for communicable diseases. For the twenty per cent of the global population that lives in poverty, 60 per cent of deaths are due to diseases such as malaria and HIV/AIDS. The disease burden associated with the two diseases is particularly overwhelming. More than 33 million people live with HIV, and 90 per cent of them live in developing countries, without access to the drugs that could prolong their lives and reduce their suffering. Similarly, every year, more than one million people in developing countries die from malaria – simply because they do not have access to effective treatment.

458.   The debate about access to, and affordability of, essential medicines has become increasingly politicized after the entry into force of the WTO agreements, in particular the TRIPS with its increased protection for patents over both products and processes. Such politicization has, to generalize an otherwise complex situation, pitted developed countries and their large pharmaceutical industries against many developing countries as well as an array of NGOs and other civil society actors. WHO does not remain immune from such politicization, as part of the debate taking place in its governing bodies on the design and implementation of what was referred to as WHO's 'revised drug strategy'. The debate has sometimes only focused on the impact of TRIPS on the price and accessibility of medicines. However, the overall issue of access is more elaborate and complex. WHO has therefore tried to adapt its strategies and programmes, and indeed its role as global health advocate, to the complexity of this topic.

459.   WHO's work on access to pharmaceuticals is currently guided primarily by the WHO medicines strategy, which was adopted by the 54th WHA with Resolution WHA 54.11, building on the consensus reached two years earlier with the adoption of Resolution WHA52.19. Within the strategy, four factors are crucial to securing and expanding access to essential drugs: (1) rational selection and use of essential drugs; (2) affordable prices; (3) adequate and sustainable financing; and (4) reliable health and supply systems. The priority areas for 2000–2003 are the major diseases of poverty, such as HIV/AIDS, tuberculosis, malaria and childhood illnesses. WHO, in particular through Director-General Brundtland, has been active and successful in ensuring that access to essential drugs remains high on the global health and development agendas. The Assembly has also tackled the specific and particularly dramatic issue of access to antiretrovirals for persons suffering from HIV/AIDS.[1] Most of these medicines have been developed and commercialized by research-based pharmaceutical companies, are patented products and their manufacturers have traditionally been very careful in maintaining the pricing powers afforded by such patents.

1. *See for example* resolutions WHA55.12, WHA54.10 and WHA53.14.

I. Rational Selection and Use

460. The aforementioned Model List of Essential Drugs is the principal instrument through which WHO influences rational selection and use of medicines by national health systems. Besides this tool, which has been reviewed *supra*, WHO carries out other activities in this regard. In particular, it has elaborated and continues to update clinical guidelines for prevention, diagnosis and treatment of specific diseases. In 2000–2001, guidelines for malaria, sexually transmitted infections, tuberculosis and antiretroviral treatment for HIV/AIDS were issued. These guidelines will eventually constitute the basis of the WHO Model List.

461. Creation of an integrated WHO essential medicines on-line library was under way as of September 2002. This collection will electronically link various sources of information such as the WHO Model Formulary, clinical guidelines, international price indicator guides, the INN database and other information.

462. International, regional and national courses have been held since 2000, for example on promoting rational drug use, on drug and therapeutics committees, on pharmacoeconomics and drug selection, and on promoting rational drug use in the community.

463. Misuse of antimicrobials and unsafe injections contribute significantly to irrational drug use. In 2001 WHO issued its global strategy for the containment of antimicrobial resistance.[1] The document summarized the evidence on interventions to promote rational use of antimicrobials and the roles of international organizations, national governments, the public, industry and other important stakeholders. WHO also hosts a secretariat for the Safe Injection Global Network, which *inter alia* addresses problems caused by unsafe and excessive use of therapeutic injections.

1. WHO Doc. WHO/CDS/CSR/DRS/2001.2.

II. Prices and Impact of International Trade Agreements

464. WHO has been working with external partners to maintain three international price information services: the *International drug price indicator guide* covering over 300 essential drugs;[1] *Sources and prices of selected drugs and diagnostics for people living with HIV/AIDS;*[2] and *Pharmaceutical starting materials/ essential drugs report.*[3] Moreover, in response to requests from Member States, regional price information services continue to be supported, in particular in the African, American and European regions.

1. Published annually by Management Sciences for Health, Arlington, Virginia.
2. Published twice a year by UNICEF, UNAIDS, WHO and Médecins sans frontières.
3. Published irregularly by the International Trade Centre, Geneva.

465. A manual for collecting data on drug prices and price composition in low and middle-income countries, developed jointly by WHO and the NGO Health Action International, was under preparation as of September 2002. It will support national policy-making by offering a global standard for producing more and better quality information on drug price variations and trends.

466. WHO actively promotes the concept of differential pricing to increase access to essential drugs, especially those under patent. Where patent protection confers pricing power for drugs of vital public health importance, differential pricing is one way of ensuring that prices in poor countries are as low as possible while higher prices in rich countries continue to provide incentives for R&D. A groundbreaking WHO/WTO workshop on differential pricing and financing of essential drugs, held in April 2001, was much cited in subsequent debates and publications, including the report of the Commission on Macroeconomics and Health. The meeting identified several options for implementing differential pricing, including: bilateral negotiations of price discounts between companies and importing governments; bulk purchasing, sound supply management; and voluntary or compulsory licensing arrangements. An example of a differential pricing strategy is also the voluntary price cuts by several pharmaceutical companies announced in the last few years, in which the price of certain antiretrovirals was reduced by 90 per cent or more. However, even at such reduced prices, the cost may still be prohibitive for the least developed countries.

467. The Health Assembly has laid particular emphasis on the impact of the uniform and strengthened protection offered by the TRIPS Agreement on the availability and affordability of essential drugs for diseases imposing a heavy burden on poor countries. Resolution WHA52.19, in particular, urges Member States 'to explore and review their options under relevant international agreements, including trade agreements, to safeguard access to essential drugs' and requests the Director-General 'to cooperate with Member States, at their request, and with international organizations in monitoring and analyzing the pharmaceutical and public health implications of relevant international agreements, including trade agreements, so that Member States can effectively assess and subsequently develop pharmaceutical and health policies and regulatory measures that address their concerns and priorities, and are able to maximize the positive and mitigate the negative impact of those agreements'. In Resolution WHA54.11, moreover, the Assembly noted 'that the impact of international trade agreements on access to, or local manufacturing of, essential drugs and on the development of new drugs needs to be further evaluated'.

468. It is not possible, within the confines of this contribution, to make even a cursory analysis of the provisions of TRIPS and their possible or perceived impact on the availability of essential medicines. The main lines of WHO's involvement in the debate on the impact of TRIPS have been the establishment of cooperation with other international agencies, in particular WTO, to arrive at sound and consensual positions on matters of overlapping competence; support to countries; and participation in major policy-making conferences to advocate for the pre-eminence of a public health perspective.[1]

1. For a thorough and action-oriented study of the implications of the WTO agreements on public health, *See WTO agreements and public health – A joint study by the WHO and the WTO Secretariat* (Geneva, WHO/WTO, 2002).

469. The perspective of WHO on this complex matter is based on a few main principles. Firstly, access to drugs has to be seen in the context of the 'right to health' as described *supra* in Part V. Secondly, while patent protection has been an effective incentive for research and development for new drugs, questions remain as to whether the patent system will ensure investment in medicines needed by the poor. Of the 1,223 new chemical entities developed between 1975 and 1996, only eleven were for the treatment of tropical disease. Thirdly, affordability of essential drugs is a public health priority. Among the four aforementioned elements needed to ensure access, the affordability of essential drugs – specifically those still under patent – is most likely to be affected by trade agreements. Patent protection awards exclusive rights to an invention and prevents generic competition. But poorer populations in developing countries should not be expected to pay the same price as do the wealthy for newer essential drugs. TRIPS-compliant mechanisms can be used to lower drug prices. Fourthly, essential drugs are not simply another commodity, thus the safeguards offered by TRIPS are crucial. WHO supports Member States in the use of TRIPS-related safeguards, as appropriate, to enhance affordability and availability of existing medicines, while not discouraging the development of needed new medicines. These safeguards include setting standards for patentability which reflect public health concerns, legislative provisions for compulsory licensing, exceptions to exclusive rights and other measures which promote generic competition, and extension of the transitional period for the introduction of TRIPS-related measures. Parallel importation of a patented drug from countries where it is sold more cheaply can also be authorized by governments.[1]

1. The use of the flexibility and safeguards provided for in TRIPS are analyzed in *ibid.*, pp. 97–103.

470. Based on these perspectives, WHO provides independent data and technical assistance to countries in order to develop informed approaches to dealing with the health implications of trade issues. WHO has provided up-to-date policy and technical support to 50 Member States through regional briefings and direct country support. Between May 2000 and January 2002, six regional briefings on TRIPS were held in China, Costa Rica, Indonesia, Poland, South Africa and Zimbabwe. These meetings brought together, often for the first time, representatives of health ministries, trade ministries, patent offices, NGOs, WTO and WIPO. A network of legal experts with specialized knowledge and understanding of public health and pharmaceutical impact of international trade agreements is being built as a resource for developing countries.

471. In June 2000 WHO was granted observer status at the WTO Council for Trade-Related Aspects of Intellectual Property Rights and is thus able to monitor all relevant issues under discussion in that Council that may have implications for the health sector. WHO was represented at the WTO Ministerial Conference, in Doha in November 2001, which produced a number of very important decisions and statements concerning the overall design and implementation of the WTO regime. In her statement on the 'Declaration on Intellectual Property Rights and Public Health' adopted by the conference, the Director-General welcomed the conclusion that the TRIPS agreement 'can and should be interpreted and implemented in a manner supportive of WTO members' right to protect public health and, in particular, promote access to medicines for all' (the declaration is reproduced in Annex 5). As instructed by the Doha Declaration, the WTO TRIPS Council is to find an expeditious solution to the problem of WTO Members with insufficient or no manufacturing capacity in the pharmaceutical sector which could face difficulties in making effective use of compulsory licensing under the TRIPS agreement. The Council must report to the WTO General Council before the end of 2002.

472. The network for monitoring the impact of globalization and TRIPS on access to essential drugs (consisting of WHO collaborating centres in Brazil, Spain, Thailand and the United Kingdom of Great Britain and Northern Ireland) formulated draft model indicators for use in studies measuring the impact of globalization and the TRIPS agreement on access to essential drugs. These indicators cover changes in pricing, generic competition, investment in research and development, and technology transfer. Case studies on trends in drug patenting have also been undertaken by the University of Buenos Aires with the support of WHO.

III. Financing

473. Published studies and national health accounts confirm that pharmaceutical expenditure in developing countries constitutes 25 to 65 per cent of total public and private health expenditure, and 60 to 90 per cent of out-of-pocket household spending on health. Because of the magnitude of drug expenditure and the unique aspects of managing this critical health resource, WHO devotes considerable attention to drug financing, treating it as an integral component of overall health care financing. WHO's efforts have included assessment of public financing for drug benefits within social health insurance schemes, a review of experience with user fees for drugs, and greater input into the planning of development bank loans for pharmaceutical projects.

474. One particularly promising trend supported by WHO is the growth in health insurance coverage and expanded drug benefits in countries as diverse as Argentina, Egypt, Georgia, South Africa and Vietnam. Some insurance programmes have special arrangements for rural and low-income populations. WHO has been working with such programmes to apply the essential drugs concept and to address the particularities of drug management within health insurance.

475. Indeed, concerns about drug costs remind us that although sustainable financing is critical, drug costs must be affordable for governments and consumers if access is to be maintained. A number of measures have been successfully developed to contain the drug prices paid by governments and the drug costs of health insurance programmes. Many of them can also be used to contain direct consumer expenditure. They include pooled procurement arrangements, generic substitution and improved price information.

476. Generic substitution, in particular, has considerable potential for contributing to increased financial access. In fact, it is a proven cost-effective strategy for containing drug expenditure. The average price of generic drugs can fall by as much as 30 per cent of the innovator drug price when the number of generic versions of the drug on the market increases. WHO is therefore actively encouraging development of drug policies based on the promotion of generic medicines of assured quality. Competition among chemically different but therapeutically similar patented drugs can also reduce the prices of patented products. It has been shown that the price of antiretroviral products fell by 73 per cent in five years once a number of antiretroviral products had become available.

477. Work on drug financing, undertaken in more than 35 countries during the biennium 2000–2001, included contribution to a publication on drug benefits in Latin American social security systems and a regional workshop on drug reimbursement in the European region. Drug donations are provided through WHO for the treatment of onchocerciasis, leprosy, trypanosomiasis and lymphatic filariasis. They are managed according to specific WHO guidelines, mentioned in Part IV.

IV. Reliable Health and Supply Systems

478. Another critical element for securing access to essential drugs is a reliable mix of public and private drug supply. In the last decade, four types of drug supply system, in addition to traditional central medical stores, and with increasing levels of private sector features, have been developed. These systems vary considerably with respect to the role of the government, the role of the private sector, and the incentives, if any, for efficiency. But whatever system is developed, it aims to ensure continued availability of essential drugs with low rates of drug stock-outs, and low total drug costs for a given level of service. Controlling costs by introducing private sector features to public systems such as outsourcing, or by decentralizing storage and distribution, helps achieve these goals.

479. Recent WHO activities to improve drug supply have included publication of guidelines and manuals, and support to international training courses and a distance learning programme (in collaboration with several organizations) to upgrade the drug supply management skills of government officials. With emergency

relief activities increasing during the last decade, WHO has also been active in drug supply programmes – for example in former Yugoslavia, Haiti and Iraq – that seek to ensure that pharmaceutical needs are met. It has also promoted the standardization of emergency health kits.

480.   International, regional or national bulk procurement can dramatically reduce costs and improve monitoring of drug quality. WHO has supported the Stop TB Secretariat to establish the Global TB Drug Facility, which has led to substantial reductions in prices for antitubercular drugs. In the Region of the Americas, a strategic fund for purchasing medicines and insecticides for targeted diseases (HIV/AIDS, leishmaniasis, tuberculosis and malaria) has been established. The fund provides for supplier prequalification, standardized criteria for inspection, harmonized drug specifications, drug quality surveillance, and technical cooperation with countries to strengthen drug selection, distribution and rational use. In the Western Pacific Region, WHO supports collaborative pharmaceutical procurement involving small Pacific island countries through a pharmaceutical bulk purchasing scheme based in Fiji.

481.   A project to increase access to high-quality HIV/AIDS drugs, including antiretroviral agents, will create a unified prequalification programme for all United Nations organizations. The first list of prequalified innovator and generic suppliers was published in March 2002 and is being updated periodically. An analysis of measures needed to correct deficiencies will help both regulatory authorities and manufacturers to improve product quality.

482.   Work on drug quality control has focused on medicines for high-priority diseases. An eight-country field study on the quality of antimalarials and the use of rapid screening techniques for drug quality control was in its final phases as of the summer of 2002. A plan of action is being implemented on the quality, safety and efficacy of the four-drug fixed-dose combination for tuberculosis. Screening tests and monographs for *The international pharmacopoeia* were being prepared as of the same period for antitubercular drugs (including fixed-dose combinations), antimalarial agents and HIV/AIDS drugs.

Chapter 4. Research and Technical Cooperation

483. For the purpose of the present contribution, only general remarks will be made on the other two functions identified above as falling within the remit of WHO. This does not mean, however, that they are of secondary importance. The list of functions in Article 2 of the Constitution makes it clear that a primary focus of the Organization is assistance to Member States in addressing their health needs. And paragraph (n) entrusts WHO with the broad mandate to 'promote and conduct research in the field of health'.

484. Several references have already been made in the previous Parts to both cooperation and research activities. In particular, the modalities of how WHO interacts with its main development partners in coordinating technical cooperation activities both at the global and country levels have been reviewed in Part IV. In the same Part, the strategy followed by WHO to encourage and stimulate research and development of medicines for a number of diseases of the poor was mentioned. In this Part, finally, the role played by collaborating centres and other sources of expertise to carry out research activities in support of WHO's programmes was referred to. All those arguments and references will not be repeated here. Moreover, there is a substantial amount of overlap among the various functions, so that activities which can be labelled as normative may also be translated into a form of direct cooperation with countries.

485. WHO embarked in activities which could be defined as technical cooperation since its inception, in particular with regard to the control or eradication of diseases and the training of national health personnel. The demand for assistance from WHO naturally increased in scope and breadth with the admission to membership of a growing number of developing countries. The implementation of technical cooperation programmes has traditionally been primarily assigned to regional and country offices, with Headquarters playing at most a policy-making or coordination role. The policy of tailoring cooperation activities to the demands and needs of individual countries, in the consideration of the specific health profiles of the various regions, has fostered the entrenchment of a considerable autonomy of regional offices in this respect.

486. WHO's technical cooperation mainly consists of advisory services rather than financial aid or operational activities (e.g. the construction of health facilities or the direct recruitment of health personnel). This, of course, has historically left open the question of whether WHO's advisory services may be effective if national infrastructures or resources are insufficient to implement them.

487.   The principles regulating WHO's technical cooperation were defined by the Health Assembly in a number of resolutions, most importantly in 1975 by Resolutions WHA28.75 and WHA28.76.[1] In the first resolution, the Assembly stated that the main ways in which assistance is given to countries are:

'(a)   assistance in establishing and strengthening national public health systems, which form an integral part of overall social and economic development;
(b)   assistance in training the national public health staff at all levels that is essential for providing the populations with adequate medical and sanitary care;
(c)   assistance in developing effective methods of disease prevention and control which should provide a scientific methodological basis for any programme to be carried out in the countries, this being a guarantee of success in disease control; and
(d)   the drawing up of recommendations for establishing norms and standards, including disease classification, criteria for evaluating the condition of the environment, methods of safeguarding the environment and making it healthier, the International Pharmacopoeia, biological preparations, etc.'

In the latter resolution, the Assembly decided that technical assistance to governments should:

'(1)   consist primarily of the types of assistance and services which have proved to be effective as well as those now being developed by the Organization;
(2)   be as flexible as possible and adapted to the specific needs, conditions and priorities of individual countries and include operational components when necessary;
(3)   be based on the experience gained and the improved understanding of the constraints limiting the development process of the developing countries.'

1. In OR 226, pp. 42–43.

488.   The conceptual and operational revolution of the HFA strategy has considerably modified WHO's approach towards technical cooperation. After the adoption of the strategy by the Assembly in 1981, it became obvious that it was necessary to focus on national health systems in a coordinated fashion, in particular to promote primary health care, community participation and interdisciplinary collaboration.

489.   One of the direct consequences of the adoption of the new strategy and of the changed climate in WHO and among its Member States, was the utilization of the concept 'technical cooperation' which replaced 'technical assistance'. The Assembly, in Resolution WHA34.24 of 1981, welcomed the rejection of the concept of 'technical assistance', 'whereby aid was provided by so-called "donors" to "recipients"', and affirmed that technical cooperation in international health work is:

'joint action of Member States cooperating among themselves and with WHO, as well as with other relevant agencies, to achieve their common goal of the attainment by all people of the highest possible level of health by implementing the policies and strategies they have defined collectively'.[1]

1. WHA34/1981/REC/1, p. 24.

490. Most recently, and in particular since the appointment of Director-General Brundtland, WHO has undertaken a re-examination of its cooperation strategy with and in countries. Strengthening WHO's country work has been a long standing concern of its governing bodies. The issue of country offices, in particular, has been discussed regularly by the Executive Board for a number of years. A Working Group on Partnership with Countries concluded in December 1998 that a number of factors within WHO were inhibiting performance at country level, such as lack of a holistic approach to health and health sector development, the fragmentation and inadequate prioritization of actitivities, and a culture of supply-driven programme delivery.

491. WHO has been working to improve its country cooperation strategy on various fronts. On the one hand, the first global meeting of WHO countries representatives in February 1999 recommended that technical cooperation focus on few priorities and that country representatives be granted additional authority as the coordinators at country level of headquarters and regional office support. On the other hand, a number of new modalities has inspired further changes in planning activities, in particular, the use of UNDAFs for a coordinated UN-system approach and the so-called 'sector-wide approach for health development', which brings together governments and donors in the development of coherent health sector policies and the negotiation of expenditure frameworks. This approach represents a significant change, moving from a situation in which key documents are produced by development agencies, particularly the international financial institutions, to a process resulting in national ownership, with governments taking the lead in formulating policies and consulting civil society.

492. As far as WHO's research activities are concerned, as mentioned earlier in this Part, there was an early decision against the establishment of substantial research facilities by WHO as such. The Organization would rely on expertise and research made available by Member States or other partners, playing a coordinating role on the overall research agenda and a validating role on the results of such research. The main exceptions to this approach are represented by IARC as well as by the two co-sponsored research and training programmes executed by WHO-TDR and HRP.

493. IARC, as it was explained in Part III, is solely devoted to cancer research. The work programme is carried out by a number of research units[1] and focuses on some fundamental areas, which cover the main aspects of cancer research. The broad areas of work are approved by the Governing Council and are selected according to criteria that were set by the Council as early as 1973. The following programmes constitute the bulk of the Agency's activities:[2]

– Cancer occurrence and outcome, which is the foundation of IARC's epidemiological studies and also monitors survival rate of cancer patients around the world;

– Environmental causes of cancer. This has been historically one of the central activities of the Agency, and focuses on the identification of agents and levels of exposure that cause cancer in humans through laboratory investigations, epidemiological studies and scientific meetings;
– Carcinogenesis by organ and mechanisms of carcinogenesis. IARC's laboratory research concentrates on the interaction of carcinogens with DNA, with the aim of elucidating mechanisms of carcinogenesis. This knowledge not only gives insight into the biology of cancer, but also helps to identify stages where it may be possible to intervene in the process to prevent progression to clinical disease;
– Prevention and early detection of cancer. The role of IARC among cancer research institutes is characterized by its focus on cancer prevention, by its emphasis on studies that combine epidemiological and laboratory approaches, and by the special forum and support it provides for international collaborations. Although the implementation of measures to control cancer is not a central part of its mission, the Agency takes part in interventions with the aim of testing their effectiveness in preventing cancers or in the early diagnosis of tumours;
– As a research institute, most of the findings and contributions of the Agency are incorporated into scientific articles, books and databases that IARC disseminates.[3] Moreover, to fulfil the training component of its mandate, IARC organizes a number of training courses and hosts visiting scientists as well as research and postdoctoral fellows.

1. According to information available on IARC's web site (<http://www.iarc.fr/pageroot/units/index.htm>), there are currently sixteen research units.
2. *See* International Agency for Research on Cancer, *Biennial Report 1998–1999* (Lyon, IARC, 2000).
3. The list of publications is too long to be mentioned in the body of this report. More information is available on-line at <http://www.iarc.fr/pageroot/GENERAL/indexgen.html>.

494.   TDR has two main objectives: (1) research and development: to improve existing and develop new approaches for preventing, diagnosing, treating, and controlling neglected infectious diseases which are applicable, acceptable and affordable by developing endemic countries, which can be readily integrated into the health services of these countries, and which focus on the health problems of the poor; and (2) training and strengthening the capacity of developing endemic countries to undertake the research required for developing and implementing these new and improved disease control approaches.[1]

1. More information on TDR's research strategy, with particular regard to the areas where the co-sponsors agreed to focus their efforts, is available on-line at <http://www.who.int/tdr/about/strategy/default.htm>.

495.   Research and training activities are organized into four functional areas, each managed by area coordinators:

– Basic and strategic research;
– Products research and development;
– Intervention development and implementation research;
– Research capability strengthening.

Cutting across these functional areas are diseases components, which are overseen by disease research coordinators.

496.   **Basic and Strategic Research** activities are divided into three areas, each of which is managed through a steering committee: (1) pathogenesis and applied genomics; (2) molecular entomology; and (3) social, economic and behavioural research. Each steering committee determines a workplan with defined targets, time frame and budget. The Basic and Strategic Research Steering Committee is responsible for the overall direction of Basic and Strategic Research. The committee meets annually to finalize recommendations on priorities, funding and future activities.

497.   **Product Research & Development** is managed in two main areas: product discovery and product development. Product discovery concerns the discovery of new compounds through to the submission of candidate molecules for preclinical and clinical development. Product discovery research is managed through two steering committees, on drug discovery research and vaccine development research. Product development concerns the development of candidate molecules through to, and including, regulatory approval and registration.

498.   As of September 2002, the task forces in **Intervention Development and Implementation Research** were terminated. Work will continue under two new steering committees – Proof of Principle, and Implementation Research – which met for the first time in October 2001. Applications and ongoing activities from the previous task forces (Malaria Home Management; Severe Malaria; Research on Drug Resistance and Policies; Filariasis Intervention Research; Intervention Research on Chagas Disease; Intervention Research on African Trypanosomiasis; Chemotherapy of Leprosy) will be incorporated in the new committees as appropriate.

499.   **Research capability strengthening (RCS)** is a cross-cutting programme area of TDR, established to strengthen the capacity of disease-endemic countries to carry out and sustain research. Specifically, RCS aims to promote and fund research training and institution development; and to increase the participation of developing countries in TDR's research and development agenda.

500.   As far as HRP is concerned, the programme has made a significant effort over the years to collaborate with countries to strengthen their capacity for undertaking reproductive health research. This has culminated in the establishment of a large network of developing country institutions active in global, regional and national reproductive health research and offering research training. Research is sustained through the provision of research capacity strengthening grants, support of reproductive health networks and assistance to centres from developing countries collaborating with the programme. Regional Advisory Panels (RAPs), comprising researchers and programme experts drawn from the region, have been established to foster, guide, monitor and evaluate research activities within their respective regions. RAPs meet annually and serve as technical and scientific advisory bodies to ensure relevance and technical excellence. Activities are undertaken in all six WHO Regions grouped together as follows: Africa and the Eastern Mediterranean, Americas, Asia and the Pacific, and Eastern European Region.

501.   The main instrument for strengthening institutional research capacity is the Long-term Institutional Development (LID) Grant. This is a technical support package covering the provision of training, expert advice, equipment, and other necessary resources to support the implementation of a well-defined research programme which responds to country needs. Other grants may be awarded to sustain the research capability established: Capital Grants to replace ageing equipment or to purchase new items required for new research areas; Small Grants to purchase scientific journals or laboratory supplies; and Research Maintenance Grants to help maintain institutional capacity to respond to national research needs or contribute to the global research effort.

502.   The main mechanism for strengthening human resource development is through the award of Research Training Grants. These enable developing country scientists to undertake training in institutions other than their own. Where such training leads to a higher degree, the trainees are encouraged to divide the training period between their home country, the field site, and the host institution. Following such training, research trainees are encouraged to apply for a Re-entry Grant, which enables them to use the newly acquired skills through the design and conduct of a research project. Other mechanisms for improving research skills include support to workshops, courses and other group learning activities, including the participation of investigators in multicentre studies.

503.   Support is also provided to the design and implementation of research proposals or programmatic activities that address reproductive health issues through coordinated multicountry studies or regional initiatives. Often, such initiatives are undertaken in collaboration with WHO Regional or Country Offices, governments, NGOs and other partners, and following their assessment by RAPs.

504.   As part of research capacity strengthening, there is also an increasing emphasis on enhancing the dissemination and utilization of reproductive health research findings as a mechanism for improving the national reproductive health care system. Continuous dialogue is being established between researchers and policy-makers, programme managers, service providers and other relevant stakeholders in the community in order to facilitate the formulation of joint research proposals and subsequent translation of research results into actions.

Part VII. Finance

Chapter 1. Legal Basis

505. Several provisions of the Constitution regulate aspects of the financial management of WHO. Article 18(f) empowers the Assembly to supervise the financial policies of the Organization and to review and approve the budget, while Articles 34 and 55 request the Director-General to prepare and submit to the Board the financial statements and budget estimates. Pursuant to Article 55, the Board has the task of considering the budget estimates and submitting them to the Assembly with its recommendations. Under Article 56, moreover, the Assembly is granted financial authority through the approval of the budget and the apportionment of the expenses among the members in accordance with a scale to be fixed by it. As mentioned in Part IV, the Assembly, or the Board acting on its behalf, may accept gifts and bequests made to the Organization. This is the statutory basis for the acceptance of extra-budgetary resources, both in cash and in kind. The regional committees are not assigned any particular budgetary function by the Constitution. However, they have always been involved in the budget process and their observations on the draft budget has traditionally influenced its finalization.

506. Besides the Constitution, the main instrument for financial management are the Financial Regulations, adopted by the Health Assembly, which contain detailed provisions on the regular budget and related appropriations, on the payment of assessed contributions, on other forms of income for the Organization, the establishment, custody and investment of funds, and the mechanisms for financial control.[1] The regulations establish the authority and responsibility of the Director-General for the financial administration of the Organization and its internal control. In addition, they provide for the appointment by the Assembly of an External Auditor[2] and regulate his/her functions. The Director-General, on the basis of Regulations 1.4 and 16.3, has established Financial Rules in order to ensure effective financial administration, the exercise of economy, and to safeguard the assets of the Organization. The rules, and amendments thereto, require confirmation by the Board for their entry into force.

1. The Financial Regulations have been amended several times. The version in force as of September 2002 is reproduced in *Basic Documents, supra*, pp. 83–94.
2. Who is, as of September 2002, the Auditor-General of South Africa.

Chapter 2. Financial Resources

§1. The Regular Budget

507. Like most international organizations, WHO was supposed to be primarily financed through a regular budget funded from contributions assessed on Member States. Besides the initial arrangement after the entry into force of the Constitution, the first regular budget was approved at a level of USD5,000,000 for the year 1949. The latest budget approved as of the time of writing was USD855,654,000, for the biennium 2002–2003. Regular budgets are calculated in US dollars while contributions should normally be paid in either dollars, Swiss francs or euros.

508. Regular budgets were initially approved by the Assembly for the following year. However, during the 1970s, the governing bodies of WHO as well as of other organizations of the UN system started debating the advantages of converting to a biennial budget cycle. The Director-General, in a report submitted at the request of the Health Assembly, noted that the advantages of a biennial cycle would be the overall reduction in workload and costs for the budget process and the promotion of longer-term planning. The main expected disadvantages would be the uncertainties and difficulty to predict exact future requirements in the light of rapid advances in the medical field, and possibly a slackening of review and control procedures.[1] The Health Assembly in May 1973, by Resolution WHA26.37, amended Articles 34 and 55 of the Constitution to introduce a biennial programme and budget. The amendments entered into force in 1977 and the Assembly, by Resolution WHA30.20 of the same year, decided that biennial budgeting would become effective as of 1980–1981.[2]

1. OR 206, Annex 14, pp. 122–123.
2. For more details, *See* Y. Beigbeder, *supra*, pp. 152–153.

509. The utilization of a biennial budget cycle requires a more articulated and longer-term approach to forecasting and programming. As noted in Part VI, the decentralization of the Organization and the entrenched independence of the regional organizations has always presented a challenge to the internal coherence of the programme budget and, more in general, to the unified nature of WHO as an organization. We have mentioned in Part VI the efforts made by Director-General Brundtland, in the preparation of the programme budget 2002–2003, to strike a balance between decentralization on the one hand, and a strategic approach to programming and budgeting as well as the reaffirmation of the Director-General's authority in the budget process enshrined in the Constitution.

510. A related issue which was the subject of long debates in the governing bodies concerned the criteria for the calculation of allocations to the regions in the regular budgets. Such allocations would then be used for country, inter-country or regional activities. In view of the difficulty and political sensitivities in devising a generally acceptable objective method for such allocations, the proportion of the regions' share of the regular budget had remained largely unchanged since WHO's inception and was empirically based on previous practice. In the light of the general dissatisfaction for such a state of affairs, the Special Group for the review of the Constitution examined three possible models and submitted them to the Board. The group noted that any model should be dynamic and flexible to respond to change in country circumstances, sensitive to a number of health determinants, and applied in a sensitive and gradual way to minimize disruptions in existing programmes.[1] The 51st Health Assembly in May 1998, by Resolution WHA51.31, took an historical decision by recommending that future budgets should be based on a model drawn upon UNDP's Human Development Index and adjusted by incorporating population statistics of countries. The resolution introduced a number of safeguards to smoothen the introduction of a new and untested allocation model and to protect in particular the least developed countries. It also requested the Director-General to monitor the impact of this new process and to report to the governing bodies. As a result of the progressive introduction of the new model, the regular budget allocations for Africa and Europe increased for the biennium 2002–2003 compared to 2000–2001, while those for the other four regions decreased. The decrease may, however, be counterbalanced by extrabudgetary resources.

1. WHO Doc. EB101/7, pp. 9–10.

511. WHO, like the United Nations and other agencies of the system, suffered a major financial crisis in the mid 1980s, precipitated by the sudden fall of the US dollar's exchange rate, by recurring delays in payments of assessed contributions, but especially by the threatened unilateral reduction of the USA's contribution, mandated by the US Congress to attain a number of financial reforms. This led to an agreement to adopt the programme budget by consensus, still complied with, which gave the major contributors a leverage they would not otherwise have from a purely numerical point of view.[1] The concerns and the renewed fiscal stringency of the major contributors, as well as the growing proportion of the budget devoted to administrative expenses and the lack of clarity of budgetary documents, led the Assembly in May 1993 to request the Director to introduce 'a clearer, simpler, more "user-friendly" proposed programme budget' and to develop 'an improved budget and accounting process'.[2] In response, the Board established in 1994 an Administrative, Budget and Finance Committee to assist the Board in budgetary matters. The concerns expressed by the governing bodies have led to efforts by the Secretariat to improve, clarify and streamline the budgeting process, in particular in the case of the 2002–2003 programme budget. An important feature of the latter exercise, moreover, has been the introduction for the first time of results-based budgeting, by which the Secretariat is held accountable for the achievement of specific results. Unlike traditional or resource-based budgeting, results-based budgeting starts by defining expected results and only after that it defines the financial and staff resources required to attain them.

1. *See* Y. Beigbeder, *supra*, p. 154.
2. Resolution WHA46.35, in WHA46/1993/REC/1, p. 37.

512. The fiscal stringency, and probably dissatisfaction by some major contributors with the implementation of parts of WHO's programme throughout the 1980s and 1990s, have led first to the approval of several zero real growth budgets and then, since the 1998–1999 biennium, to a series of zero nominal growth budgets. This has inevitably eroded the financial basis of the Organization and the centrality of the regular budget as the main programming instrument, and has driven the Secretariat to pursue with more vigour extra-budgetary resources in order to cope with increasing demands from the governing bodies and the Member States.

§2. Extrabudgetary Resources

513. Over the years, WHO's funding has changed progressively and deeply. Initially, the regular budget was the principal basis for the Organization's resources, while voluntary contributions added modest amounts. In 1971, for example, the regular budget was USD75 million while voluntary contributions amounted to USD25 million, mostly contributed by UNDP and UNFPA. However, and especially due to the freezing of real or even nominal increases in the regular budgets from the 1980s to the present time, the situation reversed itself. Extrabudgetary resources exceeded regular budget resources for the first time in the 1988–1989 biennium: about USD1 billion versus USD822 million. This reversal has remained constant and has actually increased. A comparison of the two financial sources for the biennium 2000–2001 is particularly striking: the amount appropriated for the effective working budget is USD842,654,000, while during the same biennium WHO has received extrabudgetary resources in excess of USD1.2 billion for WHO-assisted activities. The functional areas that received the highest amounts were communicable diseases (over USD116 million) and health technology and pharmaceuticals (over USD351 million). On a geographical basis, projects and programmes to be implemented in the African region received the highest level of contributions (about USD418 million from all sources).

514. The 2000–2001 Financial Report also shows graphically the broad spread of donors contributing resources for WHO-assisted activities: not only the governments of Member States, a variety of public agencies and local authorities, but a large number of associations and NGOs have contributed. To give just one example, Rotary International has been a consistent and generous donor for many years, and contributed more than USD61 million in 2000–2001. Most importantly in financial terms, several large charitable foundations (e.g. the Gates Foundation, the Fondation Merieux) and private companies, both in and outside the pharmaceutical sector, have chosen to support and cooperate with WHO. It is indicative, moreover, that the extrabudgetary resources contributed by several Member States by now exceed the level of their assessed contributions. The most remarkable examples in this connection are those of the Netherlands, which contributed over USD169 million (including in-kind contributions) in 2000–2001 against an assessed contribution of about USD13 million, and of the United Kingdom, which donated in the same period USD190 million as compared to an assessed contribution of USD41 million.[1]

1. WHO Doc. A55/25 and Add.1.

515. The Health Assembly, at its Thirteenth Session in 1960, consolidated the previously existing special funds for specific activities into a single fund, which was named the Voluntary Fund for Health Promotion (VFHP).[1] The VFHP contains a number of sub-accounts designating the functional areas for which the resources are destined, and remains to date the main fund to account for extrabudgetary resources. In addition, WHO holds and manages a number of trust funds for co-sponsored programmes, from those on onchocercisasis to those financing TDR and HRP.[2]

1. Resolution WHA13.24, in OR 102, p. 7.
2. A description of the structure of the VFHP and a list of trust funds, together with relevant finan-cial information, is contained in the Financial Report for 2000–2001, *supra.*

516. The success of WHO in raising increasing extrabudgetary resources is an important and objective indicator of its credibility in the eyes of donors as a tech-nical agency and of its ability to effectively and economically perform certain tasks. This indicator is all the more relevant if one considers the 60 per cent increase in voluntary contributions received by WHO in 2000–2001 as compared with the previous biennium. With a decreasing level of regular budget resources in real terms, the pursuit of alternative resources is seen by the Secretariat as a necessary course of action not to scale back on programmes and areas of work which remain of the highest importance for international public health. It has also been stated that the requests by donors for transparency, efficiency and accountability have accel-erated the modernization and and rationalization of management methods in certain programmes, to the benefit also of the other programmes.[1] Finally, most programmes financed by extrabudgetary funds enjoy a degree of financial and administrative autonomy which enables them to respond more quickly to change.

1. Y. Beigbeder, *supra*, p. 166.

517. On the other hand, voluntary contributions are by nature unpredictable and changing, which may hamper mid- and long-term planning. They are also costlier and more cumbersome to administer than regular budget resourcs, in view of the accounting and reporting requirements demanded by donors. More signifi-cantly, the growing importance and amount of extrabudgetary resources has led in a way to the creation of two separate budgets. The regular budget is financed collectively to carry out functions decided upon collectively, and it is subject to monitoring and oversight by the governing bodies; the voluntary one is composed of a mosaic of resources contributed by a broad and diverse constellation of donors. The destination of those resources is sometimes unspecified, i.e. they are not earmarked for specific activities, but more often they are contributed for specified programmes or projects, or for specific countries or regions. Donors, moreover, sometimes request the establishment of separate management structures dominated by them, especially for longer-term or co-sponsored programmes. This inevitable situation, it has been noted, may lead to internal tensions in the policies and management of the Organization. The Executive Board Working Group on the WHO response to global change noted in 1993 that this situation 'often creates competing policy and budgetary decisions for the Executive Board, the World Health Assembly, Regional Committees and the donor-dominated management structures of the special extrabudgetary programmes'.[1]

1. *Ibidem*, p. 167.

518. In order to rationalize the situation, the Executive Board requested the Director-General to draw up a policy on extrabudgetary resources. The draft policy presented to the 105th Session of the Board in January 2000, and endorsed by it, contains guidelines indicating the basic principles and modalities under which the Secretariat will raise and use extrabudgetary resources. Most importantly, the use of those resources shall be consistent and complementary with the goals and targets of the programme budget; funds will be raised for a limited number of programme priorities identified in the regular budget and as much as possible through longer-term contributions. The range of donors will be broadened within both the public and private sectors through a partnership approach, while the governing bodies will be kept informed through the financial report and other mechanisms.[1]

1. EB105/2000/REC/1, Annex 8.

519. A mechanism which, although outside the normal governance structure of WHO, has acquired considerable importance in the planning and monitoring of programmes and activities financed through extrabudgetary resources is the so-called 'Meeting of Interested Parties' (MIP). These meetings do not intend to formally replace separate management or review mechanisms established under co-sponsorship arrangements for extrabudgetary programmes, for example concerning tropical diseases. At the same time, WHO had been convening for many years less formal meetings to facilitate interaction between the programmes and interested parties, especially those which contributed voluntary funds. There was, however, no systematic approach. The establishment under Director-General Brundtland of clusters organized to bring together related areas of work enabled MIPs to be organized since 1999 along cluster lines, while also taking care to ensure that meetings required as part of a cosponsored programme were held within this arrangement. In practice, the Secretariat has been convening a major MIP on an annual basis.

520. At the request of the Board, the Director-General presented to the 106th Session of the Board in May 2000 draft terms of reference for MIPs. The terms of reference clarified that MIPs aim at enabling Member States and other entities contributing voluntary resources, as well as countries receiving funding, to share views, information and their evaluation of the usefulness of particular programmes and activities, including managerial issues and financial requirements for reaching the objectives set by WHO's governing bodies. The Director-General regularly submits reports on the MIPs to the Executive Board and feeds the Board's views back to the MIPs.[1]

1. WHO Doc. EB106/5, Annex.

Chapter 3. Contributions to the Regular Budget

521. As noted above, the expenses of the Organization covered by the regular budget are mostly financed through contributions assessed on Member States by the Health Assembly on a biennial basis (Article 56 of the Constitution).

522. The scale of assessments has historically been based on that approved by the UN General Assembly. Resolution WHA24.12, in particular, provides that the latest available United Nations scale of assessment shall be used as a basis for determining the WHO scale of assessment, taking account of the difference in membership and the establishment of minimum and maximum rates. Resolution WHA.26.21, moreover, in keeping with the decisions taken by the General Assembly, established a maximum rate of 25 per cent and a minimum one of 0.001 per cent. Since WHO has had up to date a larger membership than the United Nations, many countries had a slightly lower rate of assessment under the WHO scale. This difference might be virtually eliminated with the admission of Switzerland to UN membership on 12 September 2002, and the admission of East Timor to membership in the two organizations.

523. The General Assembly, by Resolution A/RES/55/5 of December 2000, adopted a scale of assessment for the period 2001–2003, reducing the maximum assessment rate from 25 to 22 per cent, while maintaining unchanged the minimum assessment rates. Based on the authority of the aforementioned resolutions, the Director-General submitted a draft scale of assessment to the 54th WHA based on that approved by the General Assembly.[1] However, dissent among Member States as to the use of the latest UN scale as the basis for the WHO scale prevented the Assembly from adopting the scale in question. In order to foster a compromise, the Director-General submitted a proposal under which countries whose contributions would be reduced under the 2002 UN scale would pay that reduced figure; contributions of least-developed countries would remain at the same level as for 2001; and countries whose contribution would be higher would benefit from a degree of relief.[2] The Health Assembly eventually adopted Resolution WHA54.17, which does not contain rates of assessment shown as percentages but rather the absolute amounts that each Member States would pay in 2002 and 2003, respectively.

1. WHO Doc. A/54/27.
2. WHO Doc. A/54/49.

524. Member States have a legal obligation under the Constitution to pay the contributions assessed on them by the Health Assembly. Pursuant to Financial Regulation

6.4, contributions are due as of 1 January of the year to which they relate. WHO, as most other agencies of the UN system, has been historically bedevilled by the recurrent and growing problem of late payment, or even non-payment, of assessed contributions. Such a situation has had on occasion political purposes. Other reasons cited for such delays or omissions are objective economic difficulties – especially for developing and transition countries – parliamentary procedures or requirements, budgetary years different from WHO's, or administrative negligence.[1] At 31 December 2001, the rate of collection for the year was 87 per cent, the highest for over ten years. This compared to 67 per cent at 30 November 2000.[2]

1. Y. Beigbeder, *supra*, p. 163.
2. WHO Doc. EB109/20 Add.1.

525. In order to tackle this problem, the Health Assembly has adopted both penalties and incentives. From the former point of view, it should be recalled that Article 7 of the Constitution enables the Health Assembly to 'suspend the voting privileges and services' of members who fail to meet their financial obligations. Article 7 is thus greatly different from Article 19 of the UN Charter, which sets directly the threshold for the application of the penalty and under which the suspension of the right to vote is automatic. By Resolution WHA8.13 of 23 May 1955, the Assembly decided that if a member is in arrears 'in an amount which equals or exceeds the amount . . . due from it for the preceding two full years' by the time the Assembly opens its session, the Assembly shall consider the suspension of the right to vote.

526. It has been reported that Resolution WHA8.13 was not consistently enforced, and that the Assembly showed great tolerance towards the defaulting contributors, until 1988. Only then, under the weight of the financial crisis of the 1980s, the Assembly set by Resolution WHA41.7 a clear procedure for the enforcement of Article 7.[1] Pursuant to that resolution, and unless it submits to the Board a clear statement of its commitment to pay its arrears, a member in arrears for more than two years at the time of the opening of the Health Assembly is subject to a resolution by a two-thirds majority to the effect that its voting privileges will be suspended as from the opening of the next Health Assembly unless the arrears have been reduced to a level below the two-year threshold. The WHO system is thus more 'generous' than the UN's since it not only requires an Assembly resolution adopted by a qualified majority, but it also grants the Member States concerned an additional year to avoid the infliction of the penalty.

1. Y. Beigbeder, *supra*, p. 164.

527. The 54th WHA, moreover, codified an arrangement which had been followed on an *ad hoc* basis for a number of years.[1] Under that arrangement, states which have lost or are going to lose their voting rights may discuss with the Director-General the rescheduling of the payment of their arrears, by committing themselves to a defined schedule of payments and a set minimum amount. Proposals in this regard are submitted to the Health Assembly and, if approved by it, the voting rights of the members concerned are restored or not suspended. However, if the Member States in question default on the payment of their instalments, their voting rights are automatically suspended without the need for an additional resolution. The voting rights of 29 Member States were suspended as of the beginning of the 55th WHA in May 2002.

1. Resolution WHA54.6, in WHA54/2001/REC/1, p. 4.

528. As for the positive measures, Financial Regulation 6.5 provides for a financial incentive scheme which rewards Member States that pay in full within the grace period set out in the Financial Rules, i.e. 30 April. The financial incentive consists of a discount in the assessed contribution equivalent to interest calculated at a defined rate for the period 1 January–30 April of the year to which the contribution relates.

Part VIII. Data and Publications

Chapter 1. Introduction

529. The dissemination of information in the field of health is part of the mission of WHO, as explicitly stated in Article 2(q) of its Constitution. WHO's publication and documentation activities not only fulfil this primary function, but are of paramount importance for the achievement of many other WHO constitutional objectives. The assistance in the development of an informed public opinion among all people on matters of health (Article 2(r)), the promotion of improved standards of teaching and training in the health professions (Article 2(o)), the development and promotion of international standards with respect to food, biological, pharmaceuticals and similar products (Article 2(u)): all of these functions cannot be achieved without creating a system that allows information and scientific data to effectively reach its addressees.

530. The importance of publications and documentation had been pointed out by the Interim Commission: in addition to fulfilling the main function of disseminating information, publications would form the prime link between WHO and professional health workers. The First World Health Assembly endorsed the main outline of the publishing programme proposed by the Interim Commission.[1]

1. OR 13, p. 343.

531. The publishing programme of WHO was in fact initially based on a few inherited functions. The origins of the WHO publications go back to the Rome Agreement of 1907 which established the Office International d'Hygiène Publique. This office had since 1909 published a monthly *Bulletin* containing information on laws relating to communicable diseases, as well as public health statistics and bibliographical notes. WHO also assumed responsibility in its first years in respect of certain publications of the Health Organization of the League of Nations.

532. In the first years budgetary restrictions made it impossible to adequately staff the publications programme. In January 1952, the Executive Board carried out a detailed study of the publishing programme. The Assembly evaluated it and approved its implementation.[1] Today, WHO's publications include periodicals, regular series of publications, official records and Annual Reports, as well as technical documents such as guidelines and reports. The overall production of technical documents has increased substantially in the last years, representing around 50 per cent of all WHO publications in 2001.

1. Resolution WHA5.24, in OR 42, p. 24.

Chapter 2. WHO's Publications

533. Among its periodicals, the *Bulletin of the WHO* is WHO's principal technical publication. It is published monthly and aims to give public health policy and practice guidance based on the best evidence available. It presents original research findings selected on the basis of their immediate or potential relevance to problems of human health.

534. The *WHO Drug Information*, launched in 1987 and published quarterly, communicates pharmaceutical information that is either developed and issued by WHO or transmitted to WHO by research and regulatory agencies throughout the world. It also regularly presents newly proposed and recommended International Nonproprietary Names (INN) for Pharmaceutical Substances. The *Weekly Epidemiological Record* has served for more than seven decades as an essential tool for the collation and dissemination of epidemiological data useful in disease surveillance on a global level. Priority is given to diseases or risk factors known to threaten international health.

535. WHO also has two regional periodicals: the *Pan American Journal of Public Health*, which communicates original research findings relevant to health problems in the Western Hemisphere, and the *Eastern Mediterranean Health Journal*, the official health journal published by the Eastern Mediterranean Regional Office of WHO, which is a forum for the presentation and promotion of new policies and initiatives in health services, for the exchange of ideas, concepts, epidemiological data, research findings and other information, with special reference to the Eastern Mediterranean Region.

536. Finally, *International Travel and Health* is an annual publication that aims at informing travellers and health professionals about the risks to which travellers are exposed and the precautions needed to protect their health.

537. Turning from the periodicals to the regular series of publications, the *Technical Report Series*, which has issued now more than 900 volumes, records the consensus reached by Expert Committees or other advisory groups commissioned to advise the world's scientific communities on the best way to tackle a selected health or medical problem.

538. The volumes of the *Environmental Health Criteria Series* issue authoritative conclusions about human and environmental risks based on a study of virtually everything ever written about a selected industrial chemical. Lastly, the *Food Additives Series* is the more recent WHO series, containing information useful to those who produce and use food additives and veterinary drugs and those involved with controlling contaminants in food, government and food regulatory officers, industrial testing laboratories, toxicological laboratories, and universities.

539. The *Official Records* series were discontinued in 1979, but WHO continues to publish the records of the World Health Assembly (three volumes: 1. Resolutions and Decisions; 2. Verbatim Records of Plenary Meetings; 3. Summary Records of meetings of the Committees and Reports of the Committees) and the Executive Board (two volumes: 1. Resolutions and Decisions; 2. Summary Records). The handbooks of the resolutions and decisions were discontinued in 1993, but all resolutions and decisions are available on-line on the Internet (www.who.int/ism/mis/WHO-policy/index.en.html).

540. The Director-General's biennial reports have been incorporated in the annual *World Health Report* as from 1995. Since 2000, it focuses on a specific theme: the 2001 report was on 'Mental health', while in 2000 the selected topic was 'Health systems'. These reports assess the current global situation in the selected area, by using the latest data gathered and validated by WHO. The International Agency for Research on Cancer has also a separate series of publications, which started in 1969.

541. WHO also publishes a wide range of other publications, mainly technical documents such as guidelines on recommended behaviours and reports on the latest research developments in the world. As an indication of the excellence of WHO publications, two WHO books have been commended at the 2001 British Medical Association Book Competition: Management of severe malaria (second edition) and Anaesthesia at the district hospital (second edition).

Chapter 3. Information on Health Legislation

542. The collection and publication of legislative health information goes back to January 1909, when the Director of the Paris-based International Office of Public Hygiene addressed a circular to the administrations of the participating states in that arrangement, requesting them to transmit to the office copies of 'general and local laws and regulations published in the different countries concerning communicable diseases'. Thereafter, the *Bulletin* of the office (which was published in French only between 1909 and 1946) carried a regular rubric devoted to significant international and national legislative instruments related to diverse aspects of health. One of the decisions taken by the Interim Commission of the World Health Organization in 1947 was that the new global health organization, WHO, would report on health legislation in an entirely new journal, the *International Digest of Health Legislation.*

543. The first issue appeared in 1948, when the Health Legislation Unit was also established. Under Article 63 of the Constitution, each Member State is required to 'communicate promptly to the Organization important laws, regulations ... pertaining to health which have been published in the State concerned'. It is essentially under the terms of that article that WHO has, in the intervening 55 years, operated a vigorous and dynamic programme in the health legislation area, with primary emphasis placed on information transfer. Since 2000, the *International Digest of Health Legislation* is not printed anymore and is published in an electronic format (www.who.int/idhl).

Chapter 4. Databases

544. WHO has progressively moved towards the development of more modern methods for handling health data in a growing number of areas. A number of data-bases have been developed and made accessible on the WHO website (www.who.int/research). The Library database WHOLIS indexes all WHO publications from 1948 onwards and articles from WHO-produced journals and technical documents from 1985 to date. An on-site card catalogue provides access to the pre-1985 technical documents.

545. Also accessible on the web, the WHOSIS database is a guide to epidemio-logical and statistical information available from WHO. Most WHO technical pro-grammes develop health-related epidemiological and statistical information which they make available on the website. Therefore, WHOSIS regroups databases con-cerning statistics on burden of diseases, causes of death, health personnel, populations, health systems performances, maternal mortality, HIV/AIDS, immunization etc.

546. In the field of health legislation, computerized databases have been devel-oped on: HIV/AIDS legislation; articles on the legal, ethical, and judicial aspects of HIV/AIDS; legislation on 'tobacco or health'; and legislation on organ trans-plantation. Reference should also be made to the LEYES database (Documentation System for Basic Legislation in the Health Sector for Latin America and the Car-ibbean), developed by the WHO Regional Office for the Americas/Pan American Health Organization, in Washington, DC. This database has been developed with the active involvement of the Hispanic Law Division of the Library of Congress in Washington, DC, and the Faculty of Law Library at the University of the West Indies in Barbados. A collaborating centre for LEYES, located at the Center for Studies and Research in Health Law, School of Public Health, University of São Paulo, Brazil, has been established.

Chapter 5. The Library

547. The growing interest in health, medical, population, and environmental data in many industrialized and developing countries has been accompanied by a veritable explosion in the number of books and journals devoted to these fields. No less remarkable has been the enormous increase in publications on bioethical issues. WHO is sensitive to these developments and over the last few years every effort has been made to build up a library containing as many such publications as possible. The vast majority of these publications have been provided to WHO at no cost.

Chapter 6. The WHO Website

548.   The website www.who.int offers constantly updated statistical, technical and practical information, including weekly alerts to disease outbreaks, daily count-downs on cases of specific diseases, country and global statistics, information for international travellers etc. An up-dated list of WHO publications is available on line, through the consultation of the WHO Catalogue (www.who.int/pub). The WHO website also provides access to a series of other research tools: the Library database WHOLIS, WHO's statistical information available through the WHOSIS database, as well as geographical information (www.who.int/research).

549.   The variety of the WHO publications cannot be reflected in such a short review. WHO publications and databases have played and still play an essential role in the information of health specialists. The significant differences between national health systems makes communication between them quite difficult. There-fore, WHO comparative studies, guidelines and report contribute significantly to the formulation of transnational solutions, and avoid waste of time and staff. WHO is also a valuable source of information for the general public, in particular through journalists who often rely on WHO publications to compare and evaluate situations at regional and global levels.

Part IX. Addresses

Headquarters
Avenue Appia 20
1211 Geneva 27, Switzerland
Telephone: (+ 41 22) 791 21 11
Facsimile (fax): (+ 41 22) 791 3111
Internet address: http://www.who.int

Regional Office for Africa (AFRO)
The Regional Office for Africa is located in Brazzaville, Congo. Due to the civil unrest which prevailed in the country in 1995–1996, the Office was temporarily relocated to Harare, Zimbabwe. Whereas the Regional Director and most of the staff have returned to Brazzaville in 2001, the office in Harare is still functioning as of September 2002.

Cite du Djoue P.O. Box 06 Brazzaville, Congo
Telephone: (+1 321) 9539100 / +242 839100
Facsimile: (+1 321) 9539100 / +242 839100

Parirenyatwa Hospital
P.O. Box BE 773
Harare, Zimbabwe
Telephone: (+263 4) 703580, 703684, 707493, 706951
Facsimile: (+263 4) 790146 or 791214
Email: regafro@whoafr.org
Internet address: http://www.whoafro.org

Regional Office for the Americas/Pan American Health Organization (AMRO/PAHO)
525, 23rd Street, N.W.
Washington, DC 20037, USA
Telephone: (+1 202) 9743000
Facsimile: (+1 202) 9743663
Telex: 248338 - 440057 - 64152 - 892744
Telegraph: OFSANPAN WASHINGTON
Email: postmaster@paho.org
Internet address: http://www.paho.org

Regional Office for the Eastern Mediterranean (EMRO)
WHO Post Office
Abdul Razzak Al Sanhouri Street (opposite Children's Library)
Nasr City, Cairo 11371, Egypt
Email: PIO@emro.who.int
Internet address: http://emro.who.int

Regional Office for Europe (EURO)
8, Scherfigsvej
DK-2100 Copenhagen 0, Denmark
Telephone: (+45 39) 171717
Facsimile: (+45 39) 171818
Telex: 15348 or 15390
Telegraph: UNISANTE COPENHAGEN
Email: fap@who.dk
Internet address: http://www.who.dk

Regional Office for South-East Asia (SEARO)
World Health House, Indraprastha Estate
Mahatma Gandhi Road
New Delhi 110002, India
Telephone: (+91 11) 3370804 or 3378805
Facsimile: (+91 11) 3379507 or 3370972
Telex: 3165095 or 3165031
Telegraph: WHO NEW DELHI
Email: PANDEYH@whosea.org
Internet address: http://www.whosea.org

Regional Office for the Western Pacific (WPRO)
P.O. Box 2932
1000 Manila Philippines
Telephone: (+63 2) 5288001 Facsimile: (+63 2) 5211036 or 5360279
Telex: 27652-63260-40365
Telegraph: UNISANTE MANILA
Email: Postmaster@who.org.ph
Internet address: http://www.wpro.who.int

International Agency for Research on Cancer (IARC)
150 cours Albert Thomas
F-69372 Lyon CEDEX 08, France
Tel: (+33 4) 72738485
Fax: (+33 4) 72738575
Internet address: http://www.iarc.fr

Short Bibliography

§1. MONOGRAPHS

Alvarez Vita, J., *El derecho a la salud como derecho humano*, Lima: Cultural Cuzco Editores, 1994.

Beigbeder, Y., *L'Organisation Mondiale de la Santé*, Paris: PUF, 1995.

Dupuy, R.-J., (Ed.), *The Right to Health as a Human Right*, Proceedings of a Workshop convened by the Hague Academy of International Law and the United Nations University, The Hague, 27–29 July 1978, Alphen aan den Rijn, The Netherlands: Sijthoff & Noordhoff, 1979.

Fidler, D.P., *International Law and Infectious Diseases*, Oxford: Clarendon Press, 1999.

Nielsen, H.K., *The World Health Organization – Implementing the Right to Health*, Copenhagen: Europublishers, 1999.

Reich, M.R. (Ed.), *Public-Private Partnerships for Public Health*, Cambridge Massachusetts: Harvard University Press, 2002.

Roemer, R., *L'action législative contre l'epidemie mondiale de tabagisme*, Genève: OMS, 1995.

Shubber, S., *The International Code of Marketing of Breast-Milk Substitutes: an International Measure to Protect and Promote Breastfeeding*, The Hague: Kluwer Law International, 1998.

Siddiqi, J.A., *World Health and World Politics: The WHO and the UN system*, Columbus, S.C.: University of South Carolina Press, 1995.

Wagstaff, A., *Measuring Equity in Health Care Financing: Reflections on and Alternatives to the WHO's Fairness of Financing Index*, Washington D.C.: World Bank, 2001.

WHO, *The World Health Report 1995 – Bridging the Gap*, Geneva: WHO, 1995.

WHO, *Macroeconomics and Health: Investing in Health for Economic Development – Report of the Commission on Macroeconomics and Health*, Geneva: WHO, 2001.

WHO, *Towards Health with Justice – Litigation and Public Inquiries as Tools for Tobacco Control*, Geneva: WHO, 2002.

WHO & WTO, *WTO Agreements and Public Health – A joint study by the WHO and the WTO Secretariat*, Geneva: WHO/WTO, 2002.

Short Bibliography

§2. ARTICLES AND CONTRIBUTIONS

Beigbeder, Y., 'Les relations des ONG avec l'OMS', in Bettati, Dupuy, Beigbeder (Eds.), *Les O.N.G. et le droit international*, Paris: Economica, 1986, 167.

Bélanger, M., 'Une nouvelle branche du droit international: le droit international de la santé', *Etudes Internationales* 13 (4), (décembre 1982), 611.

Bothe, M., 'The WHO request', in Boisson de Chazournes, Sands (Eds.), *International Law, the International Court of Justice and Nuclear Weapons*, Cambridge: Cambridge University Press, 1999, 103.

Del Ponte, K.G., 'Formulating Customary International Law: an Examination of the WHO International Code of Marketing of Breastmilk Substitutes', *Boston College International and Comparative Law Review* 5 (2), (Summer 1982), 377.

Dorfman, S.H., 'The Implementation Process of the International Code of Marketing of Breastmilk Substitutes', *Syracuse Journal of International Law and Commerce* 11 (1), (Summer 1984), 161.

Fidler, D.P., 'Trade and Health: the Global Spread of Diseases and International Trade', *German Yearbook of International Law* 40, (1997), 300.

Fidler, D.P., 'Return of the Fourth Horseman: Emerging Infectious Diseases and International Law', *Minnesota Law Review* 81 (4), (1997), 771.

Fidler, D.P., 'The Future of the World Health Organization: What Role for International Law?', *Vanderbilt Journal of Transnational Law* 31 (5), (November 1998), 1079.

Fidler, D.P., 'International Legal Implications of "Non-Lethal" Weapons', *Michigan Journal of International Law* 21 (1), (Fall 1999), 51.

Fluss, S.S., Gutteridge, F. Little, J.K., Harris, H., 'World Health Organization', in Blanpain (Ed.), *Encyclopedia of Laws*, Deventer/Boston: Kluwer Law International, 1998.

Gutteridge, F., 'Notes on Decisions of the World Health Organization' in S. Schwebel (Ed.), *The Effectiveness of International Decisions*, Dobbs Ferry, NY, Oceana, 1971.

Klein, P., 'Les organisations internationales face au Sida', *Revue Belge de Droit International* 23 (1), (1990), 153.

Klein, P., 'Quelque réflexions sur le principe de spécialité et la "politisation" des institutions spécialisées', in Boisson de Chazournes, Sands (Eds.), *International Law, the International Court of Justice and Nuclear Weapons*, Cambridge: Cambridge University Press, 1999, 79.

Lador-Lederer, J.J., 'Promotion of Health: the Making of an International Norm', *Israel Yearbook on Human Rights* 18, (1998), 121.

Leary, V.A., 'The Right to Health in International Human Rights Law', *Health and Human Rights* 1 (1), (Fall 1994), 25.

Leary, V.A., 'The WHO Case: Implications for Specialized Agencies', in Boisson de Chazournes, Sands (Eds.), *International Law, the International Court of Justice and Nuclear Weapons*, Cambridge: Cambridge University Press, 1999, 112.

Mann, J.M., 'Human Rights and AIDS: The Future of the Pandemic', in Mann, Gruskin, Grodin, Annas (Eds.), *Health and Human Rights*, New York/London: Routledge, 1998, 113.

Marmor, T., 'The Right to Health Care', in Bole & Bondeson (Eds.), *Rights to Health Care*, Dordrecht, the Netherlands, Boston and London: Kluwer Law International, 1991, 23.

Otto, D., 'Linking Health and Human Rights: a Critical Legal Perspective', *Health and Human Rights* 1 (3), (1995), 859.

Plotkin, B.J., 'Mission Possible: The Future of the International Health Regulations', *Temple International and Comparative Law Journal* 10, (1996), 503.

Schoepe, M., 'International Regulation of Pharmaceuticals: A WHO International Code of Conduct for the Marketing of Pharmaceuticals?', *Syracuse Journal of International Law and Commerce* 11 (1), (Summer 1984), 121.

Sikkink, K., 'Codes of Conduct for Transnational Corporations: The Case of the WHO/UNICEF Code', *International Organization* 40 (4), (Autumn 1986), 815.

Taylor, A.L., 'Making the World Health Organization Work: A Legal Framework for Universal Access to the Conditions for Health', *American Journal of Law and Medecine*, 1992, 301.

Taylor, A.L., 'Controlling the Global Spread of Infectious Diseases: Toward a Reinforced Role for the International Health Regulations', *Houston Law Review* 33 (5), (1997), 290.

Tietje, C., 'Die Völkerrechtswidrigkeit des Einsatzes von Atomwaffen im bewaffneten Konflikt unter Umwelt und Gesundheitsschutzaspekten: zur Gutachtenanfrage der WHO an den IGH', *Archiv des Völkerrechts* 33, Mai 1995, 266.

Toebes, B., 'Towards an Improved Understanding of the International Human Right to Health', *Human Rights Quarterly* 21 (3), (1999), 661.

Tomasevyki, K., 'Health', in *United Nations Legal Order*, Cambridge, New York: Grotius Publications, Cambridge University Press, 1995, 859.

Vignes, C.-H., 'Organisation Mondiale de la Santé: Questions juridiques', *Annuaire Français de Droit International* 9 (1963), 627.

Vignes, C.-H., 'Droit à la santé et coordination', in Dupuy, R.-J. (Ed.), *The Right to Health as a Human Right, supra*, p. 304.

Vignes, C.-H., 'Towards the harmonization of health legislation: the role of the World Health Organization', in *International Digest of Health Legislation* 40 no. 3 (1995), 422.

Vignes, C.-H., 'Mythe et réalité: Le statut des membres du Conseil exécutif de l'Organisation Mondiale de la Santé', *Revue Générale de Droit International Public* 103 (3), (1999), 685.

Vignes, C.-H., Schlenszka, H.J., 'World Health Organization', in R. Bernhardt, *Encyclopaedia of Public International Law*, Vol. 4, Amsterdam, North-Holland, 1494.

Short Bibliography

Annex 1. Constitution of the World Health Organization

THE STATES Parties to this Constitution declare, in conformity with the Charter of the United Nations, that the following principles are basic to the happiness, harmonious relations and security of all peoples:

Health is a state of complete physical, mental and social well-being and not merely the absence of disease or infirmity.

The enjoyment of the highest attainable standard of health is one of the fundamental rights of every human being without distinction of race, religion, political belief, economic or social condition.

The health of all peoples is fundamental to the attainment of peace and security and is dependent upon the fullest co-operation of individuals and states.

The achievement of any state in the promotion and protection of health is of value to all.

Unequal development in different countries in the promotion of health and control of disease, especially communicable disease, is a common danger.

Healthy development of the child is of basic importance; the ability to live harmoniously in a changing total environment is essential to such development.

The extension to all peoples of the benefits of medical, psychological and related knowledge is essential to the fullest attainment of health.

Informed opinion and active co-operation on the part of the public are of the utmost importance in the improvement of the health of the people.

Governments have a responsibility for the health of their peoples which can be fulfilled only by the provision of adequate health and social measures.

ACCEPTING THESE PRINCIPLES, and for the purpose of co-operation among themselves and with others to promote and protect the health of all peoples, the Contracting Parties agree to the present Constitution and hereby establish the World Health Organization as a specialized agency within the terms of Article 57 of the Charter of the United Nations.

Chapter I – Objective

Article 1
The objective of the World Health Organization (hereinafter called the Organization) shall be the attainment by all peoples of the highest possible level of health.

Annex 1

Chapter II – Functions

Article 2
In order to achieve its objective, the functions of the Organization shall be:

(a) to act as the directing and co-ordinating authority on international health work;
(b) to establish and maintain effective collaboration with the United Nations, specialized agencies, governmental health administrations, professional groups and such other organizations as may be deemed appropriate;
(c) to assist governments, upon request, in strengthening health services;
(d) to furnish appropriate technical assistance and, in emergencies, necessary aid upon the request or acceptance of governments;
(e) to provide or assist in providing, upon the request of the United Nations, health services and facilities to special groups, such as the peoples of trust territories;
(f) to establish and maintain such administrative and technical services as may be required, including epidemiological and statistical services;
(g) to stimulate and advance work to eradicate epidemic, endemic and other diseases;
(h) to promote, in co-operation with other specialized agencies where necessary, the prevention of accidental injuries;
(i) to promote, in co-operation with other specialized agencies where necessary, the improvement of nutrition, housing, sanitation, recreation, economic or working conditions and other aspects of environmental hygiene;
(j) to promote co-operation among scientific and professional groups which contribute to the advancement of health;
(k) to propose conventions, agreements and regulations, and make recommendations with respect to international health matters and to perform such duties as may be assigned thereby to the Organization and are consistent with its objective;
(l) to promote maternal and child health and welfare and to foster the ability to live harmoniously in a changing total environment;
(m) to foster activities in the field of mental health, especially those affecting the harmony of human relations;
(n) to promote and conduct research in the field of health;
(o) to promote improved standards of teaching and training in the health, medical and related professions;
(p) to study and report on, in co-operation with other specialized agencies where necessary, administrative and social techniques affecting public health and medical care from preventive and curative points of view, including hospital services and social security;
(q) to provide information, counsel and assistance in the field of health;
(r) to assist in developing an informed public opinion among all peoples on matters of health;
(s) to establish and revise as necessary international nomenclatures of diseases, of causes of death and of public health practices;
(t) to standardize diagnostic procedures as necessary;

(u) to develop, establish and promote international standards with respect to food, biological, pharmaceutical and similar products;

(v) generally to take all necessary action to attain the objective of the Organization.

Chapter III – Membership and Associate Membership

Article 3
Membership in the Organization shall be open to all states.

Article 4
Members of the United Nations may become Members of the Organization by signing or otherwise accepting this Constitution in accordance with the provisions of Chapter XIX and in accordance with their constitutional processes.

Article 5
The states whose governments have been invited to send observers to the International Health Conference held in New York, 1946, may become members by signing or otherwise accepting this Constitution in accordance with the provisions of Chapter XIX and in accordance with their constitutional processes provided that such signature or acceptance shall be completed before the first session of the Health Assembly.

Article 6
Subject to the conditions of any agreement between the United Nations and the Organization, approved pursuant to Chapter XVI, states which do not become members in accordance with Articles 4 and 5 may apply to become members and shall be admitted as members when their application has been approved by a simple majority vote of the Health Assembly.

Article 7
If a member fails to meet its financial obligations to the Organization or in other exceptional circumstances, the Health Assembly may, on such conditions as it thinks proper, suspend the voting privileges and services to which a Member is entitled. The Health Assembly shall have the authority to restore such voting privileges and services.

Article 8
Territories or groups of territories which are not responsible for the conduct of their international relations may be admitted as associate members by the Health Assembly upon application made on behalf of such territory or group of territories by the

member or other authority having responsibility for their international relations. Representatives of associate members to the Health Assembly should be qualified by their technical competence in the field of health and should be chosen from the native population. The nature and extent of the rights and obligations of associate members shall be determined by the Health Assembly.

Chapter IV – Organs

Article 9
The work of the Organization shall be carried out by:

(a) The World Health Assembly (herein called the Health Assembly);
(b) The Executive Board (hereinafter called the Board);
(c) The Secretariat.

Chapter V – the World Health Assembly

Article 10
The Health Assembly shall be composed of delegates representing members.

Article 11
Each member shall be represented by not more than three delegates, one of whom shall be designated by the member as chief delegate. These delegates should be chosen from among persons most qualified by their technical competence in the field of health, preferably representing the national health administration of the member.

Article 12
Alternates and advisers may accompany delegates.

Article 13
The Health Assembly shall meet in regular annual session and in such special sessions as may be necessary. Special sessions shall be convened at the request of the Board or of a majority of the members.

Article 14
The Health Assembly, at each annual session, shall select the country or region in which the next annual session shall be held, the Board subsequently fixing the place. The Board shall determine the place where a special session shall be held.

Article 15
The Board, after consultation with the Secretary-General of the United Nations, shall determine the date of each annual and special session.

Article 16
The Health Assembly shall elect its President and other officers at the beginning of each annual session. They shall hold office until their successors are elected.

Article 17
The Health Assembly shall adopt its own rules of procedure.

Article 18
The functions of the Health Assembly shall be:

(a) to determine the policies of the Organization;
(b) to name the members entitled to designate a person to serve on the Board;
(c) to appoint the Director-General;
(d) to review and approve reports and activities of the Board and of the Director-General and to instruct the Board in regard to matters upon which action, study, investigation or report may be considered desirable;
(e) to establish such committees as may be considered necessary for the work of the Organization;
(f) to supervise the financial policies of the Organization and to review and approve the budget;
(g) to instruct the Board and the Director-General to bring to the attention of members and of international organizations, governmental or non-governmental, any matter with regard to health which the Health Assembly may consider appropriate;
(h) to invite any organization, international or national, governmental or non-governmental, which has responsibilities related to those of the Organization, to appoint representatives to participate, without right of vote, in its meetings or in those of the committees and conferences convened under its authority, on conditions prescribed by the Health Assembly; but in the case of national organizations, invitations shall be issued only with the consent of the government concerned;
(i) to consider recommendations bearing on health made by the General Assembly, the Economic and Social Council, the Security Council or Trusteeship Council of the United Nations, and to report to them on the steps taken by the Organization to give effect to such recommendations;
(j) to report to the Economic and Social Council in accordance with any agreement between the Organization and the United Nations;
(k) to promote and conduct research in the field of health by the personnel of the Organization, by the establishment of its own institutions or by co-operation with official or non-official institutions of any member with the consent of its government;

Annex 1

(l) to establish such other institutions as it may consider desirable;
(m) to take any other appropriate action to further the objective of the Organization.

Article 19
The Health Assembly shall have authority to adopt conventions or agreements with respect to any matter within the competence of the Organization. A two-thirds vote of the Health Assembly shall be required for the adoption of such conventions or agreements, which shall come into force for each member when accepted by it in accordance with its constitutional processes.

Article 20
Each member undertakes that it will, within eighteen months after the adoption by the Health Assembly of a convention or agreement, take action relative to the acceptance of such convention or agreement. Each member shall notify the Director-General of the action taken, and if it does not accept such convention or agreement within the time limit, it will furnish a statement of the reasons for non-acceptance. In case of acceptance, each member agrees to make an annual report to the Director-General in accordance with Chapter XIV.

Article 21
The Health Assembly shall have authority to adopt regulations concerning:

(a) sanitary and quarantine requirements and other procedures designed to prevent the international spread of disease;
(b) nomenclatures with respect to diseases, causes of death and public health practices;
(c) standards with respect to diagnostic procedures for international use;
(d) standards with respect to the safety, purity and potency of biological, pharmaceutical and similar products moving in international commerce;
(e) advertising and labelling of biological, pharmaceutical and similar products moving in international commerce.

Article 22
Regulations adopted pursuant to Article 21 shall come into force for all members after due notice has been given of their adoption by the Health Assembly except for such members as may notify the Director-General of rejection or reservations within the period stated in the notice.

Article 23
The Health Assembly shall have authority to make recommendations to members with respect to any matter within the competence of the Organization.

Chapter VI – the Executive Board

Article 24
The Board shall consist of 32 persons designated by as many members. The Health Assembly, taking into account an equitable geographical distribution, shall elect the members entitled to designate a person to serve on the Board, provided that, of such members, not less than three shall be elected from each of the regional organizations established pursuant to Article 44. Each of these members should appoint to the Board a person technically qualified in the field of health, who may be accompanied by alternates and advisers.

Article 25
These members shall be elected for three years and may be re-elected, provided that of the members elected at the first session of the Health Assembly held after the coming into force of the amendment to this Constitution increasing the membership of the Board from 31 to 32 the term of office of the additional member elected shall, insofar as may be necessary, be of such lesser duration as shall facilitate the election of at least one member from each regional organization in each year.

Article 26
The Board shall meet at least twice a year and shall determine the place of each meeting.

Article 27
The Board shall elect its Chairman from among its members and shall adopt its own rules of procedure.

Article 28
The functions of the Board shall be:

(a) to give effect to the decisions and policies of the Health Assembly;
(b) to act as the executive organ of the Health Assembly;
(c) to perform any other functions entrusted to it by the Health Assembly;
(d) to advise the Health Assembly on questions referred to it by that body and on matters assigned to the Organization by conventions, agreements and regulations;
(e) to submit advice or proposals to the Health Assembly on its own initiative;
(f) to prepare the agenda of meetings of the Health Assembly;
(g) to submit to the Health Assembly for consideration and approval a general programme of work covering a specific period;
(h) to study all questions within its competence;
(i) to take emergency measures within the functions and financial resources of the Organization to deal with events requiring immediate action. In particular it may authorize the Director-General to take the necessary steps to combat

epidemics, to participate in the organization of health relief to victims of a calamity and to undertake studies and research the urgency of which has been drawn to the attention of the Board by any member or by the Director-General.

Article 29
The Board shall exercise on behalf of the whole Health Assembly the powers delegated to it by that body.

Chapter VII – the Secretariat

Article 30
The Secretariat shall comprise the Director-General and such technical and administrative staff as the Organization may require.

Article 31
The Director-General shall be appointed by the Health Assembly on the nomination of the Board on such terms as the Health Assembly may determine. The Director-General, subject to the authority of the Board, shall be the chief technical and administrative officer of the Organization.

Article 32
The Director-General shall be *ex-officio* Secretary of the Health Assembly, of the Board, of all commissions and committees of the Organization and of conferences convened by it. He may delegate these functions.

Article 33
The Director-General or his representative may establish a procedure by agreement with members, permitting him, for the purpose of discharging his duties, to have direct access to their various departments, especially to their health administrations and to national health organizations, governmental or non-governmental. He may also establish direct relations with international organizations whose activities come within the competence of the Organization. He shall keep regional offices informed on all matters involving their respective areas.

Article 34
The Director-General shall prepare and submit to the Board the financial statements and budget estimates of the Organization.

Article 35
The Director-General shall appoint the staff of the Secretariat in accordance with staff regulations established by the Health Assembly. The paramount consideration

in the employment of the staff shall be to assure that the efficiency, integrity and internationally representative character of the Secretariat shall be maintained at the highest level. Due regard shall be paid also to the importance of recruiting the staff on as wide a geographical basis as possible.

Article 36
The conditions of service of the staff of the Organization shall conform as far as possible with those of other United Nations organizations.

Article 37
In the performance of their duties the Director-General and the staff shall not seek or receive instructions from any government or from any authority external to the Organization. They shall refrain from any action which might reflect on their position as international officers. Each member of the Organization on its part undertakes to respect the exclusively international character of the Director-General and the staff and not to seek to influence them.

Chapter VIII – Committees

Article 38
The Board shall establish such committees as the Health Assembly may direct and, on its own initiative or on the proposal of the Director-General, may establish any other committees considered desirable to serve any purpose within the competence of the Organization.

Article 39
The Board, from time to time and in any event annually, shall review the necessity for continuing each committee.

Article 40
The Board may provide for the creation of or the participation by the Organization in joint or mixed committees with other organizations and for the representation of the Organization in committees established by such other organizations.

Chapter IX – Conferences

Article 41
The Health Assembly or the Board may convene local, general, technical or other special conferences to consider any matter within the competence of the Organization and may provide for the representation at such conferences of international organizations and, with the consent of the government concerned, of national organizations,

governmental or non-governmental. The manner of such representation shall be determined by the Health Assembly or the Board.

Article 42
The Board may provide for representation of the Organization at conferences in which the Board considers that the Organization has an interest.

Chapter X – Headquarters

Article 43
The location of the headquarters of the Organization shall be determined by the Health Assembly after consultation with the United Nations.

Chapter XI – Regional Arrangements

Article 44
(a) The Health Assembly shall from time to time define the geographical areas in which it is desirable to establish a regional organization.
(b) The Health Assembly may, with the consent of a majority of the members situated within each area so defined, establish a regional organization to meet the special needs of such area. There shall not be more than one regional organization in each area.

Article 45
Each regional organization shall be an integral part of the Organization in accordance with this Constitution.

Article 46
Each regional organization shall consist of a regional committee and a regional office.

Article 47
Regional committees shall be composed of representatives of the Member States and associate members in the region concerned. Territories or groups of territories within the region, which are not responsible for the conduct of their international relations and which are not associate members, shall have the right to be represented and to participate in regional committees. The nature and extent of the rights and obligations of these territories or groups of territories in regional committees shall be determined by the Health Assembly in consultation with the member or other authority having responsibility for the international relations of these territories and with the Member States in the region.

Article 48
Regional committees shall meet as often as necessary and shall determine the place of each meeting.

Article 49
Regional committees shall adopt their own rules of procedure.

Article 50
The functions of the regional committee shall be:

(a) to formulate policies governing matters of an exclusively regional character;
(b) to supervise the activities of the regional office;
(c) to suggest to the regional office the calling of technical conferences and such additional work or investigation in health matters as in the opinion of the regional committee would promote the objective of the Organization within the region;
(d) to co-operate with the respective regional committees of the United Nations and with those of other specialized agencies and with other regional international organizations having interests in common with the Organization;
(e) to tender advice, through the Director-General, to the Organization on international health matters which have wider than regional significance;
(f) to recommend additional regional appropriations by the governments of the respective regions if the proportion of the central budget of the Organization allotted to that region is insufficient for the carrying-out of the regional functions;
(g) such other functions as may be delegated to the regional committee by the Health Assembly, the Board or the Director-General.

Article 51
Subject to the general authority of the Director-General of the Organization, the regional office shall be the administrative organ of the regional committee. It shall, in addition, carry out within the region the decisions of the Health Assembly and of the Board.

Article 52
The head of the regional office shall be the Regional Director appointed by the Board in agreement with the regional committee.

Article 53
The staff of the regional office shall be appointed in a manner to be determined by agreement between the Director-General and the Regional Director.

Annex 1

Article 54
The Pan American Sanitary Organization 1 represented by the Pan American Sanitary Bureau and the Pan American Sanitary Conferences, and all other inter-governmental regional health organizations in existence prior to the date of signature of this Constitution, shall in due course be integrated with the Organization. This integration shall be effected as soon as practicable through common action based on mutual consent of the competent authorities expressed through the organizations concerned.

Chapter XII – Budget and Expenses

Article 55
The Director-General shall prepare and submit to the Board the budget estimates of the Organization. The Board shall consider and submit to the Health Assembly such budget estimates, together with any recommendations the Board may deem advisable.

Article 56
Subject to any agreement between the Organization and the United Nations, the Health Assembly shall review and approve the budget estimates and shall apportion the expenses among the members in accordance with a scale to be fixed by the Health Assembly.

Article 57
The Health Assembly or the Board acting on behalf of the Health Assembly may accept and administer gifts and bequests made to the Organization provided that the conditions attached to such gifts or bequests are acceptable to the Health Assembly or the Board and are consistent with the objective and policies of the Organization.

Article 58
A special fund to be used at the discretion of the Board shall be established to meet emergencies and unforeseen contingencies.

Chapter XIII – Voting

Article 59
Each member shall have one vote in the Health Assembly.

Article 60
(a) Decisions of the Health Assembly on important questions shall be made by a two-thirds majority of the members present and voting. These questions shall

include: the adoption of conventions or agreements; the approval of agreements bringing the Organization into relation with the United Nations and inter-governmental organizations and agencies in accordance with Articles 69, 70 and 72; amendments to this Constitution.

(b) Decisions on other questions, including the determination of additional categories of questions to be decided by a two-thirds majority, shall be made by a majority of the members present and voting.

(c) Voting on analogous matters in the Board and in committees of the Organization shall be made in accordance with paragraphs (a) and (b) of this article.

Chapter XIV – Reports Submitted by States

Article 61
Each member shall report annually to the Organization on the action taken and progress achieved in improving the health of its people.

Article 62
Each member shall report annually on the action taken with respect to recommendations made to it by the Organization and with respect to conventions, agreements and regulations.

Article 63
Each member shall communicate promptly to the Organization important laws, regulations, official reports and statistics pertaining to health which have been published in the State concerned.

Article 64
Each member shall provide statistical and epidemiological reports in a manner to be determined by the Health Assembly.

Article 65
Each member shall transmit upon the request of the Board such additional information pertaining to health as may be practicable.

Chapter XV – Legal Capacity, Privileges and Immunities

Article 66
The Organization shall enjoy in the territory of each member such legal capacity as may be necessary for the fulfilment of its objective and for the exercise of its functions.

Annex 1

Article 67

(a) The Organization shall enjoy in the territory of each member such privileges and immunities as may be necessary for the fulfilment of its objective and for the exercise of its functions.

(b) Representatives of members, persons designated to serve on the Board and technical and administrative personnel of the Organization shall similarly enjoy such privileges and immunities as are necessary for the independent exercise of their functions in connexion with the Organization.

Article 68

Such legal capacity, privileges and immunities shall be defined in a separate agreement to be prepared by the Organization in consultation with the Secretary-General of the United Nations and concluded between the members.

Chapter XVI – Relations with other Organizations

Article 69

The Organization shall be brought into relation with the United Nations as one of the specialized agencies referred to in Article 57 of the Charter of the United Nations. The agreement or agreements bringing the Organization into relation with the United Nations shall be subject to approval by a two-thirds vote of the Health Assembly.

Article 70

The Organization shall establish effective relations and co-operate closely with such other inter-governmental organizations as may be desirable. Any formal agreement entered into with such organizations shall be subject to approval by a two-thirds vote of the Health Assembly.

Article 71

The Organization may, on matters within its competence, make suitable arrangements for consultation and co-operation with non-governmental international organizations and, with the consent of the government concerned, with national organizations, governmental or non-governmental.

Article 72

Subject to the approval by a two-thirds vote of the Health Assembly, the Organization may take over from any other international organization or agency whose purpose and activities lie within the field of competence of the Organization such functions, resources and obligations as may be conferred upon the Organization by international agreement or by mutually acceptable arrangements entered into between the competent authorities of the respective organizations.

Chapter XVII – Amendments

Article 73
Texts of proposed amendments to this Constitution shall be communicated by the Director-General to members at least six months in advance of their consideration by the Health Assembly. Amendments shall come into force for all members when adopted by a two-thirds vote of the Health Assembly and accepted by two-thirds of the members in accordance with their respective constitutional processes.

Chapter XVIII – Interpretation

Article 74
The Chinese, English, French, Russian and Spanish texts of this Constitution shall be regarded as equally authentic.

Article 75
Any question or dispute concerning the interpretation or application of this Constitution which is not settled by negotiation or by the Health Assembly shall be referred to the International Court of Justice in conformity with the Statute of the Court, unless the parties concerned agree on another mode of settlemen

Article 76
Upon authorization by the General Assembly of the United Nations or upon authorization in accordance with any agreement between the Organization and the United Nations, the Organization may request the International Court of Justice for an advisory opinion on any legal question arising within the competence of the Organization.

Article 77
The Director-General may appear before the Court on behalf of the Organization in connexion with any proceedings arising out of any such request for an advisory opinion. He shall make arrangements for the presentation of the case before the Court, including arrangements for the argument of different views on the question.

Chapter XIX – Entry-into-Force

Article 78
Subject to the provisions of Chapter III, this Constitution shall remain open to all states for signature or acceptance.

Annex 1

Article 79
(a) States may become parties to this Constitution by:
   (i) signature without reservation as to approval;
   (ii) signature subject to approval followed by acceptance; or
   (iii) acceptance.
(b) Acceptance shall be effected by the deposit of a formal instrument with the Secretary-General of the United Nations.

Article 80
This Constitution shall come into force when 26 members of the United Nations have become parties to it in accordance with the provisions of Article 79.

Article 81
In accordance with Article 102 of the Charter of the United Nations, the Secretary-General of the United Nations will register this Constitution when it has been signed without reservation as to approval on behalf of one state or upon deposit of the first instrument of acceptance.

Article 82
The Secretary-General of the United Nations will inform states parties to this Constitution of the date when it has come into force. He will also inform them of the dates when other states have become parties to this Constitution.
IN FAITH WHEREOF the undersigned representatives, having been duly authorized for that purpose, sign this Constitution.
DONE in the City of New York this twenty-second day of July 1946, in a single copy in the Chinese, English, French, Russian and Spanish languages, each text being equally authentic. The original texts shall be deposited in the archives of the United Nations. The Secretary-General of the United Nations will send certified copies to each of the governments represented at the Conference.

Annex 2. Annex VII – The World Health Organization

In their application to the World Health Organization (hereinafter called 'the Organization') the standard clauses shall operate subject to the following modifications:

1. Article V and Section 25, paragraphs 1 and 2(I), of Article VII shall extend to persons designated to serve on the Executive Board of the Organization, their alternates and advisers, except that any waiver of the immunity of any such persons under Section 16 shall be by the Board.

2. (i) Experts (other than officials coming within the scope of Article VI) serving on committees of, or performing missions for, the Organization shall be accorded the following privileges and immunities so far as is necessary for the effective exercise of their functions, including the time spent on journeys in connexion with service on such committees or missions:

(a) Immunity from personal arrest or seizure of their personal baggage;
(b) In respect of words spoken or written or acts done by them in the performance of their official functions, immunity of legal process of every kind, such immunity to continue notwithstanding that the persons concerned are no longer serving on committees of, or employed on missions for, the Organization;
(c) The same facilities in respect of currency and exchange restrictions and in respect of their personal baggage as are accorded to officials of foreign governments on temporary official missions;
(d) Inviolability for all papers and documents;
(e) For the purpose of their communications with the Organization, the right to use codes and to receive papers or correspondence by courier or in sealed bags.

(ii) The privileges and immunities set forth in paragraphs (b) and (e) above shall be accorded to persons serving on Expert Advisory Panels of the Organization in the exercise of their functions as such.

(iii) Privileges and immunities are granted to the experts of the Organization in the interests of the Organization and not for the personal benefit of the individuals themselves. The Organization shall have the right and the duty to waive the immunity of any expert in any case where in its opinion the immunity would impede the course of justice and it can be waived without prejudice to the interests of the Organization.

3. Article V and Section 25, paragraphs 1 and 2(I), of Article VII shall extend to the representatives of associate members participating in the work of the Organization in accordance with Articles 8 and 47 of the Constitution.

Annex 2

4. The privileges, immunities, exemptions and facilities referred to in Section 21 of the standard clauses shall also be accorded to any Deputy Director-General, Assistant Director-General and Regional Director of the Organization.

Annex 3. World Health Declaration

I

We, the Member States of the World Health Organization (WHO), reaffirm our commitment to the principle enunciated in its Constitution that the enjoyment of the highest attainable standard of health is one of the fundamental rights of every human being; in doing so, we affirm the dignity and worth of every person, and the equal rights, equal duties and shared responsibilities of all for health.

II

We recognize that the improvement of the health and well-being of people is the ultimate aim of social and economic development. We are committed to the ethical concepts of equity, solidarity and social justice and to the incorporation of a gender perspective into our strategies. We emphasize the importance of reducing social and economic inequities in improving the health of the whole population. Therefore, it is imperative to pay the greatest attention to those most in need, burdened by ill-health, receiving inadequate services for health or affected by poverty. We reaffirm our will to promote health by addressing the basic determinants and prerequisites for health. We acknowledge that changes in the world health situation require that we give effect to the 'Health-for-All Policy for the twenty-first century' through relevant regional and national policies and strategies.

III

We recommit ourselves to strengthening, adapting and reforming, as appropriate, our health systems, including essential public health functions and services, in order to ensure universal access to health services that are based on scientific evidence, of good quality and within affordable limits, and that are sustainable for the future. We intend to ensure the availability of the essentials of primary health care as defined in the Declaration of Alma-Ata 21 and developed in the new policy. We will continue to develop health systems to respond to the current and anticipated health conditions, socioeconomic circumstances and needs of the people, communities and countries concerned, through appropriately managed public and private actions and investments for health.

Annex 3

IV

We recognize that in working towards health for all, all nations, communities, families and individuals are interdependent. As a community of nations, we will act together to meet common threats to health and to promote universal well-being.

V

We, the Member States of the World Health Organization, hereby resolve to promote and support the rights and principles, action and responsibilities enunciated in this Declaration through concerted action, full participation and partnership, calling on all peoples and institutions to share the vision of health for all in the twenty-first century, and to endeavour in common to realize it. (Sixteenth meeting, 27 January 1998)

Annex 4. Members of the World Health Organization (at 31 October 2002)

The Members and Associate Members of the World Health Organization are listed below, with the date on which each became a party to the Constitution or the date of admission to associate membership.

Afghanistan	19 April 1948
Albania	26 May 1947
Algeria*	8 November 1962
Andorra	15 January 1997
Angola	15 May 1976
Antigua and Barbuda*	12 March 1984
Argentina*	22 October 1948
Armenia	4 May 1992
Australia*	2 February 1948
Austria*	30 June 1947
Azerbaijan	2 October 1992
Bahamas*	1 April 1974
Bahrain*	2 November 1971
Bangladesh	19 May 1972
Barbados*	25 April 1967
Belarus*	7 April 1948
Belgium*	25 June 1948
Belize	23 August 1990
Benin	20 September 1960
Bhutan	8 March 1982
Bolivia	23 December 1949
Bosnia and Herzegovina*	10 September 1992
Botswana*	26 February 1975
Brazil*	2 June 1948
Brunei Darussalam	25 March 1985
Bulgaria*	9 June 1948
Burkina Faso*	4 October 1960
Burundi	22 October 1962
Cambodia*	17 May 1950
Cameroon*	6 May 1960

* Member States that have acceded to the Convention on the Privileges and Immunities of the Specialized Agencies and its Annex VII.

Canada	29 August 1946
Cape Verde	5 January 1976
Central African Republic*	20 September 1960
Chad	1 January 1961
Chile*	15 October 1948
China*	22 July 1946
Colombia	14 May 1959
Comoros	9 December 1975
Congo	26 October 1960
Cook Islands	9 May 1984
Costa Rica	17 March 1949
Côte d'Ivoire*	28 October 1960
Croatia*	11 June 1992
Cuba*	9 May 1950
Cyprus*	16 January 1961
Czech Republic*	22 January 1993
Democratic People's Republic of Korea	19 May 1973
Democratic Republic of the Congo*	24 February 1961
Denmark*	19 April 1948
Djibouti	10 March 1978
Dominica*	13 August 1981
Dominican Republic	21 June 1948
Ecuador*	1 March 1949
Egypt*	16 December 1947
El Salvador	22 June 1948
Equatorial Guinea	5 May 1980
Eritrea	24 July 1993
Estonia*	31 March 1993
Ethiopia	11 April 1947
Fiji*	1 January 1972
Finland*	7 October 1947
France	16 June 1948
Gabon*	21 November 1960
Gambia*	26 April 1971
Georgia	26 May 1992
Germany*	29 May 1951
Ghana*	8 April 1957
Greece*	12 March 1948
Grenada	4 December 1974
Guatemala*	26 August 1949
Guinea*	19 May 1959
Guinea-Bissau	29 July 1974
Guyana*	27 September 1966
Haiti*	12 August 1947

* Member States that have acceded to the Convention on the Privileges and Immunities of the Specialized Agencies and its Annex VII.

Honduras	8 April 1949
Hungary*	17 June 1948
Iceland	17 June 1948
India*	12 January 1948
Indonesia*	23 May 1950
Iran (Islamic Republic of)*	23 November 1946
Iraq*	23 September 1947
Ireland*	20 October 1947
Israel	21 June 1949
Italy*	11 April 1947
Jamaica*	21 March 1963
Japan*	16 May 1951
Jordan*	7 April 1947
Kazakhstan	19 August 1992
Kenya*	27 January 1964
Kiribati	26 July 1984
Kuwait*	9 May 1960
Kyrgyzstan	29 April 1992
Lao People's Democratic Republic*	17 May 1950
Latvia	4 December 1991
Lebanon	19 January 1949
Lesotho*	7 July 1967
Liberia	14 March 1947
Libyan Arab Jamahiriya*	16 May 1952
Lithuania*	25 November 1991
Luxembourg*	3 June 1949
Madagascar*	16 January 1961
Malawi*	9 April 1965
Malaysia*	24 April 1958
Maldives*	5 November 1965
Mali*	17 October 1960
Malta*	1 February 1965
Marshall Islands	5 June 1991
Mauritania	7 March 1961
Mauritius*	9 December 1968
Mexico	7 April 1948
Micronesia (Federated States of)	14 August 1991
Monaco	8 July 1948
Mongolia*	18 April 1962
Morocco*	14 May 1956
Mozambique	11 September 1975
Myanmar	1 July 1948
Namibia	23 April 1990
Nauru	9 May 1994

* Member States that have acceded to the Convention on the Privileges and Immunities of the Specialized Agencies and its Annex VII.

Annex 4

Nepal*	2 September 1953
Netherlands*	25 April 1947
New Zealand*	10 December 1946
Nicaragua*	24 April 1950
Niger*	5 October 1960
Nigeria*	25 November 1960
Niue	4 May 1994
Norway*	18 August 1947
Oman	28 May 1971
Pakistan*	23 June 1948
Palau	9 March 1995
Panama	20 February 1951
Papua New Guinea	29 April 1976
Paraguay	4 January 1949
Peru	11 November 1949
Philippines*	9 July 1948
Poland*	6 May 1948
Portugal	13 February 1948
Qatar	11 May 1972
Republic of Korea*	17 August 1949
Republic of Moldova	4 May 1992
Romania*	8 June 1948
Russian Federation*	24 March 1948
Rwanda*	7 November 1962
Saint Kitts and Nevis	3 December 1984
Saint Lucia*	11 November 1980
Saint Vincent and the Grenadines	2 September 1983
Samoa	16 May 1962
San Marino	12 May 1980
Sao Tome and Principe	23 March 1976
Saudi Arabia	26 May 1947
Senegal*	31 October 1960
Seychelles*	11 September 1979
Sierra Leone*	20 October 1961
Singapore*	25 February 1966
Slovakia*	4 February 1993
Slovenia*	7 May 1992
Solomon Islands	4 April 1983
Somalia	26 January 1961
South Africa	7 August 1947
Spain*	28 May 1951
Sri Lanka	7 July 1948
Sudan	14 May 1956
Suriname	25 March 1976

* Member States that have acceded to the Convention on the Privileges and Immunities of the Specialized Agencies and its Annex VII.

Swaziland	16 April 1973
Sweden*	28 August 1947
Switzerland	26 March 1947
Syrian Arab Republic	18 December 1946
Tajikistan	4 May 1992
Thailand*	26 September 1947
The former Yugoslav Republic of Macedonia*	22 April 1993
Timor-Leste	27 September 2002
Togo*	13 May 1960
Tonga*	14 August 1975
Trinidad and Tobago*	3 January 1963
Tunisia*	14 May 1956
Turkey	2 January 1948
Turkmenistan	2 July 1992
Tuvalu	7 May 1993
Uganda*	7 March 1963
Ukraine*	3 April 1948
United Arab Emirates	30 March 1972
United Kingdom of Great Britain and Northern Ireland*	22 July 1946
United Republic of Tanzania*	15 March 1962
United States of America	21 June 1948
Uruguay*	22 April 1949
Uzbekistan*	22 May 1992
Vanuatu	7 March 1983
Venezuela	7 July 1948
Viet Nam	17 May 1950
Yemen	20 November 1953
Yugoslavia	28 November 2000
Zambia*	2 February 1965
Zimbabwe*	16 May 1980

Associate Members

Puerto Rico	7 May 1992
Tokelau	8 May 1991

---

* Member States that have acceded to the Convention on the Privileges and Immunities of the Specialized Agencies and its Annex VII.

Annex 4

Annex 5. Declaration on the TRIPS Agreement and Public Health

Adopted on 14 November 2001

1. We recognize the gravity of the public health problems afflicting many developing and least-developed countries, especially those resulting from HIV/AIDS, tuberculosis, malaria and other epidemics.

2. We stress the need for the WTO Agreement on Trade-Related Aspects of Intellectual Property Rights (TRIPS Agreement) to be part of the wider national and international action to address these problems.

3. We recognize that intellectual property protection is important for the development of new medicines. We also recognize the concerns about its effects on prices.

4. We agree that the TRIPS Agreement does not and should not prevent members from taking measures to protect public health. Accordingly, while reiterating our commitment to the TRIPS Agreement, we affirm that the Agreement can and should be interpreted and implemented in a manner supportive of WTO members' right to protect public health and, in particular, to promote access to medicines for all.
In this connection, we reaffirm the right of WTO members to use, to the full, the provisions in the TRIPS Agreement, which provide flexibility for this purpose.

5. Accordingly and in the light of paragraph 4 above, while maintaining our commitments in the TRIPS Agreement, we recognize that these flexibilities include:

(a) In applying the customary rules of interpretation of public international law, each provision of the TRIPS Agreement shall be read in the light of the object and purpose of the Agreement as expressed, in particular, in its objectives and principles.
(b) Each member has the right to grant compulsory licences and the freedom to determine the grounds upon which such licences are granted.
(c) Each member has the right to determine what constitutes a national emergency or other circumstances of extreme urgency, it being understood that public health crises, including those relating to HIV/AIDS, tuberculosis, malaria and other epidemics, can represent a national emergency or other circumstances of extreme urgency.

(d) The effect of the provisions in the TRIPS Agreement that are relevant to the exhaustion of intellectual property rights is to leave each member free to establish its own regime for such exhaustion without challenge, subject to the MFN and national treatment provisions of Articles 3 and 4.

6. We recognize that WTO members with insufficient or no manufacturing capacities in the pharmaceutical sector could face difficulties in making effective use of compulsory licensing under the TRIPS Agreement. We instruct the Council for TRIPS to find an expeditious solution to this problem and to report to the General Council before the end of 2002.

7. We reaffirm the commitment of developed-country members to provide incentives to their enterprises and institutions to promote and encourage technology transfer to least-developed country members pursuant to Article 66.2. We also agree that the least-developed country members will not be obliged, with respect to pharmaceutical products, to implement or apply Sections 5 and 7 of Part II of the TRIPS Agreement or to enforce rights provided for under these Sections until 1 January 2016, without prejudice to the right of least-developed country members to seek other extensions of the transition periods as provided for in Article 66.1 of the TRIPS Agreement. We instruct the Council for TRIPS to take the necessary action to give effect to this pursuant to Article 66.1 of the TRIPS Agreement.

Subject Index

Subject Index

International Classification of Functioning, Disability and Health: 340
International Code of Marketing of Breast-milk Substitutes: *see* Breast-milk substitutes
Interpretation of the Agreement of 25 March 1951 between the WHO and Egypt: 10, 75–78

Joint Committee on Health Policy (JCHP): *see* UNICEF

Malaria: 341–342, 457, 459
antimalarial agents: 482
Global Fund to Fight Malaria: 374–377
Roll Back Malaria Project: 341–342
Medicines for Malaria Venture (MMV): 183, 187–191
Medicines, access to medicines: 454–482
medicines prices: 464–473
patents on medicines: 458, 470, *see also* Intellectual property rights
see also Drugs
Meeting of Interested Parties: 519–520

NGOs: *see* WHO relations with NGOs
Nomenclature Regulations: 268–274
Nuclear weapons: International Court of Justice advisory opinion on the legality of the use of nuclear weapons, 219–227

Onchocersiasis: 383–391, 477
African Programme for Onchocersiasis Control (APOC): 389–391
Onchocersiasis Control Programme (OCP): 384–389

Palestine, admission to WHO: 15, 30, 43
Pan American Health Organization (PAHO): 3, 79–80, 105
Patents: *see* Intellectual property rights
Pharmaceutical companies: *see* WHO Relations with the Private Sector
Pharmaceuticals: *see* Drugs and Medicines
Primary health care: *see* Health
Principle of speciality: 222–225
Public-Private Partnerships (PPPs): 178–193

Right to health: *see* Health
River blindness: *see* Onchocerciasis
Roll Back Malaria Project: *see* Malaria

Sanitary and Phitosanitary Measures, Agreement on the Application of Sanitary and Phitosanitary Measures (SPS): 134
Sleeping sickness: *see* Trypanosomiasis
Smallpox: 392–429
Global Eradication Programme of Smallpox: 394–396
Global Certification of Eradication of Smallpox: 420–425
Intensified Eradication Programme of Smallpox: 397–419
stock of variola virus: 426–429
Sustainable development: 337

Tobacco, *Ad Hoc* Inter-Agency Task Force on Tobacco Control: 114
tobacco companies: 195–197
Framework Convention on Tobacco Control (FCTC): 156–157, 228, 248–265, 328–329
Tobacco Free Initiative: 195, 343
Trade, Agreement on Technical Barriers to Trade (TBT): 134
and health: *see* Health
see also Intellectual property rights and Medicines, access to
TRIPS: *see* Intellectual property rights
Tropical Diseases, Special Programme for Research and Training on Tropical Diseases (TDR): 125–128, 182, 492, 494
Trypanosomiasis: 170–171, 477
Tuberculosis (TBC): 430–453
Amsterdam Declaration to stop tuberculosis: 435
antitubercular drugs: 482
Directly Observed Treatment, Short-course (DOTS): 432–450
Global Alliance on TB Drug Development (GATB): 449
Global Drug Facility (GDF): 439, 450, 480
Global Fund to Fight Tuberculosis: 374–377
Global Partnership to Stop Tuberculosis: 443–450

254

Subject Index